Making Gifts with

Woodworker

ANOTHER SELECTION FROM OVER 90 YEARS OF THE WORLD'S BEST WOODWORKING MAGAZINE

Compiled by Zachary Taylor

ARGUS BOOKS

Argus Books
Argus House
Boundary Way
Hemel Hempstead
Herts HP2 7ST
England

First published by Argus Books 1994

ISBN 1-85486-110-7

Cover photograph by Manny Cefai

Explanatory note
As the projects in this book are produced in facsimile from
the original magazine articles, some pages contain continuation text
from articles not selected for this book.
This irrelevant text has been tinted.

Due to the age of some of the material used in the production of this book,
the print quality on some pages is poor.

Printed and bound in Great Britain by BPC Wheatons Ltd., Exeter

Contents

Introduction

The Best of Woodworker is a project book compiled from the tens of thousands of articles that have appeared in past editions of *Woodworker*. Its immediate success prompted this sequel.

Whilst making my selection for that original book, I felt it should be introductory to a whole series, each part devoted to an individual theme. Many subdivisions of the general term 'woodwork' are available, some of which are very specialised and some more widely spread, and my task was to include a balance of each where possible. The decision to base the present work on gift making came about after lengthy discussions with Beverly Laughlin, who commissioned the work for Argus Books.

Included in the title, the word 'Gifts' suggested smaller items of a personal kind – some amusing, some practical, some beautiful. For the sake of variety I chose some simple pieces to encourage the less experienced woodworker, alongside others of more complex design requiring a high level of craftsmanship.

Here is a miscellany from over one thousand editions of a magazine that has occupied the place of market leader for almost a century, with contributions from some of the great names in woodworking society.

To maintain uniformity with the earlier publication, this volume is a facsimile taken from the original pages, some of which include some dated information and phrases that have become outmoded, but this adds something to its wholesome charm and gives a feeling of association with our heritage.

My intention is to continue the series with other topics – they are just waiting for me to select. I hope in your reading of this book you share the pleasure I had in compiling it.

Zachary Taylor

Design for a Moorish Table.

A MOORISH table, though quite a small article in itself, opens a wide scope for variety in work and decoration. The design here given is strictly Moorish in its feeling and treatment, but it would be quite legitimate to treat it in other ways. It might be all carved, and just incised as the top shows ; it could be inlaid with rare woods, pearl, ivory, or ebony, or even metals ; the long panels on each side could be of repoussé—*i.e.*, the hammered treatment of iron, copper, or brass ; and, perhaps, lastly, it could be made in some light wood (sycamore or white wood) and painted in geometric or natural forms, preferably the former. In all cases the construction would be the same, and it might also be made in octagonal as well as the hexagonal form.

SKETCH OF FINISHED TABLE.

In the present design the top is 18 ins. across from the two extreme corners, which will make each side 9 ins., and the panels are 20 ins. high and 8 ins. wide. A slight knowledge of geometry will soon settle the setting out of the top. But failing this, if the wood be prepared 18 ins. long and 16 ins. wide, and lines drawn through the centre both ways, points can be marked 4½ ins. on each side of the short one ; then if these are joined to the ends of the long centre line, three sides are at once given. The lines of the stand can then be marked on the under side, about ¾ in. from the edge, which will give the side about the 8 ins. The amateur would do well to make a drawing full size; and if he will remember that the angle in the hexagon is 60 degs., he will not go far wrong in the setting out.

The best wood for such a design as this is American walnut, and when finished it should be

DESIGN FOR SIDE PANEL.

simply oiled, which will make it a deep rich brown and harmonise the design. The top might

MOORISH TABLE,
DESIGNED BY
W. T. WHITEHEAD.

PLAN SHOWING
DESIGN OF TOP.

be of ¾ in. wood, and the sides not less than ½ in., but the form of construction should be considered first. If "fretted" or pierced, as the design shows, the sides should be in one piece and made as per Fig. 2, which is the cheapest and quickest method. The upright inside must be planed carefully to the right angle, and the screw bored square to the joint; there should be at least three screws up each side, and the joint must be fitted dry first, then finished with thin glue. A square piece might be screwed round the top edge (marked A), which would stiffen the side, and the top should be screwed down through it. Of course, all the carving and piercing must

be done before fixing, and the former first; the margins are about an inch wide, and it will be noticed that the design at the bottom of the panel is square. Small blocks (marked B) glued into the corner would strengthen the stand, but if the glueing and screwing is well done there should be no need of them.

Fig. 1 shows a better and more difficult mode of construction, which must be used if the panels are separate, such as copper or specially carved ones would be. The uprights are really posts, and the rails mortised and tenoned, or dovetailed as shown. Both rails and posts would have to be rebated, and if the reader will follow the articles on " Joints "now appearing in THE WOODWORKER, he will learn some valuable things to help him in construction.

The posts can be made out of 1¼ in. wood, or even 1 in., and the dotted lines show how to make them out of one piece. If mortised together, the corners should not be planed off until it is glued and dry, as they are needed for the cramping up. The rails ought to be of ¾ in. wood, and in this way the top can be fastened by screws bored through the rails from the rebate, or with grooves and a "button" (see the article on "How to Make a Kitchen Table," in the November issue of THE WOODWORKER). The top should be in one piece, if possible ; but if in two the joint should be dowelled – i.e., wooden pins, which will strengthen it for the carving.

The piercing at the bottom could be bored and

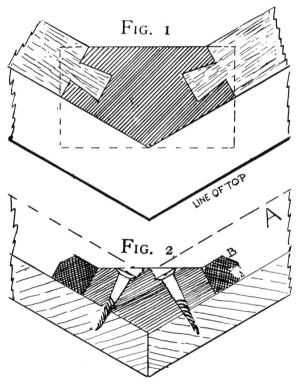

FIG. 1

LINE OF TOP

FIG. 2

finished with a file, and the designs easily varied, and the panels themselves might be of alternate designs or all different. It is easy to see how simple or how intricate the work might be, and if carried out as in the first suggestion it would be inexpensive, the wood costing about 5s. only. It would be exceedingly interesting to know what the amateur—or professional—woodworker thinks of these designs, or if any are made it would be useful and of equal interest to hear something of them. Such a table as this offers a chance for original design and good workmanship, based as it is on geometry the basis of all design. Those bought at the shops and sold as Eastern work are really made in London and are mostly a medley of pieces. This design shows what may be done in decorative detail combining a harmonious whole.

WORKSHOP WRINKLES

How to Fit Handles to Chisels and Gouges.

WHEN the handles are purchased, they will be found already bored, but the holes are never bored in far enough. They should therefore be made deeper with a gimlet ; in fact, deep enough, so that the tang of the chisel will not reach the bottom of the hole. Now take the chisel in the right hand, and the handle in the left, and placing the tang in the hole, twist the chisel round and round, thus making it enlarge its own hole. This must be continued until the flange of the chisel is up to ¼ in. from the ferrule of the handle, when a couple of taps with the hammer will force it in.

By adopting this plan the chisels are not liable to break, or the handles to split, and they are certain of being on straight and tight.

The handles should always be regulated according to the size of the chisel. Nothing looks worse than a large clumsy handle on a ½-in. chisel, unless it is a small handle on a 1½-in. chisel. In the latter case the user has no command over his tool, and bad work, if not cut fingers, is often the result.

The handles called "carver's" pattern are the most comfortable to the hand in use, and box is undoubtedly the best wood for them to be made of. These can be purchased at 2s. 6d. a dozen, in assorted sizes, at any tool dealers.

To Make Round Rods.

ROUND rods for plate-racks, large bird-cages, etc., can be easily and quickly made with a bead plane of the proper size. For ⅜-in. rods, use a ½-in. bead, and for ½ in. rods a ⅝-in. bead, and so on.

The bead must first be run on one side of the board ; then turn the latter over and run it on the other side. It will now easily break off at the quirks, and a shaving taken off with the bead-plane will remove all traces of the breakage, and the rod is complete. It is necessary for the complete success of the operation that the planes be in good working order, and that the wood be clear from knots and free from shakes.

For rods above five-eighths of an inch in diameter, the best way is to saw to the required size ; then plane up truly. Take off the corners so as to form a perfect octagon ; then again to sixteen and thirty-two squares, when glass-paper will do the rest.

If a perfect square was formed at first, and all the corners taken off evenly, a perfectly round rod will be the result, almost as true as though turned in a lathe ; but if not made true at first in the square, it will be impossible to make a true round.

A Simple Seat for a Recess.

By F. R. W.

WHEN considering how best to furnish a recess or window-bay, seating accommodation of some kind always presents a prominent claim on the score of its practical utility. Being ready to hand, compact, and convenient to move, the every-day chair is usually pressed into service in such instances ; but, mayhap, it would be as well to appreciate the fact that an opportunity' of introducing a welcome relieving note into the room furnishing is passing unrecognised. One sees the old fashioned and ugly "suite-complete" effect

FIG. I.

so frequently, that the eye is quick to note and appreciate anything tastefully departing from the ordinary run of things, and herein lies the young woodworker's opportunity of reaping a prompt reward for his individual efforts at the bench. Why should he not try his hand at a seat on the lines of the little sketch we offer herewith ?

Fig. 1 is a perspective sketch of the little notion in question, and a serviceable dimension would be from 2 ft. 6 ins. to 3 ft. long by 3 ft. 1 in. high by 16 ins. wide (back to front).

Fig. 2 offers a cut of parts showing a method of putting together.

Fig. 3 gives an alternative suggestion for seat-back, and a few details which, with the following notes, should make the setting out a matter of simplicity.

Returning to Fig. 1 for a moment, it will be noted that a wood seat is indicated ; but, as ideas of comfort vary somewhat with one and the others of us, it may be hinted that a home-made cushion, stuffed with wool or hair to a thickness of $1\frac{1}{2}$ ins., and tufted here and there to keep it from working into lumps, will soon put matters on a comfortable basis. Coming to Fig. 2, the ends at A should be got out to finish 15 ins. wide at top, with the front edge sloping out to 17 ins. at base. Thickness may show $\frac{7}{8}$ in, or for a stout job $1\frac{1}{8}$ in., in which case the edges might be finished with a cant, as at O, to lighten them in appearance. With this object, too, a small heart-shaped opening is made on the top, and another, arch-shaped, about 9 ins. by 7 ins., at the base where it enters the struts. The end is indicated as grooved for arm-rests E, mortised for rails D and C (front and back), dovetail grooved for seat, and tenoned to enter struts at H. The seat B will finish 2 ft. 11 ins. long by 16 ins. wide by $\frac{7}{8}$ in. thick, with rounded front edge to prevent uncomfortable contact with the sitter's legs, and dovetailed each end to enter corresponding grooves in A. In cutting these groovings it should be remembered to ease them slightly towards the back, as otherwise the joint has a tendency to bind when fitting up.

The rails C will come out of a piece $\frac{7}{8}$ in. thick by $2\frac{1}{2}$ ins. wide, tenoned home, as shown, and screwed up to seat. The upper backrail D may shape out of $\frac{3}{4}$-in. or $\frac{7}{8}$-in. stuff to a width of $3\frac{1}{4}$ ins. in centre, diminishing to $2\frac{1}{4}$ ins. at ends, and tenoned to A, screwed or pinned. The arm-rest at E need only be 3 ins. wide, including grooving into ends, and should have the outer edges and corner rounded for finish. It should also be slotted to receive the short tenons on the supporting brackets F, and can be either screwed or let into D. The four small brackets can be cut together to shape out of pieces $2\frac{1}{2}$ ins. by $2\frac{1}{2}$ ins. by $\frac{7}{8}$ in. (edge rounded), which allows for $\frac{1}{4}$-in. stubbing to enter E. The rail G will serve as a stop for seat cushion, as well as a finish to back, but is not really necessary to the construction of Fig. 1. It may finish $1\frac{3}{4}$ ins. wide, and is indicated as dovetailed into back edge and screwed, or it may, of course, be tenoned. The struts at H are $2\frac{1}{4}$ ins. wide, with the edges moulded to a broken ogee all round. The stuff here may be $\frac{7}{8}$ in. thick, cut to a finishing length of 19 ins., allowing ¾ in. for the moulding projection, and two mortises are cut right through for the tenons on the base of A to enter and be there wedged. If preferred, instead of two struts as at H, four shoes 5 ins. by 2¼ ins. might be fitted. These would be quite sufficient for firmness, but the former method is, of course, the stronger way.

Fig. 1 is purposely kept simple in detail, but it is possible to obtain a pleasing additional effect by fitting splats and bars, something after the manner indicated in Fig. 3. The two splats, as at I, may be cut 4 ins. by 11 ins. long by ½ in. thick, to be stub-tenoned into rails D and

alternative shaping for ends at L is selected. It works out very well to a size of 16½ ins. by 3 ft. 2 ins., allowing a height for wood seat of 18 ins., or 16½ ins. if a cushion is to be used on the seat. An enlarged section for seat joint to ends is sketched at M.

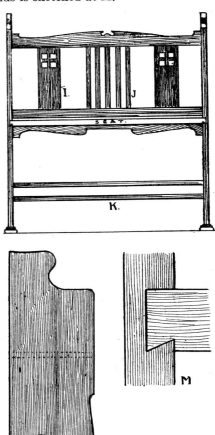

FIG. 3.

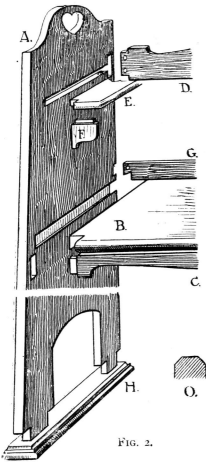

FIG. 2.

G top and bottom), and the little fret opening will assist in retaining the general effect of lightness. The bars at J (five in all) will show 11 ins. by ¾ in. by ⅝ in. stubbed in top and bottom. The splat and bar arrangement is merely suggestive, and there are several ways of alternating these with pleasing effect otherwise than sketched. Try, for instance, *two-splat - two - three - two - splat - two*; or, again, *three - one - splat - one - three*. The two rails at K, ¾ in. by ¾ in., can be introduced if the worker should happen to prefer the seat-ends A solid instead of cut out at base; or, again, if the

The following is a list of the pieces required for ready reference :—

A, two pieces, 3′ 1″ by 1′ 5″ by ⅞″.
B, one piece, 2′ 11″ by 1′ 4″ by ⅞″.
C, two pieces, 2′ 11½″ by 2½″ by ⅞″.
D, 1 piece, 2′ 11½″ by 3¼″ by ¾″.
E, two pieces, 1′ 1″ by 3″ by ¾″.
F, four pieces, 2½″ by 2½″ by ⅞″.
G, one piece, 2′ 11½″ by 1¾″ by ⅞″.
H, two pieces, 1′ 7″ by 2½″ by ⅞″.
If required :—
I, two pieces, 11″ by 4″ by ½″.
J, five pieces, 11″ by ¾″ by ⅝″.
K, two pieces, 2′ 11½″ by ¾″ by ¾″.
L, two pieces, 3′ 2″ by 1′ 4½″ by ⅞″.

In conclusion, we may add that we shall be pleased to insert in the special column reserved for reader's work any suitable photograph of the finished article that our young craftsmen may send us later on.

2 upright stiles, 8¾ ins. by 2½ ins. by ⅝ in.
2 upright stiles, 8¾ ins. by 4¾ ins. by ⅝ in.
4 cross stiles, 1 ft. 1¾ ins. by 3 ins. by ⅝ in.
2 cross stiles, 1 ft. 6 ins. by 3 ins. by ⅝ in.
2 panels, 8¾ ins. by 3½ ins. by ⅜ in.
1 panel, 1 ft. 2½ ins. by 3½ ins. by ⅜ in.
2 upright stiles, 1 ft. 3⅝ ins. by 2½ ins. by ⅝ in.
2 upright stiles, 1 ft. 3⅝ ins. by 4¾ ins. by ⅝ in.
2 panels, 1 ft. 3⅝ ins. by 8¾ ins. by ⅜ in.
1 panel, 1 ft. 3⅝ ins. by 14½ ins. by ⅜ in.

Stationery Case.

Mahogany :
4 pieces, 4 ft. 1 in. by 6½ ins.
1 piece, 1 ft. 6 ins. by 6½ ins.
3 pieces, 11½ ins. by 6½ ins.
2 drawers :
    2 pieces (front and back), 4 ins. by 3 ins. by 3-16ths in.

2 pieces (sides), 4 ins. by 4 ins.
1 piece (bottom), 4 ins. by 7 ins.
2 pieces (fillets), 3-16ths in. by 3-16ths in.

Smoker's Cabinet.

Mahogany :
2 pieces, 1 ft. 2 ins. by 6½ ins.
4 pieces, 1 ft. 0¼ in. by 6½ ins.
1 piece, 1 ft. 2 ins. by 6½ ins.
4 drawers :
    2 pieces (front and back), 7 ins. by 7 ins.
    2 pieces (sides), 1 ft. 2 ins. by 6½ ins. by 3-16ths in.
    2 pieces (bottoms), 7 ins. by 6½ ins.
    2 pieces (front and back), 1 ft. by 6½ ins.
    2 pieces (sides), 7 ins. by 6½ ins.
    2 pieces (bottoms), 12 ins. by 6½ ins.

(*To be concluded.*)

Priced Articles.

A Simple China Cabinet or Bookcase.

IN continuance of the "Priced Articles" appearing in our columns, we offer in the present issue details for a small show cabinet, which should appeal to many of our readers. It is now quite a popular hobby to collect the tiny specimens of "Goss" or crest china, decorated with arms and motto

FIG. 1.

of the particular locality, and sold in practically every town in the United Kingdom. Many of them exactly reproducing on a minor scale the lines of an antique urn-bowl or cruse—wee and dainty examples of the potter's skill—form a choice and attractive feature in any room

where suitably displayed. A friend of the writer's, an ardent cyclist, makes it a practice to purchase one or two pieces from every town he passes through for the first time a-wheel, and the circumstances of his collecting have led to many an enjoyable chat. These things, too, are just what many of the fair sex delight in purchasing, so that, given the cabinet for their display, one may be tolerably certain that the number of specimens will rapidly grow.

The dimensions of the cabinet (Fig. 1) are 23 ins. high by 16 ins. wide by 5 ins. deep outside on carcase—fitted with four shelves,

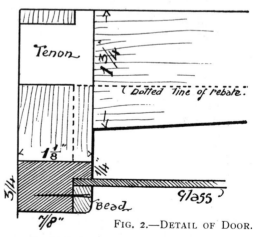

FIG. 2.—DETAIL OF DOOR.

three of which have risers or steps so that the pieces at the back may be raised well in view. The construction is just about as simple as it can be, and ought not to worry any one who can handle a tool at all. In Fig. 3 the parts are shown detached. A, the top, 19 ins. by 6½ ins.

by $\frac{1}{2}$ in., has three mortises each end to receive corresponding tenons on end B, top and bottom, 22$\frac{3}{4}$ ins. by 5 ins. by $\frac{1}{2}$ in. A mortise is also cut in each end to take the tenons on front rail C, 16 ins. by 1 in. by 1 in., round which the moulded strip D, 1 in. by $\frac{7}{8}$ in. projection, is mitred front

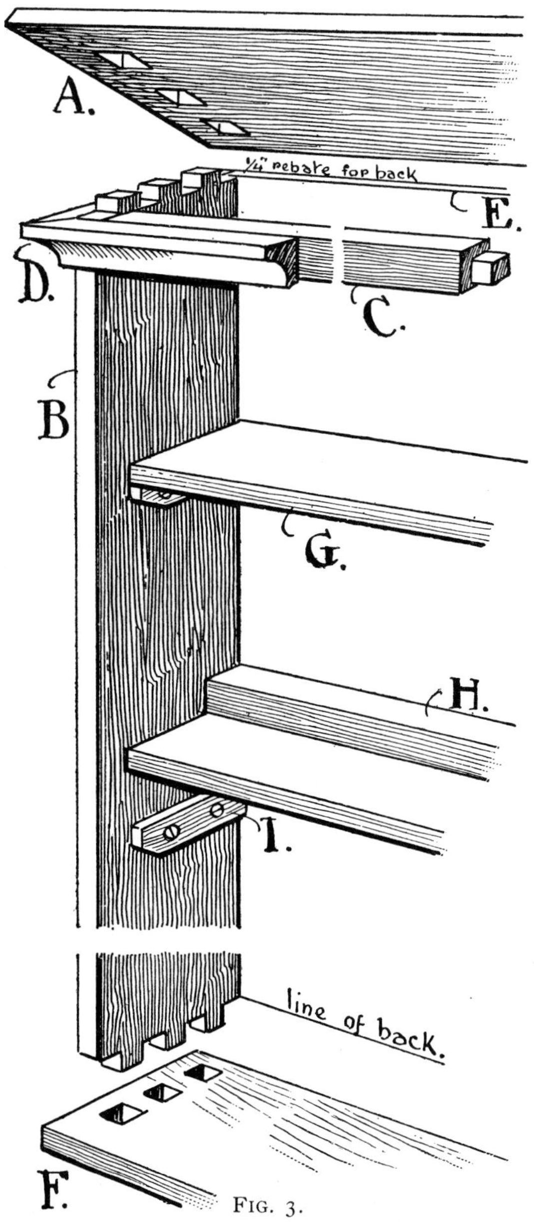

FIG. 3.

and ends. The back E is $\frac{1}{4}$-in. rebated in, size 22$\frac{1}{4}$ ins. by 15$\frac{1}{2}$ ins. by $\frac{1}{4}$ in., and screwed with fine brass round-headed screws preferably, for finish. The base F, 17 ins. by 5$\frac{1}{4}$ ins. by $\frac{1}{2}$ in., is mortised each end as indicated. The four shelves G, 4 ins. by 15$\frac{1}{2}$ ins. by $\frac{1}{2}$ in., can be $\frac{1}{4}$-in. groved into ends, and rest on slips I, 4 ins. by $\frac{7}{8}$ ins. by $\frac{1}{4}$ in., or may be tenoned to ends. The risers H are 1$\frac{3}{4}$ ins. by 1 in. high by 15 ins., glued in position, with two or three screws along line of shelves through from back. An enlarged detail, Fig. 3, is given for door, which will finish 21 ins. high by 15 ins. wide by $\frac{3}{4}$ in. thick, rebated $\frac{1}{2}$ in. by $\frac{1}{4}$ in. for the glass to be beaded in from back. Probably the cabinet would be required to stand on a side table, but if to hang had best have a couple of brass plates screwed to top as shown.

	s.	d.
Top, bottom, ends, shelves, slips:		
7-ft. oak, 10 ins. by $\frac{5}{8}$ in., at 4d. ..	2	4
2-ft. oak, 9 ins. by 1$\frac{1}{4}$ ins., at 7$\frac{1}{2}$d. ..	1	3
Risers, rail, moulding:		
4-ft. oak, 10 ins. by $\frac{3}{8}$ in., at 2$\frac{1}{2}$d. ..	0	10
(Back, beading.)		
Glass	1	6
Bullet catch and handle	0	6
Pair 1$\frac{3}{4}$-in. brass bolts, plates, screws nails	0	7
	7	0

Woodworkers' Library.

PRACTICAL WOODCARVING. By Eleanor Rowe, London: B. T. Batsford. Price 7s. 6d.; postage 5d.

As its title implies, this volume is a practical guide to woodcarvers. Beginning at the beginning, Miss Rowe introduces the student to his tools and appliances, the first chapter being devoted to the "Woodcarver's outfit." We note with satisfaction that the author says "Beware of 'Ladies' sets.' If a woman is to do good work, she should use the same tools as a man."

Another dictum of hers is perhaps not so sound. We are told to "never buy a tool maker's assorted set, as the experience of a carver is needed to know what tools will be the most useful." This will bear some considerable qualification, for tool makers who know their business always ascertain from a reliable source what tools are required to constitute "a set" for beginners, if they are not sufficiently experienced to settle the matter themselves.

Chapter II, on "The Various Woods used by the Carver," is a useful one, but later on we find that "yellow pine is only sold in planks," which we believe is a little incorrect, unless the author would have us buy direct from the importer. Chapter III, on "Construction," is a *resume* of the usual and accepted forms of construction, whilst Chapter IV deals with the possibilities of the tool. A slight omission in the reference lettering on the diagram on page 40 is merely a technical slip, and cannot possibly cause any misunderstanding. The following chapters deal with Low Relief Carving, High Relief, Gothic Tracery, Symbolism, Gothic, Jacobean and Renascence, Lettering, Pierced Carving, and, lastly, a chapter on the Treatment of Design, a glossary of a few technical terms. The illustrations number nearly 170, of which 114 are excellent reproductions from photographs, and 55 from line drawings of old and modern examples of work.

The work is in all respects practical, and its get up reflects great credit on the publishers and printers.

A Serviceable Bookshelf.

FOR the "Young Woodworker" this week we offer a suggestion for a little piece of wall furniture that, when made, is sure to prove itself of daily use in the home—to wit, a hanging bookshelf. To the craftsman who also happens to be fond of his books, a place to put them just where they can readily be found is almost as necessary as the books themselves. Not everyone can boast of, or needs, a room apart for his

FIG. I.—A HANGING BOOKSHELF.

library, yet, even from there books are misplaced, for in a family of several, the chances are that each member has a favourite volume, which—in use—is apt to be laid down haphazard in the living-room.

Here, then, a small bookshelf, thoughtfully fixed in some convenient corner, would do yeoman service, since it would invite the placing of all odd volumes upon it, and so tend to avoid the subsequent litter that the orderly housewife liketh not.

The sketch (Fig. 1) gives a fair idea of the sort of thing referred to, and the construction is of the simplest. The dimensions may be put at 18 ins. to 2 ft. in width—2 ft. 6 ins. high, with a depth to finish $7\frac{1}{2}$ ins. over all.

The parts are illustrated in Fig. 2, showing a method of putting the whole thing together, and Fig. 3 offers an alternative line for top of back, with a suggestion for some simple fret or inlay by way of relief, As the cost of material is trifling, it would be as well to use solid oak, walnut, or mahogany throughout, although bass, slightly thicker, is satisfactory for the purpose, and birch makes a nice clean job.

For the sake of making things quite clear, we refer again to Fig. 2. The ends A, shaped top and bottom, may also have the edges rounded for finish ; they are mortised to receive tenons on shelves and rebated for back. Top rail of back

B (2 ft. by 7 ins.), shaped to sketch, is grooved for matching—(this may be of deal stained to colour) and rebated, or, better still, dovetailed to ends. The three shelves C ($7\frac{1}{4}$ ins. wide), with, say, three tenons, enter each end as indicated. The bearing may be stiffened by fixing glued slips, as seen, under centre shelf, the grain, of course, to coincide with that of both ends and shelf, and the corners rounded away for neatness, so that they are as little visible as possible. Or, the shelves may be slot-dovetailed in, which makes the stronger joint, although the bookshelf will be quite strong enough with the shelves screwed through from the back and the slips. If the back D is not required, a rail (2 ins. wide) may be dovetailed to ends and screwed to back edge of centre shelf for support. The bottom rail E (say 4 ins. wide), with the lower edge shaped, is rebated or dovetailed to ends and screwed through to back edge of lower shelf. The

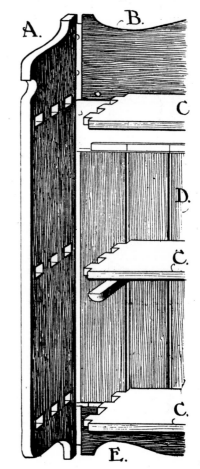

FIG. 2.—DETAILS OF CONSTRUCTION.

whole thing may be made of $\frac{1}{2}$-in. stuff (to finish $\frac{3}{8}$ in. full) if no heavy books, such as encyclopædias, are to be placed thereon, otherwise the wood had best be a trifle thicker.

A simple fret or inlaid pattern in upper part of back would not look amiss, and the three hints given are each quite easy of accomplishment. That in Fig. 1 would be a fret, whilst of those in Fig. 3 the top one F can be of pewter inlaid with a black dot in centre of each square for emphasis. That at G is a trifle more difficult to fit, but the four pewter shapes can be cut under one operation to

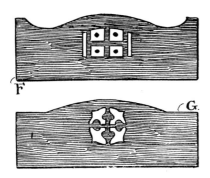

FIG. 3.—ALTERNATE DESIGNS FOR BACK.

shorten the work, or the little design might be fretted instead.

The following is an estimate for the stuff required, care being taken to secure dry stuff free from knots or shakes up to 10 ins. wide, which will allow for slips.

AMERICAN OAK.	s.	d.
Two ends, 5 ft. by 10 ins. by ½ in., at 3½d.	1	5½
Three shelves, 6 ft. by 10 ins. by ½ in., at 3½d.	1	9
One back, 7 ft. 6 ins. by 10 ins. by ½ in., at 3½d.	2	2
	5	4½
Glue, screws, brass staples	0	4
	5	9½

Workshop Hints.

PAPERING SMALL FLAT SURFACES.

A handy yet simple device for glass-papering small flat surfaces can be easily attached to an ordinary upright drilling machine. Fasten into a small flange a piece of steel or iron, shaped like the shank of a bit, to fit the machine. On the flange fasten a wooden disc of a suitable diameter. On this disc glue or tack glass-paper. Lay the work on the table, and bring the disc down with the requisite pressure. This device will be found very handy for small blocks, corner brackets, etc., and will clean up true and smooth, saving time and labour, as it can be placed in the boring machine as quickly as a bit, and is always ready for use.

In painting or enamelling a better surface is obtained by several thin coats than by a lesser number of thick ones.

How to Work Curved Mouldings by Hand.

THE working of mouldings to a curved outline in many cases is easier to do than to work the same moulding on a straight board, the only comparative disadvantage being that it is impossible to use a plane for any portion of a curve; thus the square portions, which are the easiest parts of a straight moulding, as being workable with a plane, become the most difficult to work in a curve.

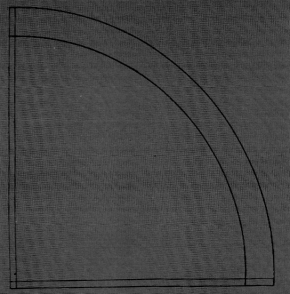

FIG. 1.—CIRCULAR BOARD TO BE MOULDED.

The successful formation of mouldings on a curved surface depends quite as much on a systematic method as the straight work, as we shall show later on.

For the first example we take a comparatively easy one, the quarter circle, Fig. 1, on which we have to work an ovolo moulding. This must

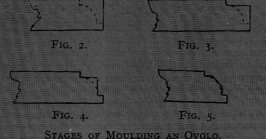

FIG. 2.   FIG. 3.

FIG. 4.   FIG. 5.

STAGES OF MOULDING AN OVOLO.

first be shaped truly, and the edge squared, that is, made a perfect right angle with the sides, and what is very important, a small portion of spare material must be left beyond the actual size required, as shown.

At the extremities of the curve mark on the outline of the moulding as dotted lines, Fig. 2, and

QUESTIONS of general interest will be answered here. Readers, however, will kindly note :—(1) As the Editor may desire to reply by post a stamped addressed envelope must be enclosed. (2) Questions will be answered in THE WOOD-WORKER as early as possible after receipt, but when sketches and research have to be made a short interval may occasionally elapse. Questions of purely personal interest cannot be dealt with in these columns. NOTE.—With each Query must be sent a Coupon (see foot of page iv. of cover). All queries to be addressed : Editor THE WOODWORKER, Montague House, Russell Square, London, W.C.1.

Toy Locomotive.

A. L. (Northampton) asks if we can give a design, with details of construction, for a toy locomotive from 18 ins. to 24 ins. long.

REPLY.—In response to your query we give here a design for a locomotive and tender, which we think will be suitable for your purpose. The base board is the first portion to be made, and should be 2 feet long by 6¾ inches wide by ⅜ inch thick. The details shown in the drawings are then made to the given measurements and may be glued and either sprigged or nailed together. The top of the cab is not shown in the detailed drawing ; this should measure 6 ins. long by 4 ins. wide, and may be ⅜ in. or ½ in. wood, according to the timber at hand. The boiler is 10½ ins. long by 4½ ins. in diameter, and it is quite possible that you may have an old piece of cornice pole, which will be quite near enough to answer the purpose. If you have not access to a foot lathe, a couple of empty cotton reels can be converted into the funnel and the steam dome, suitable holes being bored to receive them.

Two axles will be required, and washers (W) and split cotter pins (C) will effectively hold the wheels in position. The completed model is finished by giving three coats of dark green paint, and lining up the bands in vermilion colour. The axles and wheels should be of hard wood, and the axle pins should be lubricated by mixing powdered black lead and tallow to act as a lubricant.

In the December number of THE WOOD-WORKER for 1916, page 267, full particulars and drawings were given for making a much larger locomotive, which was fitted with cycle pedals and chain, and allowing for the youngster to sit in the tender and thus drive the engine similarly to a pedal motor.   418

Furniture.

J. J. B.—For a cheap book dealing generally with furniture styles we may recommend "Furniture," a 2s. 6d. handbook just published by Pitman td., Amen Corner, London, E.C.4. This will give you a brief description of the recognised furniture styles. There are numerous illustrations, and a useful feature of the volume is a list of standard books dealing with furniture. At the price, we do not know a more suitable book to recommend.

Queensland Timber.

A writer on Queensland timber says :—" We have just started to use blackbutt, crow's foot elm, spotted gum and other timbers for axe handles. We are making our own fruit cases out of pine tops previously left to waste. We are constantly getting inquiries for timber to replace imported article for saddle-trees, clothes-pegs, brushware, etc. Recently a large sale of secondary timbers was made on Fraser Island—timbers not previously used. Negotiations are now in progress for the establishment in Queensland of a

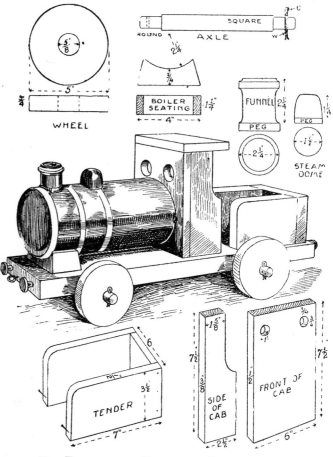

TOY ENGINE, WITH DETAILS OF CONSTRUCTION.

brushware factory capable of using half-a-million feet of timber a year—timber hitherto classed as useless."

Polishing Cement Floor.

A. G. F. (Greenock) writes :—" I want to polish a cement floor treated with oxide, which gives it a dull red appearance. Can you suggest anything which will give it a bright surface like polished linoleum ? "

REPLY.—We have discussed the polishing of a cement floor with the manager of one of the leading firms of cement makers, and the advice given was as follows :—The last coat of cement should have had a large proportion of fine granite chippings mixed in it, so as to form a hard top coating. The floor would then be finished by polishing exactly the same as mosaic floors. Seeing that the floor is already completed, we can suggest nothing better than a mixture of beeswax and turpentine. Several applications will be necesssary, and we are afraid that the process will be costly. To prevent the cement from creating an excess of dust (a fault which all cement floors possess), the following is a good remedy. Apply frequent applications of linseed oil and lime water, applied with a turk's head mop brush.   412

YOUR LETTER BOX

FIG. 1.—AN INSIDE LETTER BOX.

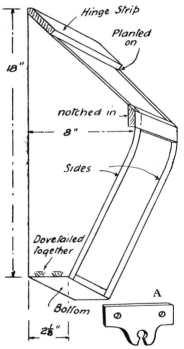

FIG. 3.—FRAME BEFORE FIXING PLYWOOD.

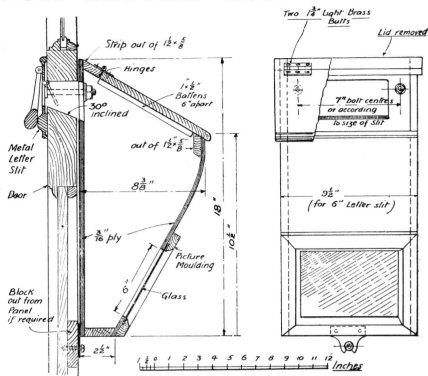

FIG. 2.—SECTION AND FRONT ELEVATION (SCALE APPLIES TO LATTER).

LETTER BOXES fitted to the inside of doors of private houses occupied by one family may be treated in quite a different manner from the containers commonly made for offices. Having experienced trouble with a dog who collected and damaged letters as they were delivered, the writer made a box on the lines of the accompanying sketches.

To facilitate the entry of long letters, the sides are made to taper from 8 ins. at the top to 6 ins. at the extreme bottom. Where drawings and other small diameter long rolls are received—as in the writer's own case—the box cannot very well be made "thick" enough to allow the packages to turn within the box. The top opening and the hinged lid are therefore inclined. The lid will lift for a long thin roll.

The construction is very simple. The sides are of $\frac{5}{8}$ in. stuff, with a narrow bottom and a hinge strip at the top dovetailed into the sides. The front and back are of $\frac{3}{16}$ in. ply. The hinged lid should be battened inside to prevent warping.

When the box is complete it should be marked out for the holes engaging the fixing bolts of the ornamental metal facing of the letter slit. These are usually left long enough to allow the extra $\frac{3}{16}$ in. under the fixing nut and washer. When drilled and fitted on the bolts, the slit in the back board may be marked out from the outside of the door.

As a rule builders do not splay the lower edge of the slit in the door, and while the job is in hand this should have attention. The lower surface should slope down to the inside to an angle of at least 30 degrees. The opening in the back board may then be cut to suit.

The bottom fixing of the box may be a notched plate of metal—a common wall-hanger plate—screwed on to the back of the box and screwed to the door with a round-headed brass screw. Filing a notch in the plate instead of using the ordinary hole allows the box to be removed without withdrawing the fixing screw.

A refinement which is shown on the drawings but which is not absolutely necessary is to pierce the lower inside face of the box with a hole and to glaze it with 21 oz. glass. This latter may be secured with a mitred frame of small and simply designed picture moulding, fixed over the opening.

In all cases the choice of material and the finishing must be made with respect to the particular door to which the box is to be fitted. (927)

"Practical Formwork and Shuttering" is the title of a new book which should be in the hands of foremen and other workers engaged in the construction of reinforced concrete. The treatise deals with modern practice relating to the design, setting-out and erection of boxes or forms for moulded columns, pilasters and similar classes of ornamental concrete work, in addition to which it covers all and every type of shuttering. The 161 illustrations, most of which are drawn from actual examples of work in progress, show walls, arch centres, vaults and ceilings, floors, stairs, domes, pendentives, etc. The joint authors are Mr. John F. Dowsett and Mr. Eric G. Bartle. The book which is well printed and bound in blue cloth measures 10 ins. by 7 ins., and the price is 18s. 6d. net from the Publishers, The Library Press, Ltd., 36 Russell Square, London, W.C.1., or from any bookseller. (931)

THE WOODWORKER

VOL. XXXVI. NOVEMBER, 1932 NO. 468

A TUDOR DOLL'S HOUSE

QUAINT IN STYLE, EMINENTLY PRACTICAL AND SIMPLY MADE

FOR centuries the doll's house has been the plaything of the little girl, and in spite of modern progress it still maintains a firm hold of the child's affection. It would be hard to find a substitute for this strong and practical toy, affording as it does so many hours of contented make-believe amusement. Needless to say, the unusual and rather quaint design suggested in Fig. 1 has been specially prepared with Christmas in view. Simple yet sturdy construction has been employed, and with a little ingenuity there is no limit to what may ultimately be achieved. The furniture in the rooms has been planned accurately to scale, and may therefore be attempted as well. At least, it will be a guide to correct proportion if purchased at the local toy stores.

House Construction.—
Commence by making a start upon the base (Fig. 3). This comprises rails, A and B, mortised and tenoned together. Allowed an overhang of ⅜ in. all round the house, the overall dimensions of the frame should be 2 ft. 9¼ ins. by 1 ft. 7¾ ins.

The next step is to proceed with the house portion. The ends (C) must be cut back, as in Fig. 3, to allow the necessary overhang of the bedroom part. The top edges must also be sawn to angles of 90 degrees to accommodate the roof. For this purpose it would be advisable to rough out a full size end view of the roof to ensure success. Grooves may or may not be necessary across the ends to receive the top (F) and shelf (H) according to the discretion of the maker. Whilst grooves are recommended to house the latter items, quite a strong effort may be obtained if these are simply glued and pinned between. Both top and shelf are allowed lengths enough in the cutting list to enter grooves ¼ in. deep if decided upon. The bottom edges of the ends should, however, be rebated continuously from front to back to receive the bottom (J).

The top front rail (E) might next be grooved (as suggested in Fig. 2) for the top, and also rebated on the under edge to act as a door stop. The top edge is bevelled to conform to the line of the ends. The angle blocking (D) is allowed in the cutting list, but will probably be

FIG. 1.—TUDOR DOLL'S HOUSE.
Width over Roof, 3 feet. Height over all, 3 ft. 4 ins.
The entire front opens for access to the apartments.

purchased in lengths.

Construct the carcase in the following manner. Glue and screw the bottom up to the ends. Insert the top and shelf into their respective grooves and glue and pin. Screw the top front rail to the edges of the ends, and between the latter secure the angle blocking.

The division (I) might next be glued and pinned between the shelf and bottom. The upper division (G) must be notched around the top rail, and should be slipped in from the back, and pinned up through the projecting portion of the shelf and down through the top. Doors should be cut out and hinged (if allowed in the divisions) before the latter are secured in the carcase. The back (K) might finally be screwed on, noting that the top edge must be bevelled to the line of the ends.

The back member of the two pieces forming the roof (S) should next be cut out to the size suggested in Fig. 2 for a door. For this, use a fine saw because the piece cut out can be trimmed up and used as the door. Hinge with a small pair of brass butts. The joint to the top of the roof may either be mitred as allowed in the cutting list, or shouldered as illustrated in Fig. 2. Screw the roof down to the front rail, ends, angle blocking and back.

The doors might next be dealt with. These may be made up separately as allowed in the cutting list, or possibly a better method is to make up each pair of doors in one piece to commence, afterwards splitting through the centre to form a pair. Thus a piece of plywood measuring 2 ft. 9⅛ ins. long and 10⅝ ins. wide might be faced up as suggested in Fig. 2, and then sawn through in the required place to form the two top doors. The extra ⅛ in. allowed over the given length in Fig. 2 is for planing up the sawn edges. The lower pair of doors might be dealt with similarly, but notice that the width in this case appears at 1 ft. ½ in.

The doors must be rebated for glass windows to the details given in Fig. 4. In the case of the top windows, rebates are on three sides of the front of the plywood. Rebates on all four sides of the lower windows are on

ELEVATIONS AND PLANS OF TUDOR DOLL'S HOUSE

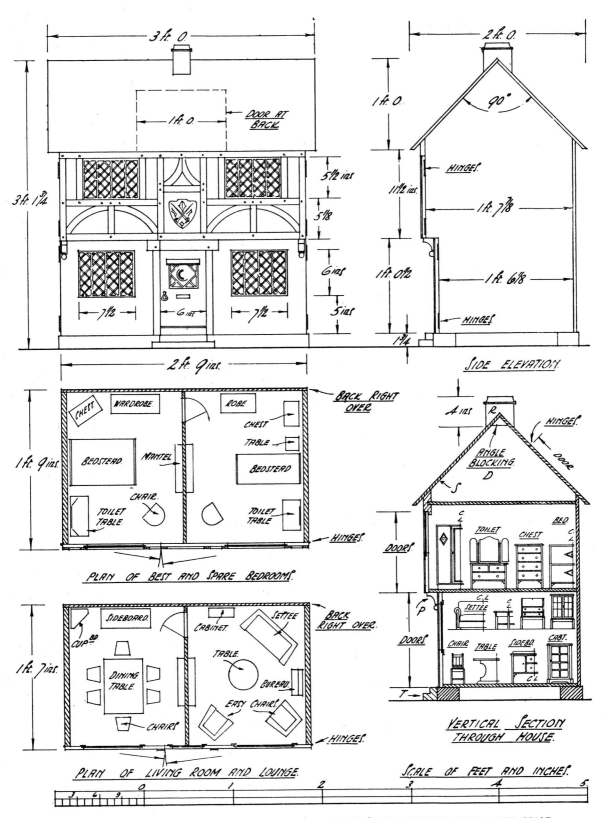

FIG. 2.—FRONT AND SIDE ELEVATIONS, PLANS (TWO FLOORS) AND SECTIONAL VIEW, WITH SCALE

the back of the plywood. Facings hold the top windows in position on three sides of each, whilst along the top edges thin card might be glued. The lower windows are held in position by means of beads pinned to the ply, but glued veneer strips might be used if available. The glass panel to the false front door can be secured in a similar manner. The facings to upper and lower doors should be shouldered as suggested, with dowel pegs driven through the supposed tenons. The corbels (P) are glued to the lower doors and open with them. Finally hinge the two pairs of doors to the carcase, as shown in Fig. 2.

The step (T) might be glued to t e base rail, and chimney cut to fit down over the roof. An odd length of moulding that may be at hand can be mitred around to give a shaped top edge. Shape up a piece of plywood or cardboard to give a shield and coat of arms effect to the top door. All screws used throughout should be of brass, with the heads sunk slightly below the surface. Fill up with putty or wax preparatory to laying tile papers. Remove all sharp edges with glasspaper, and ensure that no splintered corners are passed over.

Furniture, etc.—Lengths of wood, $\frac{1}{4}$ in. square, may be used for the legs of all furniture, with tops, doors and so on of $\frac{1}{8}$ in. plywood. Small glass beads can be utilised for knobs, and bright lead foil glued to plywood for mirrors. Foil may also be used to give the leaded light finish to the windows. Cut several narrow strips and paste on to the glass, letting them overlap where necessary at the joints. This will give a bright and effective finish to the windows.

Tiles for the roof might be cut from $\frac{1}{8}$ in. cardboard and laid on in the proper manner, afterwards colouring to a suitable shade. Alternatively, use printed tiling paper. Brick papers may be adopted for the lower doors, ends, back and base. A roughcast effect can be obtained on the top doors by sprinkling sand on a glued surface, and then painting cream. If the rooms are to be papered, attempt this before glueing up the carcase. The joints in the papers can then be concealed between the meeting places of the shelves and divisions, etc. Finally fit a pair of bullet catches to the top edges of the upper doors, and to the bottom edges of the lower doors.

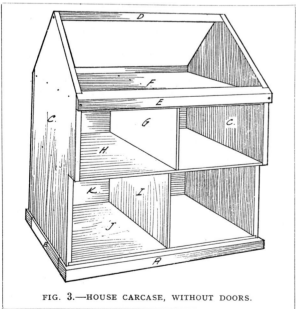

FIG. 3.—HOUSE CARCASE, WITHOUT DOORS.

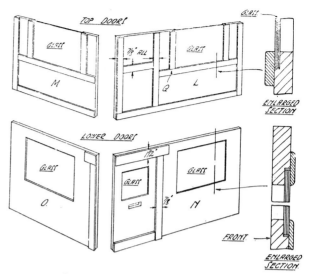

FIG. 4.—SHOWING CONSTRUCTION OF DOORS.

Cutting List—

			Long. ft. ins.	Wide. ft. ins.	Thick. ins.
A	2	Base rails	2 9¾	3	1¼
B	2	Ditto	1 3¾	3	1¼
C	2	Ends	2 11½	1 7⅞	⅝
D	1	Angle blocking	2 7¾	2	1
E	1	Front rail	2 9	3¾	1⅛
F	1	Top	2 8¼	1 8	⅜
G	1	Division	11¼	1 7⅞	⅜
H	1	Shelf	2 8¼	1 7⅞	⅜
I	1	Division	1 0¼	1 6⅛	⅜
J	1	Bottom	2 8½	1 6¼	⅜
K	1	Back	2 9	2 1⅜	⅜
L	1	Door	1 7¾	10⅝	¼
M	1	Ditto	1 1¼	10⅝	¼
N	1	Ditto	1 7½	1 0¼	¼
O	1	Ditto	1 1½	1 0½	¼
P	2	Corbels	2½	1⅞	¼
Q	1	For facings	3 6	9	¼
R	1	Chimney	4	4	2¾
S	2	For roof	3 0	1 5½	⅜
T	1	Step	8½	2	1¼

All given sizes are strictly net, excepting item Q. The latter in length and width is full for splitting and cleaning up, but the thickness given is net. Select good, clean birch or pine plywood for items C, F to O inclusive and S. Whitewood or pine may be used elsewhere. (234)

The Christmas "Woodworker."—Among features for the December number are designs for a new Kitchen Cabinet and (with Christmas specially in view) a Model Farm. In addition to these we have designs in readiness for Radio and Gramophone Cabinets, a Needlework Cabinet, a Sideboard, and several small articles of lighter furniture. Incidental features will be on polishing, workshop hints, etc., and we have also ready some novelties which have been specially designed for Christmas. Here, too, we may mention that, for the new volume (beginning in January), we have in preparation a series of practical articles which will cover the whole art of veneering. With the December number will be included the index for the present volume. Will readers kindly send us the name and address of any interested friend to whom we might post a specimen copy ?

TOY FARMYARD FOR CHRISTMAS

FIG. 1.—A TOY FARMYARD CAN BE MADE TO ANY SCALE AND FURNISHED WITH MODELS OF FARMHOUSE, OUTBUILDINGS, FENCING AND FITTINGS AS REQUIRED.

OF late years the place of the leaden soldier has been largely taken by the more peaceable farmyard character, and some really excellent little models of farmers, farm hands, milkmaids, dogs, cattle, horsemen, and so on are now available. This in turn has given rise to a demand for suitable model farmyard buildings—barns, cowsheds, farmhouses, etc. They can be obtained cast in lead, but they are necessarily rather expensive, and no better than (and certainly not so strong as) models made in wood.

The success of a complete set of models is dependent chiefly upon the ingenuity of the worker : there are so many scraps of material and various odds and ends that can be used, things which ordinarily would find their way to the dustbin. These, and a few tins of paint and stain, and possibly one or two special materials such as miniature brick and tile paper, are really all that are needed to make an excellent model which will delight the youngsters.

Stand.—As a rule there is no need to start with fixed ideas as to what is to be made. Often enough real farmyards have grown gradually at odd times, so that a lack of regularity lends realism. One good plan is to start with a main baseboard on which the models can be moved about in any position the youngster fancies. This can suitably be of thick plywood, say, $\frac{1}{2}$ in. stuff, and could be of any size from 2 ft. square upwards. The sharp edges should be taken off with glasspaper, and one side painted in green and brown to represent grass and pathways. The reverse side can be treated similarly, but have a different layout, giving an alternative. Oil paint is the most suitable to use as it wears well.

Material.—The accompanying illustrations give suggestions for the various buildings. There is no need to follow them closely. In fact, the reader will probably prefer to use his own ideas in accordance with the scraps he has by him. One of the most valuable materials is plywood as it is much stronger than ordinary wood. Cardboard, too, can be used for large surfaces, whilst for smaller parts, stripwood is handy. Commercial stripwood, however, is not so suitable as wood which is sawn by

hand, because its surfaces are usually too regular. A certain amount of roughness, providing it is not liable to cause splinters, is an advantage.

In all cases the use of glue as well as nails is an advantage. For such parts as the gabled ends of the barn or the farmhouse (Figs. 2 and 3) where both are the same shape, two pieces of ply can be nailed together temporarily, and separated after being cut out. In the case of the farmhouse, Fig. 2, the two sides can be prepared in this way, and, after separating, one of them can be cut in two, the smaller piece acting as the wall of the small wing.

If the reader has the time and patience, he can add a touch of realism by actually fretting out the windows, and backing them with cellophane. A simpler alternative is to paint them in. Roof windows can be made from short lengths of triangular moulding. Doors should certainly be cut out as it appeals to a child to be able to open a door. Short strips of tape glued on forms an excellent means of hingeing.

Buildings such as barns are generally of timber, and the simplest way of imitating them is to paint in a main ground work, and paint in the lines of the boarding afterwards. A strip of imitation brick paper at the bottom looks well. The sides of the farmhouse could be covered with stone paper, or it could have a coat of white paint and a few pieces of stained stripwood nailed on to give a timbered effect. An excellent imitation of a thatched roof can be given by glueing on pieces of coconut fibre.

The latter is also useful for making hay ricks. That suggested in Fig. 4 is made from two discs of $\frac{3}{16}$ in. wood, one smaller than the other, with thin plywood ($\frac{1}{32}$ in.) fixed around the edges. The top, also of $\frac{1}{32}$ in. plywood, is cut out as indicated. A circle is drawn in with compasses, and a segment cut from it. An overlap is allowed so that it can be glued up easily.

Pond.—An addition that always pleases a child is a pond. This can either be fitted to the main base, or it can be made up separately. A piece of stout glass, preferably of the kind with a wavy surface can be fixed with glue to a piece of plywood. Around the edges some plaster of paris is modelled, partly to hide and protect

TOY FARMYARD—DETAILS OF MODELS

the edges of the glass, and partly to give a natural earth-like appearance. The plaster can be carried over the glass in places so that the pond is of irregular shape. The plaster is painted afterwards. Pieces of fibre matting glued here and there make splendid water rushes. Odd pieces of sponge with a few dabs of paint come in for bushes.

Fencing, etc.—A fair amount of fencing is needed,

and it is as well to adopt some standard method to enable it to be made quickly and easily. As it is an advantage to be able to move it about, some method of making it able to stand by itself should be used. Fig. 6 shows how this can be done. A quick method of making the strips is to use the cutting gauge. Materials for the rustic bridge too can be made in this way.

(*Continued on page* 17).

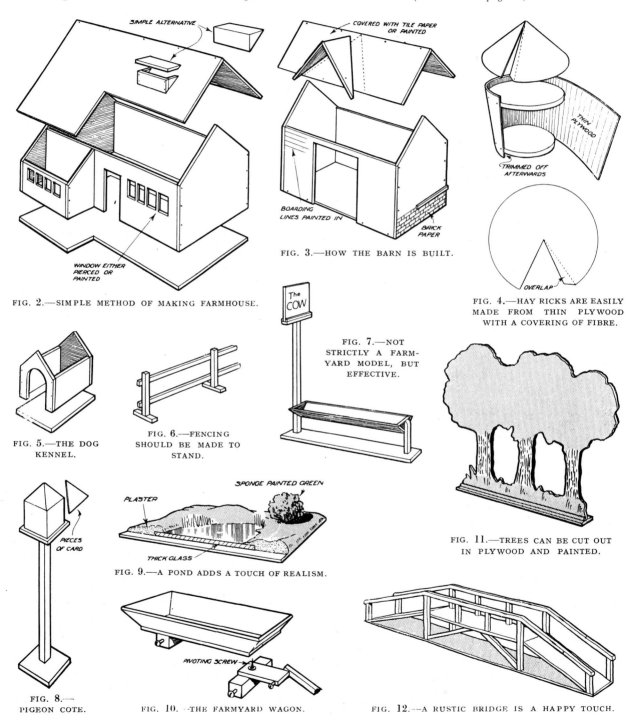

FIG. 2.—SIMPLE METHOD OF MAKING FARMHOUSE.

FIG. 3.—HOW THE BARN IS BUILT.

FIG. 4.—HAY RICKS ARE EASILY MADE FROM THIN PLYWOOD WITH A COVERING OF FIBRE.

FIG. 5.—THE DOG KENNEL.

FIG. 6.—FENCING SHOULD BE MADE TO STAND.

FIG. 7.—NOT STRICTLY A FARM-YARD MODEL, BUT EFFECTIVE.

FIG. 11.—TREES CAN BE CUT OUT IN PLYWOOD AND PAINTED.

FIG. 8.—PIGEON COTE.

FIG. 9.—A POND ADDS A TOUCH OF REALISM.

FIG. 10.—THE FARMYARD WAGON.

FIG. 12.—A RUSTIC BRIDGE IS A HAPPY TOUCH.

ARTISTIC CRAFTSMANSHIP IN GERMANY

THE last thirty years in Germany have seen a great revival of artistic handicraft. This has led to an increased realisation of the value of craft work, and demonstrated that it will continue to exist despite all industrial mass production. At the present day there are something like eight million Germans, or about one in every eight, who earn their living by handwork.

A summer exhibition was organised by the Commission for Folk Art in the Wertheim House in Berlin, under the name " Volkskunst, Hausfleiss und Handwerk," bringing together a great many articles produced by artistic craftsmanship, and above all the products of old peasant art, which has maintained itself much better than had been generally supposed. One finds large sections of the country which furnish their art products not merely to Germany but also for the world market. Here old traditions of artistic handicraft have been handed down from one generation to another and even strengthened.

The distribution of these sections and their products is still similar to that which existed in the Middle Ages. The best products of hand weaving still come from the old weavers' districts on the North Sea and in the Baltic Sea districts as far eastward as East Prussia. Sonneberg in Thuringia, the heart of Germany, is still the world-famed city of toys and dolls. The Christmas toys for millions of children of all races and lands are made in the villages around Sonneberg, and glass ornaments for the Christmas trees of the whole world come from the district of Lauscha, which is not far away. Here the men, women and children work all their lives chiefly for one holiday in the year. Artistic glass-blowing is a home industry which has been carried on here for centuries.

The subjects are the same that have been used for many hundreds of years—trees, hunters, stags and dogs, birds and flowers. The objects produced are dainty, almost as light as bubbles, of no intrinsic value, but highly prized for their artistry. They have recently become popular in America as table decorations. A new Lauscha product is spun glass tapestry to take the place of wallpaper. It is but little dearer than wallpaper, and much more beautiful with its changeable shimmering hues.

The Thuringian Forest and the Franconian forest district along the Main have been the home of woodworking from ancient times. Here are made the beautiful wooden tankards—without a nail—from which the students of the University of Jena drink the famous Lichtenhain beer. Other products of these districts are carved or turned cake forms, butter forms, kitchen utensils, boxes, etc. On the Main, especially in the district around Lichtenfels, one finds villages where all the inhabitants weave baskets and furniture from willow. Artistic woodwork is found also in other wooded districts of Germany. From the Erzgebirge, on the border between Germany and Czechoslovakia, come wonderful chests of toys,

villages with people, animals and trees, brightly coloured angels and candlesticks. Here is also the home of bobbin-lace, now coming into fashion again.

One famous region of folk art known throughout the world is, of course, Oberammergau. Religious wood-carving is here intimately connected with religious folk plays, so that the Oberammergauers are artists in a double sense. The new carvings from the workshops of Georg Lang's heirs are beautiful products of an old art and a new spirit. The art of woodcarving has also been preserved in Berchtesgaden, on the Königssee.

In older days the potter, like the weaver, was an important handicraftsman in every village and city. The industrial mass production of enamel and aluminium vessels has made serious inroads on hand pottery, but peasant pottery still exists. Here and there it is possible to find potters who bake an ovenful of wares two or three times a year for the surrounding villages and airs. This peasant pottery has survived especially well in Hessia. Near Marburg or Cassel one can make interesting visits to village potters, particularly in the so-called " Schwalm," where the bright old folk costumes are still worn.

BEAUTIFUL WOODEN TANKARDS MADE WITHOUT A NAIL.

In Munich charming figures are still made of wax ; in the Luneburger Heath, the paradise of bee-keepers, fragrant candles are made of beeswax ; and in Erbach in the Odenwald (Oden's Forest) a whole city is busy carving tiny ivory roses.

The persistence of these and many other regions of artistic craftsmanship in Germany is an encouraging indication of an enduring love for traditions and a craving for the beautiful. (309)

TOY FARMYARD *(Continued from page 16)*

Wagons and carts are easily made. The wheels can be formed by cutting off thin strips from various sizes of dowel rod, or they can be fretted out from plywood. Fig. 10 shows a simple way of arranging the front wheels to pivot.

Various things can be used to increase the boy's interest in the model. For instance, short lengths of dowel painted brown make excellent logs to be loaded into the cart ; a box of sawdust makes splendid meal food ; fibre is just the thing for hay. The provision of a few extras of this kind give the child something actually to play with, apart from the arranging of the models.

Farmyard animals can be bought at any toy store. The larger type may be costly, but these are not wanted for a model—as a rule, indeed, they are too big. The small painted wood animals are inexpensive, whilst at Messrs. Woolworth's stores an excellent type of more realistic animal can be purchased at a very low figure. On the other hand, those who use the fretsaw may cut out the animals in stout plywood. Published designs are available, but frequently the patterns may be taken from a child's picture book. (331

GARDEN ARM CHAIR
WITH ADJUSTABLE SEAT AND RECLINING BACK

FIG. 1.—THE IDEAL GARDEN ARM CHAIR, WHICH GIVES YOU AN ADJUSTABLE SEAT AND A RECLINING BACK. (SEE FIGS. 2 TO 9 ON NEXT PAGE).

A COMFORTABLE garden seat of new and improved pattern, light in weight and appearance, having an adjustable seat and reclining back, is sketched at Fig. 1. The construction is both simple and economical to carry out; deal finished by enamelling a bright and attractive colour is recommended, and it is chiefly used in 2½ in. by 1 in. section, which is easier to procure and work than the larger sections commonly used. No great amount of skill will be needed, for most of the parts are just screwed together, the only exception being the back, which is framed up.

The chair is shown in section at Fig. 2, and a sketch of the frame is given at Fig. 3. The two sides (Fig. 4) are each made with two legs 2 ft. long, a top rail 2 ft. long, and a bottom rail 2 ft. 7½ ins. long. The rails are screwed outside the legs, and a brace 2 ft. 10 ins. long is screwed outside the rails, a small filling block being placed between the back leg and brace. Three cross-framing rails are used to join the sides, two 1 ft. 11 ins. long are half-lapped and screwed to the front legs, and one 2 ft. 3 ins. long is half-lapped and screwed to the braces. It should be noticed that the top edge of the top cross rail which is fixed to the legs requires to be rounded over as shown in the detail at Fig. 2. The frame is completed by preparing two front facing pieces (Fig. 5) 2 ft. long by 4½ ins. wide, and nailing them to the edges of the front legs level on the inside; and two elbows (Fig. 6) 2 ft. 6 ins. long by 4½ ins. wide, and nailing these to the top rails level with the inside edges of the legs.

NEXT month we are publishing a splendid model design of Nelson's famous flagship, the "Victory." It will have a hull length of 19 ins., a total over all length of 28 ins. and on stand reaches a height of 20 ins. The detail has been simplified, so that even a novice can undertake this fascinating piece of work. H.M.S. "Victory," on which Nelson fought the Battle of Trafalgar and on which he died, was the pride of the Navy. Of 2,162 tons, she has a gun deck of 186 feet, her broadside discharge of shot was 1,160 pounds and at Trafalgar she carried 104 cannon. Be sure you order your June number well in advance, so as not to miss this fine model.

MODEL OF
H.M.S. "VICTORY."

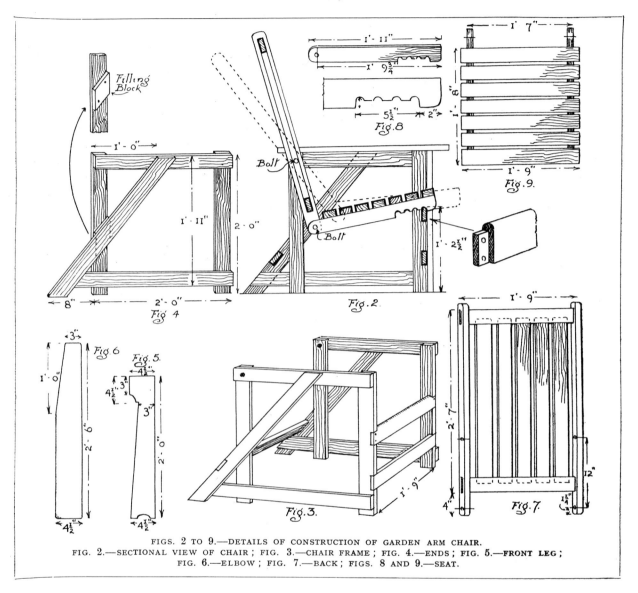

FIGS. 2 TO 9.—DETAILS OF CONSTRUCTION OF GARDEN ARM CHAIR.
FIG. 2.—SECTIONAL VIEW OF CHAIR ; FIG. 3.—CHAIR FRAME ; FIG. 4.—ENDS ; FIG. 5.—FRONT LEG ;
FIG. 6.—ELBOW ; FIG. 7.—BACK ; FIGS. 8 AND 9.—SEAT.

The back (Fig. 7) is framed with two stiles 3 ft. long, two cross rails 1 ft. 9 ins. long, and five back rails 2 ft. 4 ins. long, the cross rails being tenoned into the stiles, and the back rails into the cross rails.

The seat (Figs. 8 and 9) is made with two bearers 1 ft. 11 ins. long, preferably of hardwood such as ash or birch, having a series of four notches cut in the bottom edge according to the details shown. Seven battens 1 ft. 9 ins. long are screwed above the bearers, the latter being spaced 1 ft. 7 ins. wide.

The seat and back are fixed to the frame with $\frac{5}{16}$ bolts, two being fitted through the top back corners of the frame and the sides of the back, and two through the bottom ends of the back and the back ends of the seat, thin iron washers being placed in these positions

to give a slight clearance. The seat and back are adjusted by moving the seat bearers on the front top cross rail of the frame. (516)

GESSO

ONE or two readers have recently inquired how to make gesso, used by picture framers for repairs to the ornamental corners of pictures and for filling up small defects and nail-holes in composition picture framing. Take ten tablespoonfuls of dry whiting and mix it to a thick cream with lukewarm water. Mix into this creamy paste six tablespoonfuls of ready-made liquid glue. Into a separate dish mix one tablespoonful of best clear copal varnish with four tablespoonfuls of linseed oil. Stir the second mixture into the first and then boil them, glue-kettle fashion, for twelve minutes.

This mixture may be applied cold and will keep fairly soft and pliable if well sealed up. This gesso ornamentation may be stained with wood dye, paint which is thinned with turpentine, or may be bronzed or gilded where necessary. Another good recipe is six tablespoonfuls of ready-made liquid glue, three teaspoonfuls of linseed oil and three teaspoonfuls of best oil varnish (not spirit varnish). Some workers add a teaspoonful of glycerine to the latter mixture to prevent it from drying too rapidly and cracking. (520)

———

WOOD PESTS.—Among special articles ready for next month is one dealing with timber pests—dry rot, the common furniture beetle and the "death watch" beetle.

WOOD BLOCK PUZZLES

READERS are familiar with the many variations of the six-piece block puzzles which have appeared in these pages during the last twenty-five years, but few will have attempted to construct a twelve-block or a sixteen-block puzzle. Take a glance at Fig. 1, where we give a sketch of a completed twelve-block puzzle and then set about making it as follows.

Plane up very accurately a piece of hardwood (such as birch, beech, or American black walnut) so that it measures on its ends ½ in. by ½ in. The length of the rough wood required should be about 26 ins. so as to allow for cutting and trimming-off the ends after they are severed.

Take a piece (2) and stand it up with the two recesses facing you as at Fig. 3. Now take up pieces (4) and (5) and, placing them back to back, fit them into the upper half-inch recess. on piece (2), with piece (5) at the top. Take up another piece (4) and another piece (5) and, placing them back to back, fill up the lower half inch cut of piece (2), this time with piece (5) at the bottom.

Take up a second piece (2) and place this over the already assembled pieces in such a way that the two pieces (2) grip and hold (5), (4), (4) and 5. Fig. 2 shows this assembly.

Now push the two blocks (4) to the left hand, sufficiently to admit another piece (4) and another piece (5) which are

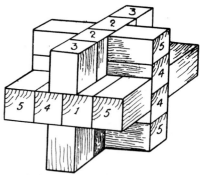

FIG. 1.—THE TWELVE-BLOCK PUZZLE.

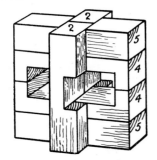

FIG. 2.—BEGINNING TO ASSEMBLE.

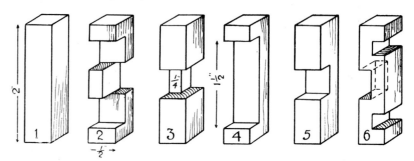

FIG. 3.—THE SIX PIECES SHOWN SEPARATELY. THESE ARE ALL 2 INS. BY ½ IN. BY ½ IN., THE CUTS BEING IN MULTIPLES OF ¼ IN.

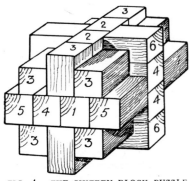

FIG. 4.—THE SIXTEEN BLOCK PUZZLE.

After the planing is completed set out and make : one block like No. 1 ; two blocks like No. 2 ; two blocks like No. 3 ; three blocks like No. 4 ; and four blocks like No. 5. The shapes of these blocks are shown at Fig. 3, and it will be noticed that all the cuts are multiples of a quarter of an inch. The blocks should be set out with a fine penknife blade and a small try square, after which they should be gauged to the required thicknesses with a marking gauge and then sawn and pared out with a bevelled edged chisel to their respective shapes.

After the twelve blocks are completed set to work to assemble them as follows :

placed in the slot back to back with a (5) piece on the outside. Push the two (4)'s back to their original position and fix two (3)'s into the slots that will be observed for them, placing one piece on each side of a vertical (2) block. This leaves an opening, ¼ in. by ½ in., which can be seen in the partly assembled puzzle at Fig. 2.

The remaining piece (5) is inserted into this opening with the ½ in. cut facing to the right hand. Immediately this cut engages the ends of (4) (4) at the right hand, the remaining opening is formed for the ½ in. square key block (1), and when this is pushed into position the twelve-piece puzzle is completed and will appear as at Fig. 1.

To make the sixteen block puzzle (Fig. 4) prepare the following pieces : One block No. 1 ; two blocks No. 2 ; six blocks No. 3 ; three blocks No. 4 ; two blocks No. 5 ; and two blocks No. 6. The puzzle is fitted together in a somewhat similar manner to the twelve-block one, but its assembly is rather more difficult. Try it. We are not giving detailed sketches because this would detract from the charm of the puzzle. A strip of wood which measures 34 ins. by ½ in. by ½ in., will give ample allowance for cutting and trimming off the ends of the blocks. (86)

Furniture Reviver.—Here is a tried and trusty recipe which may be safely used by the inexperienced polisher : 3 oz. English beeswax, 1 oz. white soap, 1 oz. Castile soap, 1 pint turpentine, 1 pint boiling water. Shred the wax and cover it with the turpentine, and when this emulsion has softened add the other ingredients. Lastly add the water *very* slowly, beating the mixture with a wooden spoon.

If the furniture is dirty it should be washed with luke-warm water and a spot of soap so as to remove all the old furniture cream, dirt and dust. Make a pad of soft rag and apply a little of the cream to its surface. Rub the cream well into the surface and then wipe off and polish with a soft duster. Do not use a furniture cream on carvings because a much better method is to take a penny bristle nail brush of the oblong pattern and rub the bristles of this brush on to a piece of beeswax ; then apply the brush and vigorously rub it over the carved portions. .

Another good reviver is made by mixing 4 ozs. of malt vinegar, a teaspoonful of sulphuric acid, 2 ozs of butter of antimony (this is a liquid), and 2 ozs of medicinal paraffin oil. Mix these ingredients in the order given and then add as much vienna chalk as will stand on a shilling. (80)

C

MAKING A TABLE LOOM

FULL DIRECTIONS FOR THE CONSTRUCTION OF THIS USEFUL TYPE OF HAND-WEAVING LOOM

THE table loom is a thing of recent invention. It has been developed in its present form through the need of a loom which will produce the same type of material as the foot-power loom, but which will take up less space and be cheaper. For the amateur and the handicraft class it will do all that is required of a loom. The cycle of operations is carried out with the hands in a definite order, instead of being shared between hands and feet, which is often confusing to the beginner.

Of course, an obvious drawback is the extra time taken up in doing with the hands that which the feet could be doing while the hands are also engaged ; but, where space, cost and convenience are of more importance than time (usually the case with the amateur) the table loom is to be preferred. There is also the consideration that if it is intended only to make scarves, cushion squares and similar things of narrow width, each probably with a variation of colour and pattern, a small compact loom is just as serviceable as a large treadle loom capable of weaving much wider than will ever be required.

Features.—There are two points in which this loom differs from the usual table loom, and which the designer has found of some use. The warp roller is large in diameter, suspended above the warp level, and there is a spring loaded roller which serves as a guide for the warp.

The large warp roller was adopted because, for a given length of warp, there are fewer layers on the roller than with a roller of smaller diameter, thus avoiding the necessity for a lot of careful packing with sticks or heavy paper to prevent the warp from becoming soft and cushion-like. The roller was suspended over the warp level because, with the tensioning system advocated, the extra height is useful. Reference to the diagram (Fig. 5) of the working parts will make this system clear. The heavy weight box with its backward pull on the roller keeps the warp always at an even tension, and allows elasticity. It has the further advantage that, when winding off the woven cloth every inch or so, it is only necessary to turn the cloth roller the required amount and go on weaving. Once in every foot the weights are dropped again merely by lifting the small weights suspended over the front of the roller, which releases the friction on the brake rope.

For those who prefer the simple ratchet, and perhaps a smaller diameter roller, it will be necessary to provide enclosed bearings for the roller spindle, instead of the drop-in type shown. It is admitted that the ratchet does not make the loom heavy, but it makes it difficult to keep an even warp tension. The problem cannot be solved by having ratchets with equal numbers of teeth on each roller, because, as the warp roller becomes thinner with unwinding, the cloth roller becomes thicker.

> *For the construction of a foot-power Loom, 3 ft. wide over front, by 5 ft. 1 in. high, see the January number of this year.*

The spring-loaded guide roller has been introduced to lighten the strain on the warp when the shed is opened. With such a short distance between guide roller and breast beam the strain of lifting and depressing can easily break the threads, but if the distance can be lessened as the shed is opened the strain is not so great. The spring loading can be dispensed with if the guide roller is fastened to the back uprights so that it will revolve very freely, and the warp roller bearings and spindle are of metal and well greased, so that the shedding strain is taken up, *via* the guide roller, by the weighting system which will allow the warp roller to rock back and forth with the shedding.

In Constructing the Loom, make the two sides first, taking care to make them right and left hand (See Fig. 4). The front upright is halved right across the horizontal member, the middle upright only half across, and the back upright screwed on the outside. The oblique side member is halved to the outside of the front, screwed across the middle, and let into the inside of the back upright. The inside of this member has to be cut away at the back upright to accommodate the end of the warp roller, as indicated in Fig. 1. Note that the right hand middle upright is shorter than the left-hand, to allow room for the rocking levers which lift the heddles. All this framing is made from 2 ins. by 1 in. stuff, planed to $1\frac{7}{8}$ ins. by $\frac{7}{8}$ in. This dimension has been allowed for in the drawings. All the square section stuff is $\frac{7}{8}$in. first quality straight deal, without knots.

Cramp the two side frames together so that each pair of members coincides, and mark off and drill the $\frac{3}{8}$ in. holes for the cloth roller, batten and the rod which carries the guide roller and the six side-levers at the back of the loom. Drill also the $\frac{7}{8}$ in. holes for the warp roller bearings, and cut down to them with the tenon saw. Separate, then, make and fix the breast beam and the crossed struts at the back, which are halved to the uprights. The ends of the breast beam are dowelled to the inside of the uprights ; then a screw is put through from the front so that it goes through the dowels. The top rails which support the rocking levers are screwed to the left-hand middle upright, and supported on the right by square pieces bridle jointed to them and screwed to the uprights, back and front. Before fixing, drill a $\frac{5}{32}$ in. hole in each to take the spindle upon which the rocking levers are fulcrumed.

The heddles are operated by six side-levers which work in the frame shown on the right side of the loom in the drawings. All the levers are not shown, to avoid confusion (see Fig. 5), but a glance at the drawings will make the principle clear. The lever frame is made from square stuff carefully jointed together. The lower rail of it is halved into the lower horizontal rail of the side framing and mortised into the outer upright. The top rail has a piece of 2 ins. by 1 in. as stiffening, and the oblique side member is notched to take its inner end. Five $\frac{1}{4}$ in. dowels are inserted after six cuphooks of suitable size have been screwed into the lower rail near the front edge. This frame must be rigid, and is firmly glued and screwed to the loom, being further braced by the metal rod upon which the batten swings.

Guide Roller.—The spring-loaded guide roller (Fig. 8) is fitted next. The springs are fairly stiff and can be of any convenient length from 3 ins. to 5 ins. Most ironmongers stock a selection. The stops are short lengths of 1 in. round stuff, bored $\frac{1}{4}$ in. to slip over the dowel, and are fastened in place by glue and a light pin driven right through. The front ends of the dowel are lodged $\frac{1}{2}$ in. deep in $\frac{3}{8}$ in. holes in the back of the middle uprights, and the other ends pass through holes close to the ends of the cross member of the roller support.

The tension should not be adjusted till the loom has been set up. Then, when the tension of the work is right, the springs should be adjusted so that the roller moves forward about $\frac{1}{4}$ in. when the shed is open. In Fig. 4 the roller is shown in about the position it would occupy when the loom is set up and under tension. With the tension off, or with no

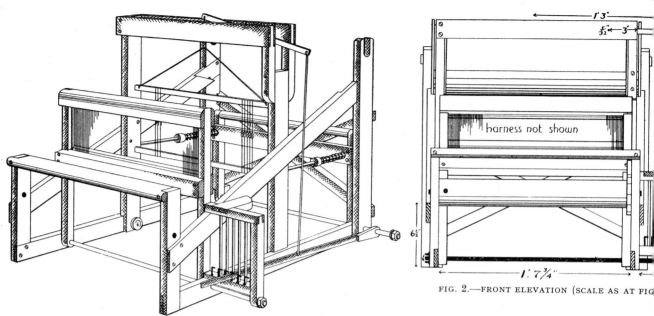

FIG. 1.—GENERAL VIEW OF LOOM. FOR CLEARNESS, THE ROLLERS ARE OMITTED, AND ONLY ONE HARNESS IS SHOWN.

FIG. 2.—FRONT ELEVATION (SCALE AS AT FIG

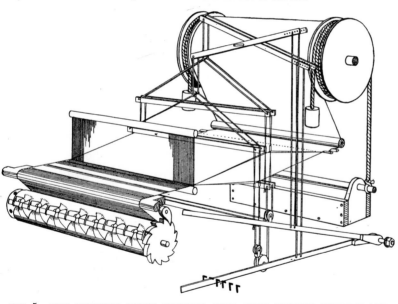

FIG. 5.—THE WORKING PARTS, SHOWING SHED OPEN, TENSION WEIGHTS AND METHOD OF ATTACHMENT OF WARP ENDS TO CLOTH ROLLER. FOR CLEARNESS, ONLY TWO SIDE LEVERS ARE SHOWN.

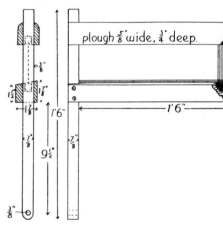

FIG. 6.—DETAIL OF BATTEN AND RE

FIG. 7—DETAIL OF THE HEDDLE B AND METHOD OF USE.

warp on the loom at all, it would be firmly pressed against the cross-stays at the back of the loom.

The batten (Fig. 6) should be made next, and fixed in position. Care must be taken to make it square, with the supports (or swords) dead parallel. The lower member, the shuttle race, must have its top carefully planed and the edges sand-papered. The angle of the top has been designed so that, when the batten is swung back and the threads

opened in the shed, the lower " leaf " of the shed will just rest on this inclined surface, and the shuttle will actually rest on the wood beneath the threads on its passage across, so that it is not likely to break through before it emerges at the other side. In practice, the loom must be adjusted till this is so. The swords are glued and screwed into the shuttle race, but the cap is just a firm fit, so that the reed, which fits in the grooves, can be taken out and another one put in if

necessary.

Front Roller.—The front or cloth roller is planed or turned up from a piece of 3 ins. square stuff. If it is planed, it should be dead parallel throughout its length—perfect roundness does not matter so much. Carefully mark and drill the holes in the ends for the spindles, 4 in. lengths of $\frac{3}{8}$ in. steel rod. The ratchet is cut from $\frac{3}{8}$ in. or $\frac{1}{2}$ in. plywood, slipped over the spindle, and screwed with long screws to the end of the roller.

22

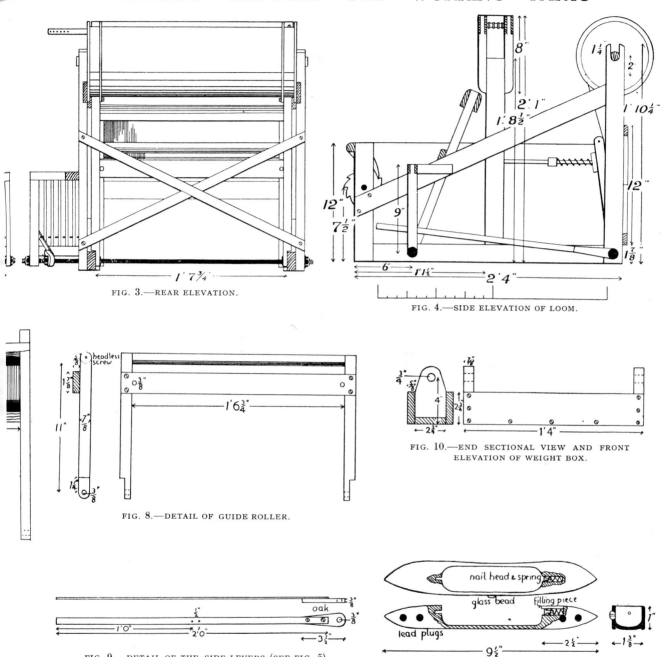

FIG. 3.—REAR ELEVATION.

FIG. 4.—SIDE ELEVATION OF LOOM.

FIG. 8.—DETAIL OF GUIDE ROLLER.

FIG. 10.—END SECTIONAL VIEW AND FRONT
ELEVATION OF WEIGHT BOX.

FIG. 9.—DETAIL OF THE SIDE LEVERS (SEE FIG. 5).
SIX OF THESE LEVERS ARE REQUIRED.

FIG. 11.—ENLARGED DETAIL OF SHUTTLE.

The pawl is a piece of hard oak cut to suitable shape, and is a loose fit on a stout round headed screw : no spring is necessary, as its own weight will cause it to engage the ratchet teeth. Tacked and glued to the roller is a length of stiff calico, 18 ins. wide and 15 ins. long ; the outer end is hemmed and has loops of stout tape attached to it, through which is passed a stick or metal strip.

The ends of the warp, after having been brought through the reed, are tied in groups round this stick, which will be held just in front of the breast beam. The piece of calico thus economises in warp, which would otherwise be wasted if it were taken over the breast beam and down to the roller before it were fastened. The sketch of the working parts of the loom (Fig. 5) shows the stick with the warp ends tied round it, after the calico has been wound back on to the roller. At the left hand end of the roller, bore four ⅜ in. holes equidistantly spaced around, with their centres 1in. in from the end, and make them 1¼ ins. deep. A short rod inserted into these holes will facilitate turning on the woven cloth.

In the original loom, the large warp roller was made from a thick cardboard cloth bale, about 7 ins. diameter, and ½ in. thick. Some doubts were entertained about this at first, but finally it was given several coats of size until the cardboard would soak up no more, then it was veneered with oak. The veneer

23

THE TABLE TYPE OF HAND-WEAVING LOOM

thickness was $\frac{1}{16}$ in., and the finished roller, glass-papered and varnished, looked like a solid beam of oak. The roller and veneer were well warmed, both given a coat of hot thin glue, and then the veneer was wrapped round with the application of a cloth dipped in hot water, working towards the joint and the ends, and forcing out as much glue as possible. It was then tied round firmly with thick good string, starting from one end and making the windings one inch apart. The string, secured at the other end, was then well wetted with hot water, and the job left for two days, when the string was unwound and the roller cleaned up. The ends were plugged with discs of $\frac{5}{8}$ in. wood, glued in and drilled to take the $\frac{7}{8}$ in. rod which acts as spindle.

Finally, fretcut plywood rings were slipped over the ends and glued and pinned in place. Thin plywood discs were screwed to the plugging discs on the ends, and a very robust roller was the result. A solid roller would be much too heavy for a light loom this size. A hollow one could be built up by coopering. But another alternative is to make a skeleton roller with solid disc ends, and a central supporting disc, the discs being joined by $\frac{3}{8}$ in. by $1\frac{1}{8}$ ins. straight stuff, fitting into notches in the discs. However the roller is made, it should have the same arrangement of calico, tapes, and sticks as the front roller, so that the tail end of the warp can be drawn forward and as much of it used as possible.

The Harness building is the last job. There will be required :—

8 pieces $\frac{1}{2}$ in. by $\frac{1}{8}$ in. mild steel $18\frac{1}{2}$ ins. long for heddles.

4 pieces $\frac{1}{2}$ in. by $\frac{1}{8}$ in. mild steel 15 ins. long for rocking levers.

6 pieces $\frac{1}{2}$ in. by $\frac{1}{8}$ in. mild steel 24 ins. long for side levers.

With a $\frac{5}{32}$ in. twist drill bore holes in the eight heddle pieces, $\frac{1}{4}$ in. from each end, in the rocking lever pieces, one in the centre and six at one end, in a row at $\frac{3}{8}$ in. centres, and in the side lever pieces, two in the centre and two at one end.

Suspend the rocking lever pieces in the top cross rails, by means of a short meccano rod, and with a meccano spacing washer between each. Make the wooden ends for the side levers and thread the levers on the metal rod, keeping them there with a washer and nut. The front ends of the levers pass through the frame which holds the dowels and cuphooks, so that the innermost lever passes between the loom and the first dowel, and the others in order fill the remaining spaces. The cuphooks should be so arranged that the end of the lever will pass down between the dowel and the end of the hook, and slide nicely under the hook.

The heddles, or leashes, are now placed on the eight rods, an equal number on each, which should not be less than one quarter of the number of threads in the whole width of the warp. For example, if it is desired to make a cloth 18 ins. wide, with twenty threads or ends per inch, there will be 360 threads and therefore 90 heddles on each harness or pair of rods.

Now make from wire $\frac{1}{16}$ in. thick the links by which the harnesses are suspended from the ends of the rocking levers. A little care is necessary here, but once one set is made, the others can be made from it. It is desirable that, when the rocking levers are horizontal, the harnesses should hang so that the eyes of the heddles are in a line with the top of the breast beam and the bottom of the guide roller : a piece of cord stretched across at each side will establish this. Reference to Figs. 1 and 5 will show the arrangement of the compensating pulleys which, when two harnesses are lifted, will depress the remaining two. A pulley is screwed to the bottom of each middle upright, with a piece of packing behind it ; a small clothes line pulley would do. Four other pulleys are required. These could be $\frac{1}{2}$ in. meccano type, with a piece of brass bent round to make the bracket. The whole thing is rigged up with good cord.

Rocking Levers.—The outer ends of the rocking levers are now tied to the side levers, with stout cord, in the following order :—

Side lever	1	to rocking levers			1.3
,,	,, 2	,,	,,	,,	2.4
,,	,, 3	,,	,,	,,	1.2
,,	,, 4	,,	,,	,,	2.3
,,	,, 5	,,	,,	,,	3.4
,,	,, 6	,,	,,	,,	4.1

The rocking levers are numbered from the front, and the side levers from the outside. The two outer levers will weave plain, or " tabby " cloth, the other four, taken in different orders, will weave various types of twill. The length of the connecting cord can be obtained by locking one side lever under a hook, and pulling down the two rocking levers, so that the bottom of the eyes of the heddles in the lifted harnesses are just visible below the top rods of the depressed harnesses. When released, the side lever should be about half-way up the side of the dowel.

In actual weaving, a lever is hooked down, the batten pushed back, the shuttle thrown through the shed and caught, the weft thread beaten up with the batten, and the lever released by a sideways push with the thumb. If preferred, the levers could be given wooden handles, or lengthened, so that they project beyond the front of the loom.

Heddles are made in the heddle board, illustrated (Fig. 7), using good strong linen thread, tied in loops round the nails as shown, and cut off at the point end of the board. Leave about an inch of end and, when placing the heddles on the rods, have these ends at the top. It does not look very tidy, but it is more convenient if a knot comes loose : a reef knot is not expected to become loose, but it sometimes happens. Wear on the heddles can be prevented by enamelling or cellulosing the metal rods to give them a hard, smooth surface.

Shuttles (Fig. 11) can be an expensive item to the weaver, but with care they can be made from a good close grained wood. Boxwood is preferable, but hard beech or mahogany would do. The sketch of a shuttle is mainly suggestive, since opinions differ as to the best type. The holes for the bobbin wire can be burnt in with a hot wire if difficulty is experienced in drilling them (47)

BUREAU (*Continued from page 227*).

Wide hinges let equally into the fall and the writing top are used to pivot it.

The drawers call for no special mention. Dovetailing is easily the best construction. The fronts are veneered, but even so it is advisable to use lap-dovetails at the front, as the veneer would not hold well over the end grain of the dovetails. A walnut slip at the top of the fronts is advisable so that there is a neat finish when the drawers are opened.

Fig. 6 gives details of the stationery nest. A simple method of butting the ends to the top and bottom with the front corners mitred is shown. A rather stronger method is to dovetail them. The partitions are V-grooved in. It slides in as a whole from the back and is screwed. Leave the final fixing until after polishing.

Cutting List—

		Long. ft. ins.	Wide. ins.	Thick. ins.
2 Ends	.	1 $7\frac{1}{4}$	$14\frac{1}{4}$	$\frac{5}{8}$
1 Top	.	1 $8\frac{1}{4}$	$6\frac{3}{4}$	$\frac{5}{8}$
1 Bottom	.	1 8	14	$\frac{5}{8}$
1 Writing top	.	1 8	$11\frac{1}{2}$	$\frac{1}{2}$
1 Top rail	.	1 8	4	$\frac{5}{8}$
1 Drawer rail	.	1 8	$2\frac{1}{4}$	$\frac{5}{8}$
2 Bottom rails	.	1 8	$3\frac{1}{4}$	$\frac{5}{8}$
2 Runners	.	1 $0\frac{1}{2}$	$1\frac{1}{2}$	$\frac{1}{2}$
2 Kickers	.	$10\frac{1}{2}$	$1\frac{1}{4}$	$\frac{1}{2}$
1 Back	.	1 8	$17\frac{1}{2}$	$\frac{3}{16}$ ply
1 Fall	.	1 $5\frac{1}{4}$	$8\frac{3}{4}$	$\frac{1}{2}$

		Long. ft. ins.	Wide. ins.	Thick. ins.
2 Clamps	.	$8\frac{3}{4}$	$2\frac{1}{4}$	$\frac{1}{2}$
4 Cabriole legs 16 ins. high.				
Drawers—				
1 Front	.	1 7	$3\frac{1}{2}$	$\frac{3}{4}$
1 Ditto	.	1 7	$4\frac{1}{2}$	$\frac{3}{4}$
2 Sides	.	1 2	$3\frac{1}{2}$	$\frac{3}{8}$
2 Ditto	.	1 2	$4\frac{1}{2}$	$\frac{3}{8}$
1 Back	.	1 7	$3\frac{1}{4}$	$\frac{3}{8}$
1 Ditto	.	1 7	4	$\frac{3}{8}$
2 Bottoms	.	1 $6\frac{1}{4}$	14	$\frac{3}{16}$ ply
Stationery Nest—				
2 Pieces	.	1 7	$5\frac{1}{4}$	$\frac{1}{4}$
2 Ditto	.	$6\frac{1}{2}$	$5\frac{1}{4}$	$\frac{1}{4}$
4 Ditto	.	6	$5\frac{1}{4}$	$\frac{3}{16}$
3 Ditto	.	$10\frac{1}{2}$	$5\frac{1}{4}$	$\frac{3}{16}$

(73)

GARDEN WOODWORK

CHILD'S FITMENT : COMPRISING SWING, SEE-SAW AND CLIMBING LADDER

FIG. 1. A CHILD'S GARDEN FITMENT : SWING, CLIMBING LADDER, AND ADJUSTABLE SEA-SAW

IF space only a few yards square can be reserved and fitted up in the garden for the use of the children it will result in their lasting contentment while adding considerably to their health. A suitable fitting, taking but a few hours to build at the cost of as many shillings, is shown at Fig. 1. The space occupied need not be greater than about three yards by four, and the fitting comprises a swing, adjustable see-saw, and a climbing ladder. With such a choice the children are not likely to soon tire, and all helps to their physical development.

While the dimensions may be adapted to conform with any requirements, it is suggested that the swing should be 8 ft. high, but some consideration should be given to the ages of the children when deciding on the height of the climbing ladder. That shown has ten rungs with a total height of 7 ft. 6 ins., but for very small kiddies it may be advisable to omit a few at the top at first and add them as they grow older. It will be noticed that the see-saw rests on the lower rungs of the ladder, and by moving it up or down it may be adjusted to suit children of various ages. Deal could be used for all the framing, although some may prefer hardwood for the first three rungs of the ladder.

Figs. 2 and 3 show details of three uprights framed to bearers, stayed with braces, and joined by the swing headpiece and the ladder rungs. The uprights are 11 ft. long, tenoned into bearers 6 ft. long, the latter being placed on the flat. Braces are tenoned through the bearers and notched and stub-tenoned to the uprights. All joints through the bearers could be fixed with bolts, and long bolts are used to fix the braces on each side of the uprights. Full details of the joints are given in Fig. 4. It takes about an eighty-six foot run of $4\frac{1}{2}$ ins. by 3 ins. deal for the main framing.

The swing head-piece is bridle-jointed to the top ends of the uprights, and should be fixed with $\frac{5}{16}$ in. bolts to enable it to be easily removed should occasion demand. All the ladder rungs should be 3 ft. 6 ins. long, the three bottom ones could be of hardwood 3 in. wide by $1\frac{1}{4}$ in. thick, and those above of deal 2 ins. wide by 1 in. thick. Most of the rungs need only be tenoned $1\frac{1}{2}$ in. into the uprights, but one at the top and another at the bottom could be tenoned right through and pinned.

Trenches for the bearers and uprights must be prepared in the ground, the bearers being sunk to a depth of 3 ft., and the wood treated with tar, thick paint, or patent preservative. The two uprights carrying the swing should be placed in the trenches and the head-piece fitted and bolted. A plumb-line could be used for truing up as the frames are firmly embedded. The remaining ladder upright is then placed in its trench, and the rungs fitted and fixed.

The best means of attaching the swing ropes to the head-piece is with strong hooks, having spills to carry through the head-piece and nuts for fixing. It is necessary, however, to see that the hooks themselves are well formed, and that their points are turned around sufficiently to give safe attachment. Metal thimbles such as those used in ship and boat work should be provided

BIRD SHELTER AND BATHS.
FIG. 1 (A) Roof Bird Shelter.
(B) Rustic Pedestal Bird Bath.

CHILD'S GARDEN SWING AND SEE-SAW FITMENT

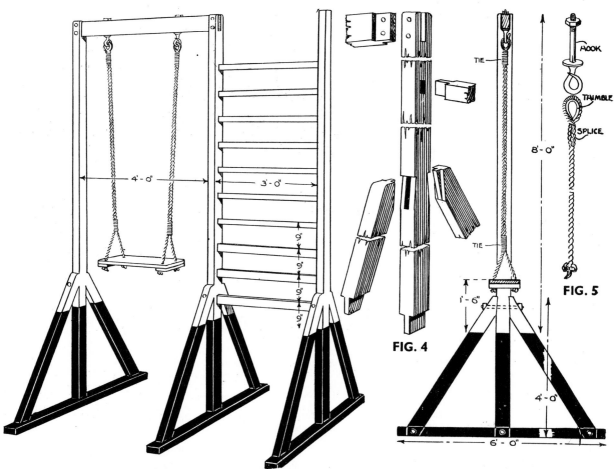

FIG. 2. SKETCH VIEW OF SWING AND LADDER.   FIG. 3. END VIEW OF UPRIGHT.
FIG. 4. DETAIL OF JOINTS.   FIG. 5. DETAIL OF SWING FIXING.

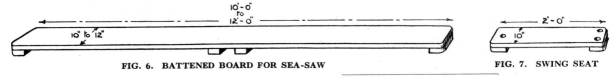

FIG. 6. BATTENED BOARD FOR SEA-SAW   FIG. 7. SWING SEAT

for fitting the swing ropes. There may be a single rope at each side, with the thimble spliced in, as shown at Fig. 5, or a double rope may be used and the thimble tied in without a splice. A rope of the latter kind could be brought down to within about 1 ft. from the seat where it is tied again, and the free ends passed through two holes in the seat board and knotted. The latter (see Fig. 7) should be 2 ft. long by 10 ins. wide, strengthened with battens at the ends.

The board of the see-saw may be from 10 ft. to 12 ft. long by from 10 ins. to 12 ins. wide. A thickness of 1¼ in. is essential, and it should be strengthened by screwing battens across the ends as shown at Fig. 6. Two battens are also screwed across the middle, with a space of about 2 ins. between, their object being to keep the board from slipping on the rungs when in use.   (506)

GARDEN BIRD SHELTER AND BATHS
(See perspective sketches (Fig. 1) on previous page).

IN addition to the interest created by the presence of the birds, fittings of this kind give a distinctive touch and are of ornamental value in the garden, while from the handy woodworker's point of view they cost next to nothing to make. Fig. 1 (previous page) shows at (A) a hanging bird rest and bath, and at (B) a pedestal bath. In both some of the parts are nailed up from rough material, but to harmonise with the garden surroundings they are finished externally by nailing on short lengths cut from the unbarked branches of trees.

THE HANGING SHELTER and bath at (A) is made with a gable roof from which the bath is suspended with four chains, full details and dimensions being shown in Figs. 2 to 5. The gable ends should be cut from ½ in. or ¾ in. stuff, and are 1 ft. 10 in. long with a rise of 6 in. Weather boards make a good roof, especially if V-grooves are cut across the face to give a representation of tiles, but ordinary boards finished by nailing pieces of rustic wood outside are also very suitable. It should be noticed that, while the roof boards are 2 ft. long, the gable ends are fixed 5 ins. in as shown in Fig. 3.

A shallow earthenware or enamel bowl of any shape, measuring about 10 ins. across, could be used for the bath. It should be carried in a wood case made by nailing up four sides about 2 ins. deep to form a frame 1 ft. 2 ins. square. This is covered at the bottom

BIRD SHELTER AND BATH FOR THE LAWN

with four slats, spaced about ¼ in. apart and nailed on. The covering piece should be 1 ft. 4 ins. square, with an opening cut for inserting the bowl, and it also is nailed on to overhang equally all around.

Small branches of oak or chestnut may be easily split down the middle for the purpose of ornamentation. This material could be nailed to a flat board roof (to the gable ends) around the sides of the bath casing, and also to its bottom (*see* Fig. 5), where slits should be left under those in the boards to allow surplus water to drain away. The bath is hung from the roof with small chains fitted with eyes screwed into the gable ends and bottom frame. A perch could be arranged as shown in Figs. 1 and 3, and chains should be provided for suspending the shelter and bath from a convenient tree or other support. The roof could be painted red, and the joints picked out white. The chains also, unless they are galvanised, should be painted, and it would be an advantage to use brass pins for fixing the split rustic wood.

THE PEDESTAL BATH (B), details of which are shown in Figs. 6 and 7, may be preferred to that just described, and is quite as easy to make. It should be carried on a wood upright about 3 ins. diameter, buried 1 ft. in the ground, and standing 2 ft. above.

The bath may be contrived with a loose fitting bowl as before, or it may be formed from concrete as shown in Fig. 7. For this a wood case must again be provided; only the bottom should have close fitting joints. It is nailed down to the end of the upright, and four supports are carried out from the upright to the corners of the bottom. The case is filled with concrete, say, about three parts sand to one of cement, and the cavity for the bath is formed by pressing in any suitably-shaped object. A soup plate or the bottom of a round bowl gives a very good shape. It should be plunged to a suitable depth and the top of the concrete levelled off. Pains should be taken to obtain a well-moulded shape, and it may be advisable to soap or grease the mould. Drying should not be allowed to proceed too rapidly, a piece of damp sacking being

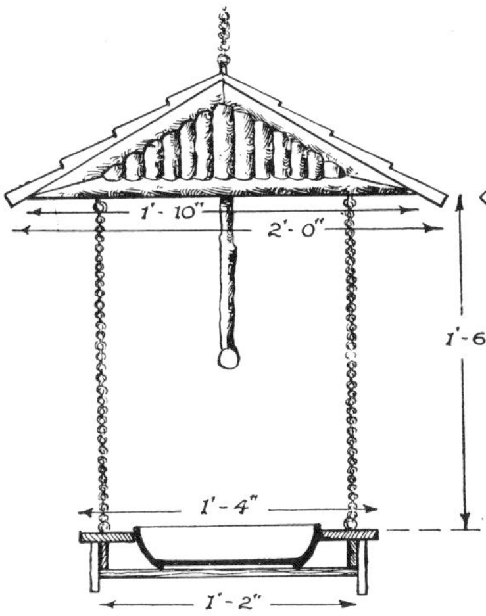

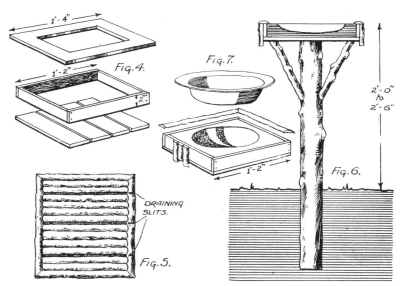

FIG. 2. BIRD SHELTER

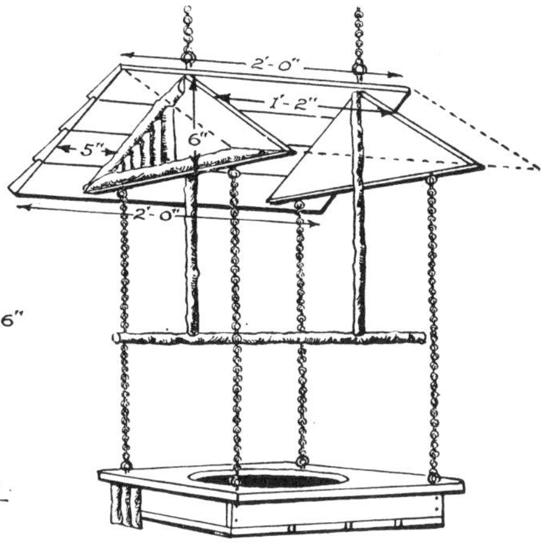

FIG. 3. DETAIL OF ROOF, Etc.

DRAINING SLITS.

FIGS. 4 and 5. BATH, Etc.

FIGS. 6 and 7. PEDESTAL BATH

placed over the concrete.

Split rustic wood is used to finish the sides of the casing, and pieces of the same material are mitred around the upper edges to cover the joints between the casing and concrete. (505)

YOUR GARDEN PLANT TUB

PLANE up the four legs to a length of 18 ins., 1¾ in. square. Point the top ends, and slightly chamfer off at the foot. Cut mortises for the upper and lower rails. Note the section, which shows the rails set in ¼ in. from face of legs. The rails are 1½ ins. wide by ¾ in. thick.

The bottom, of ¾ in. boards, is tongued to enter grooves cut in the lower rail. The legs might also be slightly notched to receive it.

The slats, it will be observed, are fixed *inside* the rails, resting on the bottom. This is seen in the section. At the top they may be gently chamfered and allowed to finish flush with the upper edge of top rail. They are nailed to both rails. The slats may be equally spaced if so desired, but the elevation shows the three end ones 1½ ins. wide and the centre one about 2½ ins.

All joints should be fixed with paint, the edges of the slats being painted before nailing. For finish, give a coat of priming and then two coats of oil paint. Alternatively a wood preservative might be used. The sizes of parts are :—

	Long ft.	Long ins.	Wide ins.	Thick ins.
Four legs	1	6	1¾	1¾
Eight rails	1	2½	1½	¾
Bottom	1	1½	13½	¾
Twenty-four slats	1	0¼	1½	½
Four centre slats	1	0¼	2½	½

The sizes given include joints. Allow for cutting. (719)

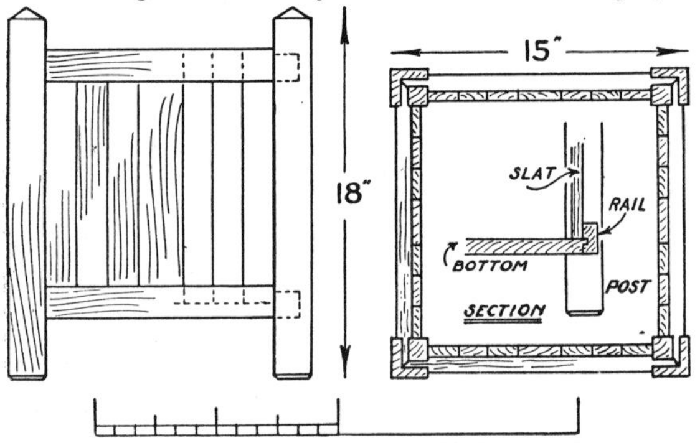

ELEVATION OF SIDE. SECTIONAL PLAN.

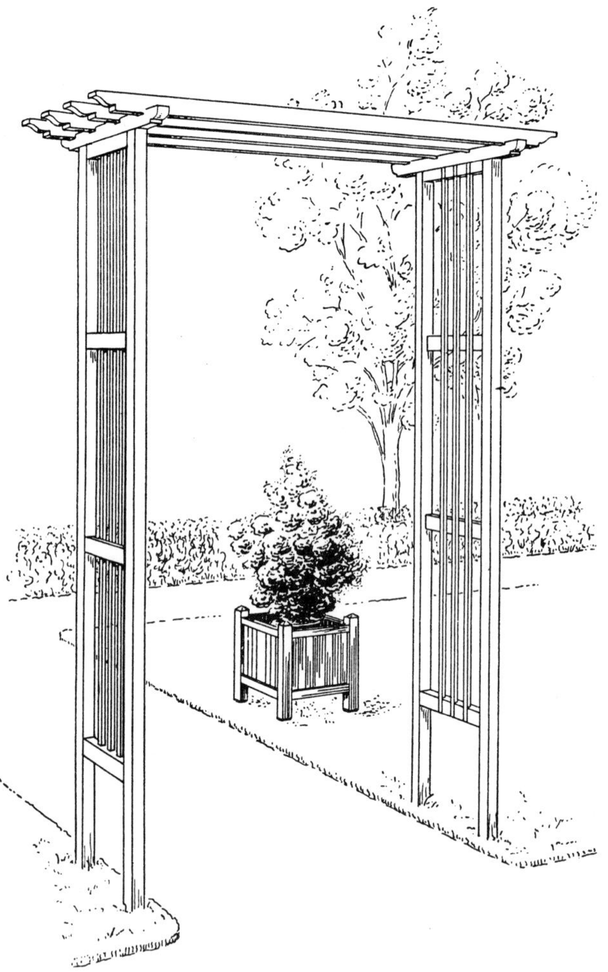

GARDEN PLANT TUB, 18 INS. HIGH BY 15 INS. WIDE.

HINTS ON MAKING CRAZY PAVEMENT

CRAZY PAVEMENT, which is sometimes difficult to obtain locally, can be manufactured at home if the following instructions are followed. Make or obtain a wooden frame about, say, 3 ft. by 2 ft. and from 3 ins. to 4 ins. deep. The frame is laid upon an existing floor and a layer of sand 1 in. deep deposited in it; the sand should be well damped after placing. A pointed stick is used for marking the surface of the sand to resemble strata of natural rock; the identations should not be too deep. A better plan is to obtain a slab of stone having an irregular surface, lay it upon the sand and lightly press. This will give an impression, a replica of the rock face. Move the stone and repeat until the whole of the sand is marked.

A thin paste of cement and sand is then mixed—suitable proportions for the mixture would be 1 part cement to 1 of sand by volume. This is then poured gently over the sand to a depth of ¼ in.

The ordinary concrete is composed of clean, sharp sand, ½ in. stone chippings, or gravel and Portland cement, in the proportions as follows: 1 part cement, 1½ parts sand to 3 parts stone or gravel. The whole should be well mixed dry, until of a uniform colour throughout, then water added until the mixture is plastic but not too wet. While placing the concrete in the mould, care should be taken to disturb the facing mixture as little as possible.

To obtain the irregular shapes common to crazy paving, strips of stiff cardboard, tin or zinc, are pressed into the concrete immediately after placing, until they reach the sand. In this way slabs of any shape or size can be made. The mould should be left for a week or more to allow the concrete to harden.

A much stronger concrete will result if, while the concrete is setting, the mould is covered with wet sand or sacking. When the mould is removed, it will be seen that, besides being irregular and indented, the face of the paving will also be sand covered. (684)

Lac is a resinous substance which is deposited by the lac-bugs on the twigs of trees. The twigs are broken off by the natives and dried in the sun, and the insect is entombed within the lac. At this stage the gum in its crude state is called *stick-lac*. When the lac is removed from the twigs it is called *seed-lac*, and after being finally melted, purified, bleached and stretched it is called *shellac*.

CHAIR STEPS

INVALUABLE FOR FIXING UP AND
TAKING DOWN A.R.P. CURTAINS

FIG. 1. EASILY MADE FROM ODDMENTS
The joints are of the simplest type.

NOW that nearly all of us are faced with the necessity of fixing up curtains and screens every night and taking them down the next morning, this pair of chair steps will prove invaluable. It can be made up at a cost of from 4s. 6d. to 5s. Much of the $\frac{7}{8}$ in. thick wood may be selected from clean packing cases which may be purchased at from 3d. to 6d. each ; and even if it is necessary to purchase new white deal and the steel back flap hinges the completed article should not cost more than the stipulated price.

The steps may be left " in-the-white," so that they may from time to time be scrubbed clean ; or they may be given one coat of glue size, followed by one coat of shellac spirit varnish and a final coat of Degrah water and acid-proof oil varnish. A little ordinary joiners' hot glue run down with warm water will answer for sizing purposes.

For the inexperienced worker we advise the making of the step portion first : that is the lower part of Fig. 2. When this is completed he should make the upper portion of Fig. 2 to agree with the lower half, and he will thus run little or no risk of going astray with his work. When making the upper portion or chair back, the worker will be well advised to secure the various parts together in a temporary manner by the use of a few panel pins which should not be driven quite home. This will enable him to withdraw the fine nails and to make any slight adjustment to the joints and the hingeing position before he finally glues up and nails and screws his work.

For the final assembly it is best to use wrought or cut nails because they hold much better than the polished surfaces of round or oval nails. All nail heads should be punched down and the holes filled up with plastic wood. The screws should be fixed nice and flush and all the sharp edges of the woodwork should be

removed with No. Middle 2 glasspaper. For those of our readers whose pocket is deeper we suggest that they use clean straight grained beech, birch, or American oak. The various angles to which the joiner's bevel should be set are shown by the thick black lines beneath each drawing.

(936)

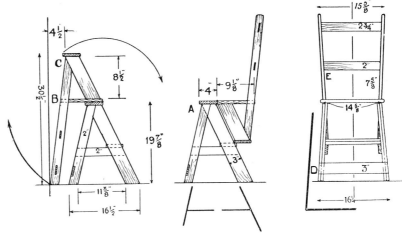

FIG. 2. USED AS STEPS.   FIG. 3. IN USE AS CHAIR.   FIG. 4. FRONT ELEVATION.

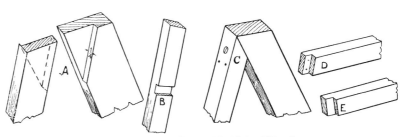

FIG. 5.   ENLARGED DETAILS OF JOINTS.
Notched joint at A.   B. Notch for seat.   Butt joint at C.   Rails at D and E.

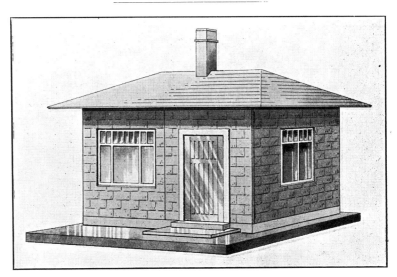

THIS DESIGN FOR A DOLL'S HOUSE WILL APPEAR NEXT MONTH.

29

DOLL'S CRADLE

Use $\frac{3}{8}$ in. whitewood, except for rockers which may be $\frac{3}{4}$ in., and the $\frac{3}{16}$ in. plywood bottom. Sizes are : Head end (A) 8 ins. by $6\frac{1}{2}$ ins. ; Foot end (B) 7 ins. by $6\frac{1}{2}$ ins. ; Two rockers (C) $8\frac{1}{2}$ ins. by $1\frac{3}{8}$ ins. ; Two sides (D) $14\frac{5}{8}$ ins. by 3 ins. Bottom (E) $14\frac{1}{4}$ ins. by $6\frac{1}{2}$ ins. ; Rod (F) $14\frac{5}{8}$ ins. by $\frac{1}{2}$ in. diameter.

FIG. I. DOLL'S CRADLE.
Size 15¼ ins. by 8½ ins.

Ends are tenoned to rockers right through, the sides being housed or simply nailed. Bottom is nailed on from below. A $\frac{1}{2}$ in. dowel rod (F) let into rockers helps to stiffen the whole. The little piercings shown are optional. The cradle could be enlarged to 18 ins. or 24 ins. as required.

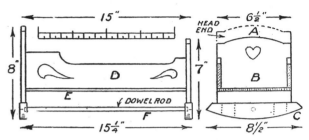

MADE IN ANY WOOD TO BE PAINTED OR ENAMELLED.

MAGAZINE STAND

Parts are : Four legs (G) 7 ins. by $1\frac{1}{4}$ ins. square ; Two uprights (H) 13 ins. by 9 ins. by $\frac{3}{8}$ in. ; One upright (J) 13 ins. by $10\frac{1}{2}$ ins. by $\frac{3}{8}$ in. ; Bottom (K) 13 ins. by $7\frac{3}{4}$ ins. by $\frac{3}{8}$ in. ; Fan pieces (L) $3\frac{3}{4}$ ins. by $1\frac{3}{4}$ ins. by $\frac{7}{8}$ in.

Legs taper to $\frac{7}{8}$ in. and at top are cut down 2 ins. by $\frac{3}{4}$ in. to take the outer uprights (H). These

FIG. 2. MAGAZINE STAND.
Size 13 ins. by 8¾ ins. by 15½ ins.

latter are rebated for the bottom. Uprights could be of $\frac{3}{8}$ in. stuff and are strongest if clamped at ends with $1\frac{3}{4}$ in. wide clamps. They are held by the fan blocks (L) fitted behind the legs. Uprights and blocks are screwed through the bottom. Glue-blocks could be fitted inside as per dotted lines.

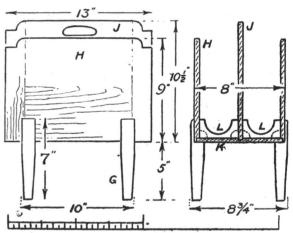

PREFERABLY IN OAK OR OTHER HARDWOOD.

SET OF FOUR TRAYS

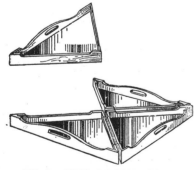

These could be made any size to form a square. The parts for a set of four are : Four sides (M) $18\frac{1}{4}$ ins. by 2 ins. by $\frac{3}{8}$ in. ; Eight sides (N) 13 ins. by $1\frac{1}{2}$ ins. by $\frac{3}{8}$ in. ; Four bottoms (O) which can all be cut from a $\frac{3}{16}$ in. or $\frac{1}{4}$ in. plywood board 48 ins. by 9 ins. Alternative shapes for sides are shown at P, Q, these being a shade wider than M, N. If preferred they may be straight.

FIG. 3. NEST OF FOUR TRAYS.
Size (grouped) 18 ins. by 18 ins.

Sides are rebated $\frac{1}{4}$ in. by $\frac{1}{4}$ in. for the plywood bottom. It will be noted that the main angle is a right angle, requiring a mitre of 45 degrees. The other two angles are *half* right angles, with mitres of 22½ degrees. Corners are glued and held each with a pair of veneer keys which should be fitted wedge-wise.

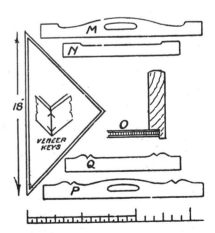

CAN BE MADE IN ANY HARDWOOD.

30

FROM ODDMENTS

of the family • • •

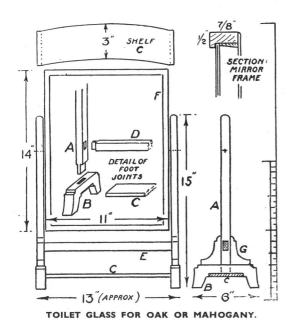

TOILET GLASS FOR OAK OR MAHOGANY.

TOILET MIRROR

Sizes : Two posts (A) 14 ins. by $\frac{7}{8}$ in. by $\frac{5}{8}$ in. (on face), tenoned through to feet ; Two feet (B) 6 ins. by 2 ins. by $\frac{7}{8}$ in. ; Shelf (C) 12 ins. by $3\frac{1}{2}$ ins, by $\frac{5}{16}$ in. If straight instead of shaped, width is only 3 ins. Shelf is let into feet and screwed from below. Cross bar (E) $12\frac{3}{4}$ ins. by $\frac{3}{4}$ in. by $\frac{1}{2}$ in., tenoned to posts ; Frame (F) : two lengths 14 ins. and two 11 ins. by $\frac{7}{8}$ in. by $\frac{1}{2}$ in. wide on *face* ; preferably dovetailed at corners; but could be mitred, glued and nailed like a picture frame. Rebate for glass. Brackets (G) for posts are $2\frac{3}{4}$ ins. by $1\frac{3}{4}$ ins. by $\frac{1}{2}$ in. or $\frac{3}{8}$ in. tongued in.

FIG. 4. TOILET GLASS.
Size 19 ins. by 13 ins.

BOX FOR WRITING TABLE

Sizes : Two sides (H) $9\frac{1}{2}$ ins. by 3 ins. by $\frac{3}{8}$ in. ; Two (ends) $6\frac{1}{2}$ ins. by 3 ins. by $\frac{3}{8}$ in. ; Bottom (J) 10 ins. by 7 ins. by $\frac{3}{8}$ in. ; Top (in two parts) $10\frac{1}{4}$ ins. by $6\frac{1}{2}$ ins. by $\frac{3}{8}$ in.

FIG. 5. HANDY DESK BOX.
Size $9\frac{1}{2}$ ins. by $6\frac{1}{2}$ ins.

This is intended for jotting paper, stationery, or correspondence, and has a double hinged lid which, when open as indicated, holds a calendar pad. Corners of box 'are shown as dovetailed, but might be rebated, glued, and panel-pinned. Notches are cut in sides to engage the front fold of lid when open.

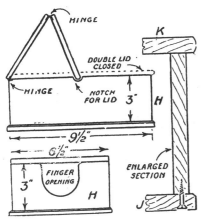

PREFERABLY MADE IN OAK.

BOY'S TROLLEY

Sizes : Two sides (K) 21 ins. by 4 ins. by $\frac{3}{4}$ in. ; Two cross-boards (L) $9\frac{1}{2}$ ins. by 4 ins. by $\frac{3}{4}$ or $\frac{7}{8}$ in. ; Top (M, boarded) 23 ins. by 13 ins. by $\frac{1}{2}$ in. ; Two side rails (N) 17 ins. by $1\frac{1}{4}$ ins. by $\frac{1}{2}$ in. ; Back rail (O) 13 ins. by 2 ins. by $\frac{1}{2}$ in. Two wheels (P) 5 ins. diam. ; two 4 in. diam. by $\frac{3}{4}$ or $\frac{7}{8}$ in. thick.

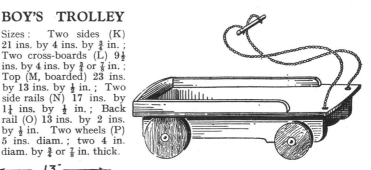

FIG. 6. TROLLEY A BOY WILL ENJOY.
Size 22 ins. by 13 ins.

The two main sides (K) are connected by the cross-boards (L), the parts being screwed. Top is nailed on above, and the sides and back rails (N, O) nailed or screwed from underneath. Wheels should be of hardwood, held by long round-head screws driven through sides and cross-boards. Metal washers are fitted on both sides of each wheel. (437)

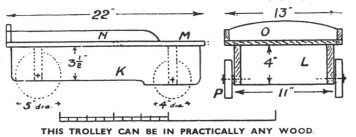

THIS TROLLEY CAN BE IN PRACTICALLY ANY WOOD.

THE HIGH-LOW CHAIR

FIG. I. ESSENTIAL IN EVERY HOME IN WHICH THERE IS A BABY

Special skew hinges can be obtained for pivoting the upper part on the slanting legs. The seat height is 2 ft. 2 ins. when in the high position, and about 9½ ins. when folded.

● *This is easily the most convenient type of child's chair. It is neither difficult nor costly to make, and, whilst it fulfils all the functions of a high chair and is fitted with an hinged tray, it may be quickly turned into a low chair by unlocking the hinged legs and turning up the lower portion which then serves as a play table. In this low position a child may be left quite safely, and the chair is supported on four wheels which enables it to be easily moved.*

THE sketch (Fig. 1) shows the chair in both the high and low positions. It is important that all the dimensions shown in the detail drawings should be observed if the chair is to fold properly. The four legs after being framed up with their various rails into the seat board, are separated at the point indicated. The upper and lower portions of the leg framework are then hinged together at the front, and two pair of small wheels are fitted through the back legs in such a manner that, when the legs are swung round on the hinges, the wheels rest on the ground at the front and back of the leg framework. In this position the panel which is fitted over the lower rails then forms a play table, and the hinged tray used in the high position is swung round at the back. It is advisable to use hardwood in constructing a chair of this kind.

Legs.—The four legs are fully 2 ft. 2 ins. long by 1⅛ ins. square. They are first framed in pairs as shown in Fig. 4, joined with three rails 1 in. wide by ¾ in. thick, the two upper ones being 1 ft. and 1 ft. 2 ins. long, and the bottom one 1 ft. 7 ins. long. In setting out the legs and rails, the line at which the legs will be divided and hinged should be carefully marked. The two upper rails are set an equal distance above and below this line, the measurement over the rails being 5 ins. For these rails the tenons are cut the full width, but, as the bottom rail must have its top edge bevelled to the splay of the legs to allow a thin panel to be fitted over it, the tenon should be haunched down to ¾ in., as shown in Fig. 5.

The framing of the legs is continued by taking the two pair of framed legs and connecting them at the back with three rails, as in Fig. 6. The two upper rails are tenoned into the legs to stand

above and below the corresponding rails at the sides; that is, the distance between them will be 5 ins., while the bottom rail is kept in line with those at the sides. Its top edge is also bevelled. At the front the legs are joined by a foot-board 1 ft. 2 ins. long by 4 ins. wide by ½ in. thick, and a bearing rail 1 ft. 2 ins. long by 1⅞ ins. wide by ½ in. thick.

Foot board.—To fit the foot-board in place it will be necessary either to bevel the bottom edges of the rails to which it is fixed, or to cut slightly bevelled incisions at the ends of the board to allow it to fit on the edges of the rails to which it is screwed. The bearing rail is fitted in the position indicated under the uppermost side leg rails, and is screwed to the legs. It may be necessary to remove this rail when the legs are separated and hinged as its bottom edge, which should be rounded, is intended to project about ⅜ in. below the separated ends of the legs. A piece of plywood or thin ordinary wood should be used for the bottom panel. If of plywood it could eventually be glued and pinned in place, or ordinary wood could be fixed with a few round-head screws, but final fixing should not be done at this stage.

Seat Joints.—Before separating and hingeing the legs it is advisable to frame the legs into the seat-board and fit up the wheels on which the leg frame runs when the chair is in the low position. The seat-board is 1 ft. 1 in. long by 1 ft. wide by 1 in. thick, and the legs are tenoned up into it as indicated in Figs. 2, 3, 4 and 6, the tenons being square with the bevelled shoulders. Grooves ⅝ in. wide by ¼ in. deep are cut in the upper face of the seat-board, ⅜ in. from the side and back edges to

receive the seat sides and back (see Fig. 9).

Castors.—Wood wheels, or rubber tyre castors (the latter being of course preferable) should be used for the chair to run on when in the low position. Iron or mild steel rods ¼ in. diameter are bored through the legs ¾ in. above and below the line of cut to carry the wheels, and wood blocks are fitted inside the legs above the cut, and outside below to provide flat bearings for the wheels. Details are shown in Figs. 6, 7, and 8.

The positions in which the rods are bored through the legs will allow 2½ in. diameter wheels to project ½ in. beyond the ends of the legs, and a turned wood spindle is used to hold them apart and against the wood blocks fitted inside the legs (see Fig. 7). The ends of the rod could be screwed and fitted with nuts f r fixing the wheels, or iron washers could be slipped over and the ends riveted. The wheels below the cut fit outside the legs (see Fig. 8), and it is advisable to fit nuts on the rod in this case for fixing the wheels. Before separating the legs the line of cut should be carefully marked on two sides of each leg. Skew hinges are used to hinge the two portions of the chair frame together, and they are screwed outside the legs.

Seat Back and Sides.—The sides of the seat, which are ⅝ in. thick, shaped as shown in Fig. 10, fit in the grooves in the seat-board. Grooves are also cut near the back edges of the sides (see Fig. 9) to receive the seat back, which projects 3 ins. above the sides and also fits down into the grooves in the seat-board. The seat could be left quite plain and a loose cushion used to make it comfortable, or it may be lightly upholstered.

If this is done, the simplest method is to make separate pieces of upholstery for the seat, sides and back, and tack them in place before finally fixing the portions of the seat together. These pieces of upholstery should be made with calico lining inside, and leather or similar material outside; they need to be only lightly stuffed, and a few buttons could be introduced to hold the stuffing in place.

Pivoting.—At this stage the chair should be tested to see that it folds properly. When the lower portion is swung round on the hinges into the low position, the front edge of the panel of the play table should rest against the front edges of the sides of the seat, with the wheels running freely, and the lower rounded edge of the bearing rail just clearing the ground. Adjustment by planing the front edge of the panel may be necessary.

To make the chair safe in the high position, it is advisable to fit a locking catch at the back. This consists of a piece of thin metal about $\frac{3}{4}$ in. wide, with a screw hole for fixing at one end, and a notch at the other, as shown in Fig. 11. The catch is fixed to the uppermost rail at the back of the chair frame with a screw, and the notch in the other end engages with a screw driven into the rail below.

Tray.—The hinged tray for use when the chair is in the high position is made as shown in Fig. 12. The frame consists of two sides 1 ft. 6 ins. long by 1 in. wide by $\frac{1}{2}$ in. thick, and two cross pieces roughly 1 ft. $1\frac{1}{2}$ ins. long, the front one being 1 in. wide, and the inner one $\frac{7}{8}$ in. wide by $\frac{1}{2}$ in. thick. The inner cross piece is tenoned into the sides and its top edge is rounded, while the front cross piece is joined to the sides with open mortise and tenon joints as shown in Fig. 13. A thin panel is then fixed under the sides and cross pieces to form the tray. It is advisable to hinge the tray to the sides of the seat with small bolts and wing nuts.

On completion all sharp edges should be removed, and the chair may be finished by staining and varnishing, or enamelling. (480)

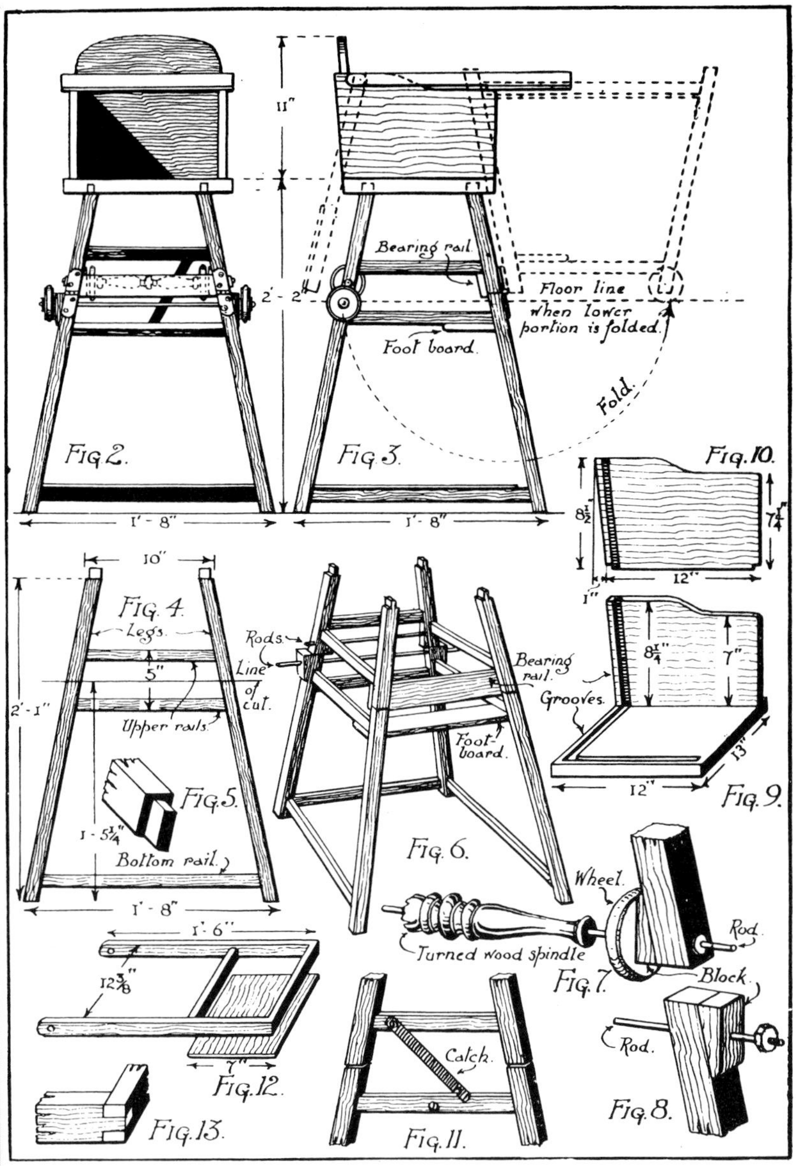

SCALE ELEVATIONS AND DETAILS OF CONSTRUCTION, JOINTS, Etc.

TEA TROLLEY

(Continued from page 67)

to the tray bottom, Fig. 3. The tray runners (O) which are screwed underneath the side rails (D) should be a suitable width to clear the leg and leave enough to engage the grooved tray sides, the ends being rounded to enable the tray to be pushed in easily, Fig. 2. Soften all corners and add finger pulls at each end, corresponding pieces being placed under each side to give stability when the tray is placed upon a table.

CUTTING LIST

Trolley with Detachable Tray

		Long ft.	Long ins.	Wide ins.	Thick ins.
A	4 Legs ..	2	$3\frac{1}{2}$	$1\frac{3}{8}$	$1\frac{3}{8}$
B	2 End rails ..	1	$3\frac{1}{4}$	$1\frac{1}{2}$	$\frac{3}{4}$
C	2 do. ..	1	$3\frac{1}{4}$	$1\frac{1}{8}$	$\frac{3}{8}$
D	2 Side rails ..	1	$9\frac{1}{4}$	$1\frac{1}{2}$	$\frac{3}{4}$
E	2 Side rims ..	1	$4\frac{1}{2}$	$1\frac{1}{8}$	$\frac{3}{8}$
F	1 Lower deck	1	10	16	$\frac{1}{2}$ or $\frac{3}{8}$
G	1 Top deck ..	2	0	18	$\frac{1}{2}$
H	2 Top rims ..	2	0	1	$\frac{7}{16}$
I	2 do. ..	1	6	1	$\frac{7}{16}$

Separate Tray. *(These sizes must be adjusted to suit any existing trolley.)*

		ft.	ins.	ins.	ins.
K	1 Tray bottom	1	10	$13\frac{1}{8}$	$\frac{5}{16}$
L	2 Rims ..	1	7	$1\frac{1}{2}$	$\frac{1}{2}$
M	2 do. ..		$10\frac{1}{8}$	$1\frac{1}{2}$	$\frac{1}{2}$
N	4 Fillets ..		8	$\frac{1}{2}$	$\frac{1}{2}$
O	2 Runners ..	1	$7\frac{1}{4}$	$1\frac{11}{16}$	$\frac{7}{8}$

Note.—All sizes are net excepting (A) which is carried to floor and cut to suit any sized castor. 1 in. long tenons are allowed for, being mitred in the mortises. (481)

TIMBER BORING WASPS

ALL OVER the country at present much timber is being felled, and in saw-mills complaint is frequently heard of large wasp-like insects which emerge from the logs. Flying around with an ominous whirr, their black and gold streaks and threatening tail stings arouse natural apprehension. In reality they are harmless—to us, at least, though not to timber. There are two kinds of wood wasp; one, less common, the *sirex cyaneus*, steel-blue in colour; the other, our foe the *sirex gigas*, which more nearly resembles the wasp with which we are familiar.

The wood wasp is often seen in woods, and favours trees such as larch, spruce, pine, and silver fur. It makes use of its sting to pierce the bark and, in a hole which takes no more than ten minutes to cut, it deposits its eggs. The sting is in the form of a saw and the eggs pass down through a tube. For three years the larvae hatched from these eggs carry on their boring and tunnelling operations, and in time the tree becomes worthless. The presence of the pest is really due to the inadequate thinning of plantations. It is the weak, not the healthy tree that the wood wasp invades, and if systematic thinning were adopted the insect would disappear from our forests. When encountered in saw-mills the larvae have reached the stage when they are ready to emerge from the tree. They thus appear as fully-fledged wasps. (372)

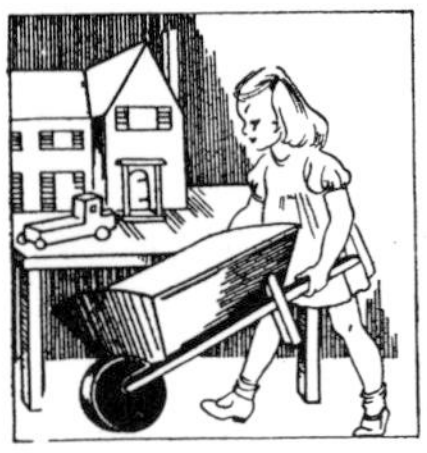

TOYS FOR CHRISTMAS

Kiddies' Roller

FOR roller ends (A) take two pieces a full 9 ins. by 9 ins. and $\frac{3}{4}$ in. thick and cut to a circle of from $8\frac{1}{2}$ ins. to 9 ins. diameter. These are connected by the axle bar (B), 10 ins. by $1\frac{1}{8}$ ins. square, and by the

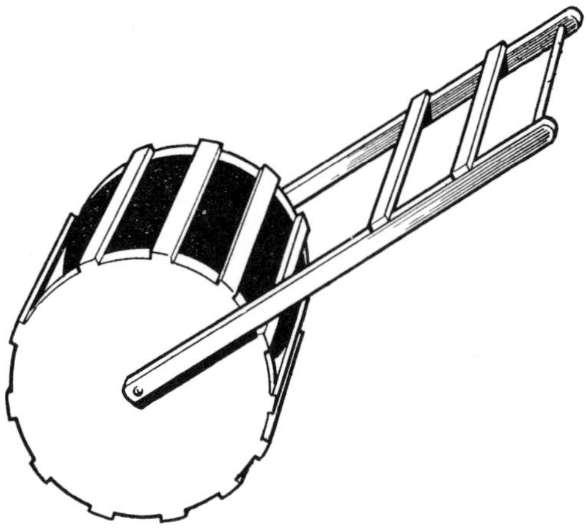

FIG. 1 *(right).* **TOY ROLLER Painted in bright colours a youngster will enjoy playing with this roller. Size 10 ins. long, 9 ins. diam. Handle length, 18 ins.**

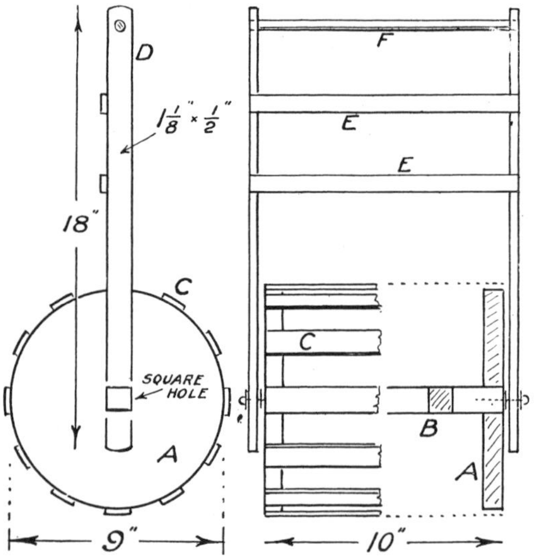

twelve circumference laths (C) which are 10 ins. by 1 in. by $\frac{1}{4}$ in. thick. Bar (B) enters square holes cut in ends and is glued; the strips (C) are equally spaced and are nailed on. Nail aslant.

The handle consists of two arms (D), 18 ins. by $1\frac{1}{8}$ ins. by $\frac{1}{2}$ in., these being joined by two cross strips (E), about $11\frac{1}{2}$ ins. by $\frac{3}{4}$ in. by $\frac{1}{4}$ in., and the hand rod (F) which may be a $11\frac{1}{2}$ in. length of $\frac{1}{2}$ in. dowel rod. This rod enters the arms (D) to which it is glued, the strips (E) being nailed on.

The handle is connected to the roller by two 2 in. round-head screws which pass through a free hole bored in arms (D) into the axle bar (B). At each side fit two thin metal washers. (561)

FIG. 2 *(left).* **ELEVATIONS WITH PRINCIPAL SIZES**

Doll's Basket Cradle

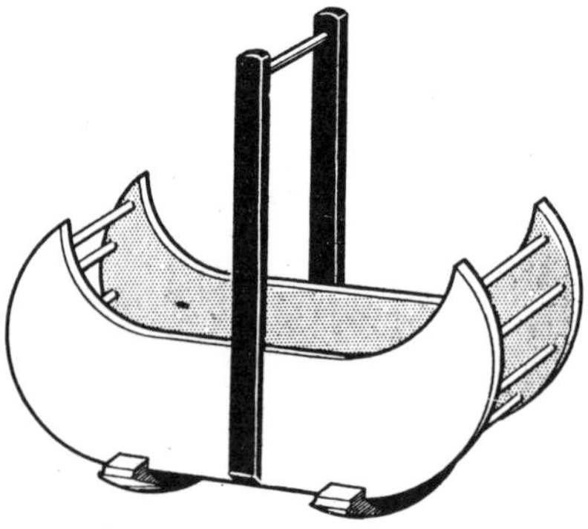

FIG. 1. NOVEL TYPE OF BASKET CRADLE FOR A SMALL DOLL 12 ins. long by $8\frac{1}{4}$ ins. over rockers.

FOR a small doll of some 8 ins. or 10 ins. this type of cradle is appreciated, as it may be carried about by hand. The size may, if desired, be increased to 12 ins. or 15 ins. For the cradle shown these few parts may be noted :—

		Thick ins.	Wide ins.	Thick ins.
(A)	2 Sides . .	12	$5\frac{1}{2}$	$\frac{5}{16}$
(B)	Bottom . .	6	$5\frac{3}{8}$	$\frac{3}{8}$
(C)	10 pieces dowel rod . .	6	$\frac{1}{4}$ diam.	
(D)	2 Rockers .	$8\frac{1}{4}$	$1\frac{3}{8}$	$\frac{3}{4}$
(E)	2 Handle bars .	10	$\frac{3}{4}$	$\frac{1}{4}$
(F)	Handle rod .	$6\frac{1}{2}$	$\frac{3}{8}$ diam.	

The sides (A) are easily set out from the plotted diagram (Fig. 2). The centres for the outer and inner curves are marked at ×. If the outer curves (with a 3-in. radius) are first drawn, with the centres 6 ins. apart, the two parallel horizontal lines are at once obtained. It is then easy to find the centres of the short inner curves which have a radius of $2\frac{1}{2}$ ins.

Cut both pieces together, and at the same time bore small holes for the $\frac{1}{4}$ in. dowel rods (C). In this way the sides will be uniform. Glue in the bottom (B) and the dowel rods, additionally fixing the bottom with panel pins. Later glasspaper all flush.

The rockers (D), of $\frac{3}{4}$-in. stuff, are cut to fit over the batten as at Z (Fig. 3). They are glued on and screwed down through the bottom. Handle bars (E) are glued and panel-pinned to the sides, the $\frac{3}{8}$-in. dowel rod (F) being tightly fitted at top by gluing into holes bored for it in the bars. (562)

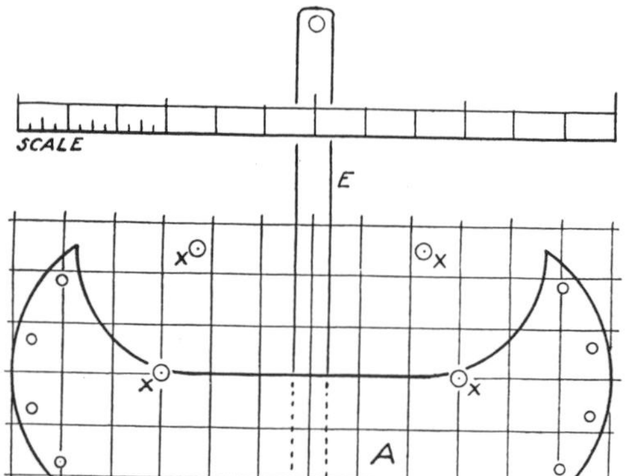

FIG. 2. SIDE VIEW MAPPED INTO 1 in. SQUARES.

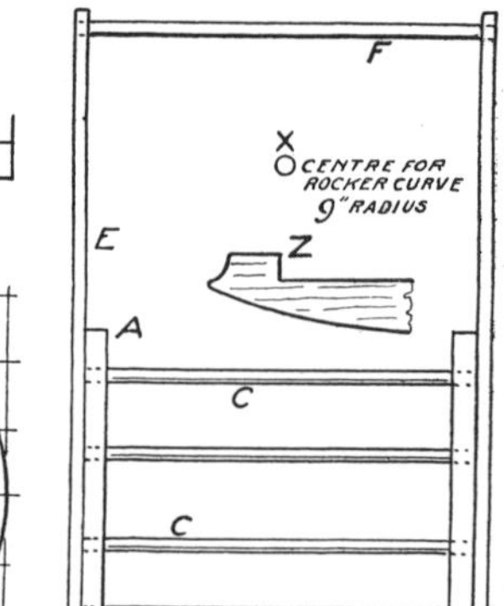

FIG. 3. END VIEW

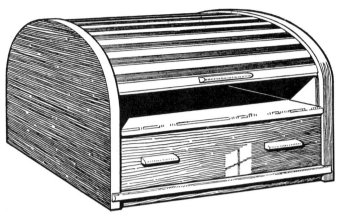

FIG. I. HANDY GENERAL-UTILITY BOX FOR THE TABLE
Useful for smoking requisites, papers, or for ladies' work. Sizes are : 12 in. long, 12 in. deep, and 8¾ in. high. Small oddments of choice hardwood can be used

TABLE CABINET
WITH
TAMBOUR TOP

Apart from making a useful item for the sideboard or table, this cabinet box is extremely interesting to make. The tambour top in particular makes an absorbing piece of work. It could be carried out in two different woods, as suggested in Fig. 1, or a single wood could be used throughout

PREPARE the two ends A to the finished over-all size, making them rectangular. Mark out with square and gauge the positions of the various members and joints. So far as the top shaping is concerned, this is elliptical, and the best plan is to mark out half the shape in thin card, cut it out, and use this as a template for marking the wood. It can be reversed each side of a centre line to give the complete shape.

Tambour track.—Clearly the groove which forms the track for the tambour must run round parallel with the edge, until at the back it passes inwards and so down to the bottom, where it runs right through, emerging at the front. A gauge can be used to mark the groove where it runs around the curve and the short straight part at the front. The gauge can also be used at the straight part along the bottom, but the rest can be struck out with compasses from the centres shown in Fig. 2, or it can be drawn in free-hand. Special care is necessary in both marking out and cutting this groove in order to ensure free running.

The simplest way of cutting the groove is to use a small gouge of the type used by wood-carvers. The U form of gouge is specially handy. This will remove the bulk of the waste. You can then cut down each side of the groove with gouges and a chisel, selecting a gouge which best lines up with the curve being cut. Cut in the side as upright as possible, and ease away the waste with a small chisel. As

the groove finishes $\frac{3}{16}$ in. wide, you can comfortably use a $\frac{1}{8}$ in. chisel. Carry this down nearly to the finished depth ($\frac{3}{16}$ in.) and finish off with a small router. It will be found simpler to work this groove before the edge is shaped. It eliminates any risk of the grain chipping away, especially where this runs crosswise.

Construction.—The bottom B is lap-dovetailed into the ends, and it is advisable to leave the pins wide because the grain of the ends runs from back to front. Back C is also lap-dovetailed. Note from Fig. 3 how the top edge is chamfered at the inside so as to enable it to clear the groove in which the tambour runs. Note here that, as the tambour itself is shouldered at the outside, the chamfer must be cut sufficiently deep to allow for this. At the bottom the back is rebated to hold bottom B.

Shelf D is grooved into ends A, and you can either allow a shoulder at the top or it can fit in its full thickness. An inner back E is attached as shown in Fig. 3, the purpose of this being to prevent articles from catching against the tambour.

All the joints being cut and the inner surfaces cleaned up, the whole can be assembled. Fix back E to shelf D, screwing upwards from beneath and put the two as whole into ends A. Knock up bottom B and finally add back C. Clean off any glue at the inside before it sets.

Tambour.—It will be seen from Fig. 3 that the tambour groove runs right out at the front. This is necessary to enable the tambour to be fed in after the cabinet has been assembled. The ends of the groove are concealed later by the piece F which is applied above the bottom. To make the tambour a series of strips about $\frac{3}{8}$ in. or $\frac{5}{16}$ in. wide by $\frac{5}{16}$ in. thick are needed. The number depends on the width of the pieces, but it is advisable to prepare one or two extras

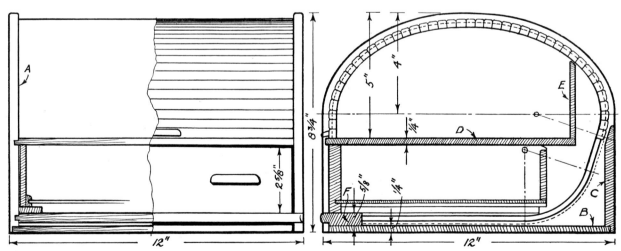

FIG. 2. FRONT ELEVATION IN PART SECTION, AND SECTIONAL SIDE VIEW WITH MAIN SIZES

in case of any mischance. Cut them off about 3 in. extra in length so as to enable them to be handled with ease when being polished. Otherwise it would be almost impossible to grip them. Take off the extreme outer corners to form a slight round and rub a little candle grease along the adjoining edges of each. This is a precaution against their becoming stuck together when being assembled on the duck or canvas. No candle grease, of course, must be allowed on the bottom surface, which is directly attached to the material.

To assemble the whole, cut a piece of duck sufficiently large to complete the entire job, and stretch as far as possible by drawing it back and forth over the rounded edge of a piece of wood. Now place it upon a piece of flat wood and tack down the far edge. Strain it as taut as possible, and tack the front edge. Equalise the strain as far as possible by holding a piece of wood beneath and levering it over when strained. Otherwise distortion may occur later. Fix down temporarily a straight edge at the back, as a guide to keeping the back tambour strip straight. The strips can be glued down in packs of about 4 or 5, gluing the underside and rubbing down on to the duck. Put any convenient weight on the top to maintain close contact with the material. When the glue has set, open out the tambour to make sure that every joint is free.

Fitting.—Mark the over-all width of the tambour including the portion projecting into the grooves, and cut off square. There should be slight clearance in length when offered into into grooves. Mark in the shoulders at the front with the cutting gauge and trim away to fit the groove, using a bull-

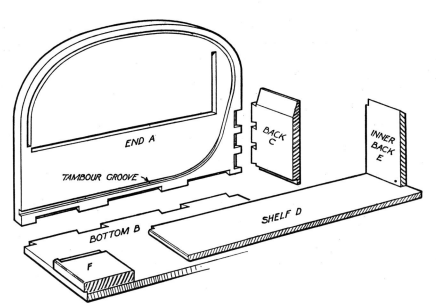

FIG. 3. THE PARTS SEPARATED SHOWING CONSTRUCTION

nose or shoulder plane. To ensure free running, candle grease can be run over all bearing surfaces as a lubricant, but this should not be done until after the whole job has been stained (if required) and polished. When the tambour is in place, the rail F can be cut and fitted. It is advisable not to glue it but merely to screw either from top or bottom. Then, if any attention to the tambour should later be necessary, it can be withdrawn easily. Fig. 2 shows how the drawer fits. Note that the bottom is set up rather more than usual so that it rests upon the runners. Handles can be of either wood, plastic, or metal. (162)

EASILY MADE BENCH VICE

A READER has sent us a description and sketch of a simple and inexpensive vice he has made and he thinks that the idea will interest readers.

The screw was obtained from an old wood-and-wire mattress, but the screw from an extensible table would do just as well. For guides, he used 8 in. by ⅜ in. bolts, the heads being sawn off, Fig. 1. The vice cheek comprises a beech block about 1⅛ in. thick which is drilled to take the screw and bolts. As the corresponding holes in the bench apron must align with the holes in the vice cheek, the latter, after being drilled, is clamped to the apron so as to serve as a drilling template. The screw is revolvably secured to the vice cheek by two washers, the inside washer being held in place by a split pin, Fig. 2. The guides are fixed by square nuts let into the vice cheek and clamped by nuts and washers on the inside. If the vice is required to tighten up closely to the bench, it may be necessary to recess the nuts and washers on the interior of the vice. The nut for the screw is let into a hardwood block, Fig. 3, the block being screwed to the inside of the apron.

It may be that the squared end of the screw will be found to be too small to permit of its being drilled for a handle, in which case the original key or spanner could be adapted to serve as a handle. In order to secure the key or handle, the end of the screw could be drilled and tapped to take a screw so that a washer can be positioned over the end of the screw to hold the key or spanner in place.

It is an advantage if the guides can be arranged to slide in tubes fixed under the bench. The tubes could be supported at the front by the apron, but

at the rear it would be necessary to mount them on blocks secured to the underside of the bench. Ordinary pipe clips could serve to secure the tubes to the blocks. Both screw and guides should be kept lubricated with oil. In the case of a wood screw the best lubricant is black lead and water, this being allowed to dry out.

(164)

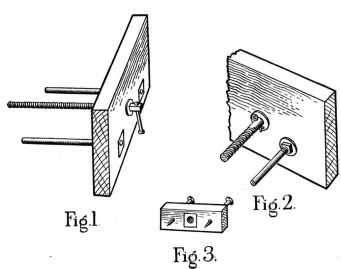

Fig.1. Fig.2. Fig.3.

DETAILS OF THE VICE AND HOW IT IS FITTED UP

—————————— TOY FORT

The present of a toy fort with its garrison of men and guns is one that invariably arouses the enthusiasm of the growing youngster. Approximate dimensions for the fort itself, Fig. 1, are 1 ft. 6 in. wide, 12 in. high in centre, and depth back to front as required

THE fort is built on to a box which will contain the toy garrison, and the space necessary to house the latter when not in use will govern the size of the box. The parade ground itself might be allowed a depth of 12 in. and the parapet enclosure will give the whole a finished appearance. It may also be made in one piece with the fort frontage but, to conserve space, it is suggested that it be made loose to stand vertically when the toy is not in use.

Towers.— A start may be made with the four towers, Fig. 2. These are of plywood, square in shape glued and panel-pinned up round two blocks of 1 in. wood. The use of a small fine-toothed saw for cutting will give a good edge and also reduce the amount of cleaning up later. It will be noticed that these are built to face in reversed directions as an additional effect. The method of fixing them is shown on plan of box, Fig. 5.

Box.—It will thus be convenient to make this next, and, assuming that its depth can be 4 in., either 5-ply or ⅜ in. whitewood can be used with the bottom in one piece. The top of box is allowed three pieces about 2¼ in. wide. The longer back piece is tongued or halved to the two end pieces and glued. The box portion can be glued and panel pinned clear of the positions of towers.

To complete, each tower in turn can be stood upon the back edge and marked round with a pencil or scratch, and these parts cut cleanly away. This gives a correct fixing for all four, as Fig. 2 indicates.

The wall between each pair of canted towers is about 2¼ in. wide and will be fitted into position on the back of box after the towers have been fixed thereon, and all of these will have their top edges cut for the battlements as they occur.

Battlements.—These can be made more important in appearance by planting a facing on them, as Fig. 3. Between the towers also is a panel of tiles enclosed top and bottom in moulding which can easily be prepared from ply. The tiles can be drawn in indelible ink and coloured red for relief. When cutting the slit window openings these can be about

⅜ in. by 1⅛ in. high with a moulded surround which conveniently could be cut from ordinary smoking spills. The centre of the fort showing a full 3½ in. wide is in one flat piece of 3-ply relieved by an arched piece with moulding and battlements cut. This could be of thicker wood so that it presents a projected appearance with bracketed ends.

The lower part of centre has the semi-circular portion cut out as a depth effect, and a separately made fret glued on behind this to form the portcullis. The panelled drawbridge again will be easy to draw in indelible ink colouring, the structure black and the panels a dark brown. A tower above is included for flag display. The parade ground may project about 12 in. and will be of 5-ply.

Parapet.— The parapet can be built up of ⅜ in. wood in lengths 2½ in. wide with a ledge cut in for the parade ground to be panel pinned down. The moulded capping can be of two over-laid strips of ply, with panel facings and plinth of ply glued on. The steps can be in lengths of ⅜ in. wood full cut to fit in

FIG. 1. THE OLD TYPE OF FORT WITH SPACE FOR DISPLAY IS STILL POPULAR
Odds and ends of material could be used for this, including plastic board, hardboard, and even stout cardboard. Oil paints of the artist's kind will give a good durable finish. Alternatively poster colours are satisfactory if the whole is given a following coat of clear varnish

position and should be glued and pinned. This parade ground is intended to clip on to the ends of fort, and, being about the same size as the latter, can be loose so that all will stand compactly together when the toy is not in use.

Moat.—At this stage it will be realised that the fort itself is limited to a frontage only which may answer all needs. An appropriate development, however, would be to include a moat and this could be made, as in Fig. 6. The sides of the fort are continued to the limits of the toy box and an additional tower built in, all in agreement with the frontage but leaving sufficient space for the posting of guards. The parade ground is extended in width by a few inches, each end cut to leave a clear space of 2 in. or 2½ in., the edges being supported here by lengths of notched fillet as indicated Fig. 8. Upon these ledges lengths of glass (preferably builders' roofing glass for the sake of its strength and tint) can be laid loosely for removal when packing up. The parapet is then completed to include a narrow ledge for sentry placing. (192)

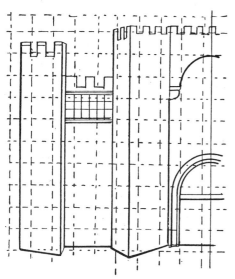

FIG. 2. TOWERS DRAWN IN 1 IN. SQUARES

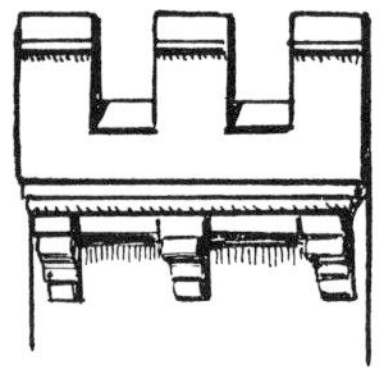

FIG. 3. APPLIED BATTLEMENTS

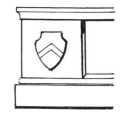

FIG. 4. PARADE GROUND PARAPET

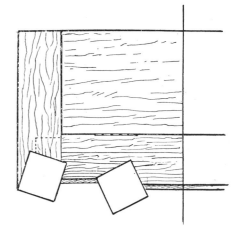

FIG. 5. PLAN OF FORT FRONT AND BOX

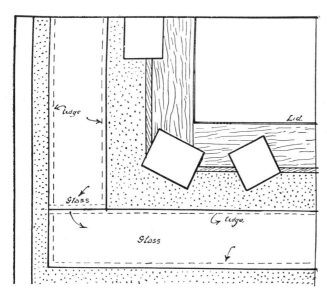

FIG. 6. ALTERNATIVE PLAN WITH MOAT

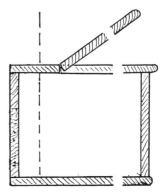

FIG. 7. SECTION OF TOY BOX

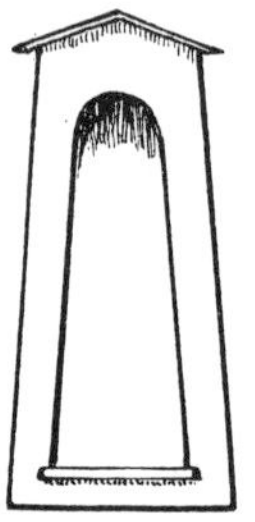

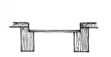

FIG. 8. MOAT DETAIL

FIG. 9. SENTRY BOX

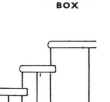

FIG. 10. STEPS

BENCH SANDER

(Continued from page 185)

top edge so that the sanding top is dead square with the disc when the latter drops down on to it. The hinges are let wholly into the support. The addition of the slotted strut to the sanding table and upright completes this part of the work.

Fence.—This finishes 5 in. by 1⅜ in. by ¼ in. and the protractor is screwed to bottom edge. For the protractor either a piece of metal about $\frac{1}{16}$ in. thick can be fitted, or a piece of plastic board can be used. Good quality plywood is an alternative. Note that the centre from which the semi-circle is struck is position of the hole for the main pivoting bolt. Near the edge a semi-circular slot is cut, and the other bolt passes through this. Thus, the protractor can be secured at any required angle.

Clearly the bolts in the slide have to finish flush at the underside. A simple method of fixing which avoids tapping the hole is to use ordinary round-head bolts which have a small square beneath the head. Cut off the head, and having bored the hole in the brass the same size as the bolt ($\frac{3}{16}$ in.) pass the bolt in from beneath. The square will stop it from passing right in, but if this is hammered the square will cut into the brass. This will hold it and prevent it from turning round. Place washers beneath the fly-nuts.

Sanding Disc.—Remove the stone from the spindle and prepare a piece of reliable ¾ in. hardwood. Plane it flat and cut to circular shape. Fix this on the spindle, and tighten the nut, using a rather smaller washer at the front so as not to cover up too much of the surface. Revolve the handle, and placing a chisel across the sanding table, gradually bring up edge so that it cuts the wood. In this way the disc can be made dead flat. Remove the disc, glue the abrasive paper to it, and replace once again. (199)

When punching in a nail it is advisable to look at the head of the punch, not the nail. You are not so liable to miss, especially when using a hammer with a small face.

BOY'S RUNABOUT

MADE FROM ODDMENTS

For a good wearing runabout a pull car of this type is cheap and easy to make. The over-all dimensions could be modified as required, and the experienced worker may alter the adjustment of the front wheels so that they pivot for steering. For quite young children the body of the car shown will serve the purpose, and is so built that it can be fitted with either wooden or rubber-tyred wheels. (Iron wheels are very noisy.)

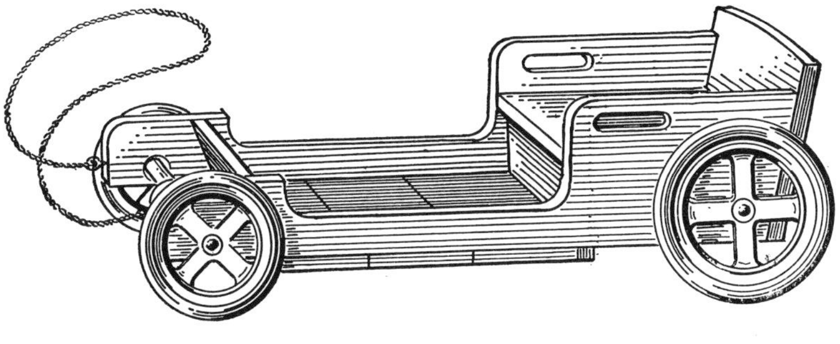

FIG. I. SOMETHING TO GIVE THE YOUNGSTERS NEVER-ENDING PLEASURE
Size (over body) 24 in. by 14 in. Either wooden or rubber tyred wheels can be used. Old discarded pram wheels are excellent

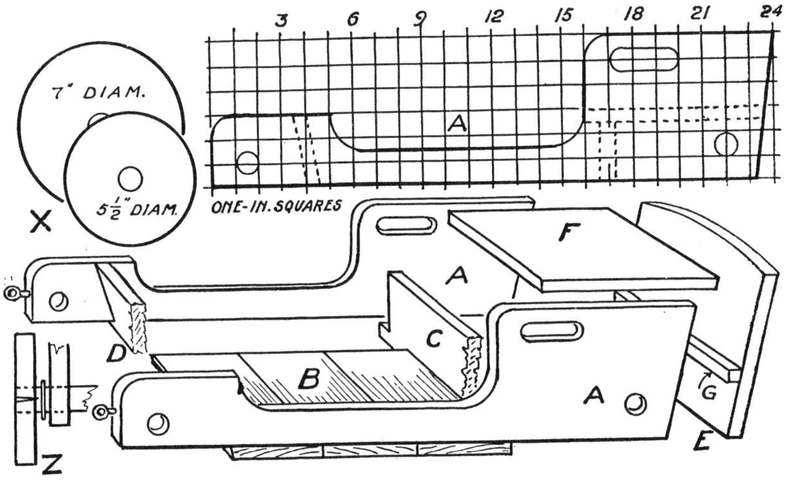

FIG. 2. MAIN SIZES AND CONSTRUCTION. THE SIDE IS SHOWN IN 1 IN. SQUARES

THE two sides (A), each 24 in. by 6 in., can be cut from one board $9\frac{1}{2}$ in. wide and about 33 in. long. The shaping is shown (Fig. 2) mapped into one-inch squares, and is so simple that it may be set out direct on the wood. The width of car (over body) is 14 in., the sides being connected by the three bottom boards (B), the two cross bars (C, D) and the back (E). These, preferably, should be screwed, but may be nailed. Note that the cross bars (C, D) look better if cut in at sides so that they may butt against (and be nailed to) the bottom (B). The slight curving of the back (E) is also an improvement. Before assembling, the centres for the wheel axles should be marked and the hand holes cut in sides. The seat (F) rests on bar (C) and on a fillet (G) nailed to back.

Wheels.—If wooden wheels (X) are made choose a hardwood $\frac{7}{8}$ in. thick. All may be the same diameter, but it gives a touch of variety if the front ones are smaller. If the sizes chosen are 7 in. and $5\frac{1}{2}$ in. note that the front axle holes must be centred $\frac{3}{4}$ in. lower than those at rear. Use axles of 1-in. or $1\frac{1}{8}$ in. diameter, these fitting tight into wheels and being wedged. Allow about $\frac{1}{4}$ in. clearance between wheel and side and place thin metal washers between (see Z).

Should rubber-tyred wheels (with axle fittings) be procurable these should be obtained *beforehand*, otherwise the worker runs the risk of a misfit.

All woodwork should be attractively painted, this being completed before the wheels are added.

CUTTING LIST

			Long ft. in.	Wide in.	Thick in.
(A)	2	Sides, cut from one length ..	2 9	$9\frac{1}{2}$	$\frac{5}{8}$
(B)	3	Bottom boards	1 $2\frac{1}{2}$	4	$\frac{1}{2}$
(C)		Seat bar	1 $2\frac{1}{2}$	$3\frac{1}{4}$	$\frac{5}{8}$
(D)		Foot bar	1 $2\frac{1}{2}$	$3\frac{3}{4}$	$\frac{5}{8}$
(E)		Back	1 $2\frac{1}{2}$	8	$\frac{5}{8}$
(F)		Seat	1 $0\frac{1}{2}$	8	$\frac{1}{2}$
	2	Wheels		7 diameter	$\frac{7}{8}$
	2	Wheels		$5\frac{1}{2}$,,	$\frac{7}{8}$
	2	Axles	1 $2\frac{1}{2}$	$1\frac{1}{8}$ diam.	

CARPENTRY AND JOINERY. John Lee. Tradesmen, students, and those seeking a fuller knowledge of the timber work involved in a house should see this book. It is essentially practical and gives the basic principle of its subject. It contains over 170 pages and is well illustrated with clear line diagrams. The chief subjects with which it deals are: Tools, timber, common joints, floors, roofs, doors, windows, mouldings, setting-out rods and lists, scheme of practical work. It is a book we can recommend to readers. Published at 6s. 6d. net by English Universities Press Ltd., St. Paul's House, Warwick Square, London, E.C.4.

HANDICRAFTS IN PLASTICS. Benjamin T. Richards. Plastics are coming in for increasing use, both by themselves and in conjunction with other materials. Readers wanting a practical and inexpensive book on the subject will find this extremely useful. It opens with notes on the tools required and general working of plastics and follows with a series of designs for small items to make—boxes, stands, serviette rings, spoons, bowls, etc. Published at 3s. 6d. net by G. Bell & Sons Ltd., York House, Portugal St., London, W.C.2.

Intarsia is a term applied to inlaying in which the design is cut out in thin wood and inlayed into cavities chopped in the solid wood. It is thus different from marquetry in which both inlay and background are in veneer, and the whole glued down on to a groundwork of solid wood.

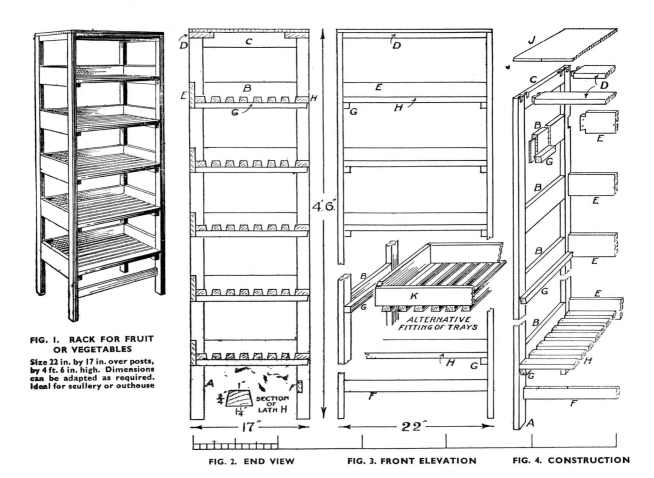

FIG. 1. RACK FOR FRUIT OR VEGETABLES

Size 22 in. by 17 in. over posts, by 4 ft. 6 in. high. Dimensions can be adapted as required. Ideal for scullery or outhouse

FIG. 2. END VIEW   FIG. 3. FRONT ELEVATION   FIG. 4. CONSTRUCTION

FRUIT AND VEGETABLE RACK

Racks for fruit and vegetables must be open to permit of the free passage of air. Thus, although we may have a plywood top, the sides and back are open ; whilst, instead of solid shelves or tray bottoms, space laths are used

IN height the rack may vary from 3 ft. 6 in. to 5 ft. ; in width from, say, 18 in. to 24 in. ; in depth (front to back) from 15 in. to 18 in. An average size is shown (22 in. by 17 in. over carcase and 4 ft. 6 in. high), but the dimensions given may be altered according to the number of shelves or trays desired. Fixed lath shelving is indicated, but if sliding trays are preferred a method of providing for these is shown in Fig. 3.

If for outdoor or outhouse use the corner posts (A) may be of 2 in. by 1¼ in. softwood, but if to be employed indoors it is better to select hardwood such as birch, 2 in. by ⅞ in., other parts (except where noted) being ⅞ in. For a rack of the size shown the following are the timbers :

CUTTING LIST

				Long ft. in.	Wide in.	Thick in.
(A)	4 Posts	..	.. ..	4 6	2	⅞
(B)	10 Side rails	..	.. ..	1 5	3½	⅞
(C)	2 Top side rails	..	.. ..	1 5	2	⅞
(D)	2 Top bearer rails	..	..	1 10	3½	⅞
(E)	5 Back rails	..	..	1 10	3½	⅞
(F)	1 Front rail	..	..	1 10	1½	⅞
(G)	10 Shelf fillets	..	..	1 5	1	1
(H)	10 Shelf laths (outer)	..	..	1 9½	2¼	¾
	30 Ditto	..	..	1 9½	1¼	¾
(J)	Top (plywood)	..	..	1 10	17	5⁄16

The number of shelf laths might be reduced by cutting them 1½ in. wide and spacing them further apart.

Construction.—The two ends are first completed by tenoning the side rails (B and C) to the posts (A). In a quite simple way they might be half-lapped and screwed instead of tenoned. To each side rail (B) screw on the fillet (G) on which the shelf laths (H) will rest, the fillet being kept flush with rail at bottom (see Fig. 4).

The ends are connected by the two top bearer rails (D), which are lap-dovetailed, and by the back rails (E), also lap-dovetailed. Here again, for a quite simple job, the rails (E) might be screwed direct to back of posts. At front a stiffening rail (F) is let into posts 4 in. from bottom and screwed.

The screwing down of the shelf laths (H) and the plywood top (J) completes the work. It will probably be found simpler to fix the shelf laths to their fillets (G) before screwing the latter to the ends. The laths are usually bevelled in section as shown in detail (Fig. 2).

Trays.—These involve considerably more work ; but, if preferred, a method of fitting them is shown in Fig. 3. In this case the side rails (B) may be reduced to a width of 2 in. Fillets (G), which will form the runners, are screwed on as before. Trays (K) could have 2½ in. by ¾ in. fronts and 3½ in. by ¾ in. sides and backs, these being either dovetailed or rebated and screwed together. The laths, it will be seen, lie from front to back, the two outer ones being fitted to clear the runners. The trays will stop against the back rails (E) which will be kept to the same width as side rails—that is, 2 in.   (297)

Put waste blocks of wood beneath the shoes of a cramp. It saves the wood from being damaged by the pressure.

Simple yet reliable . . . .
WEATHER INDICATOR

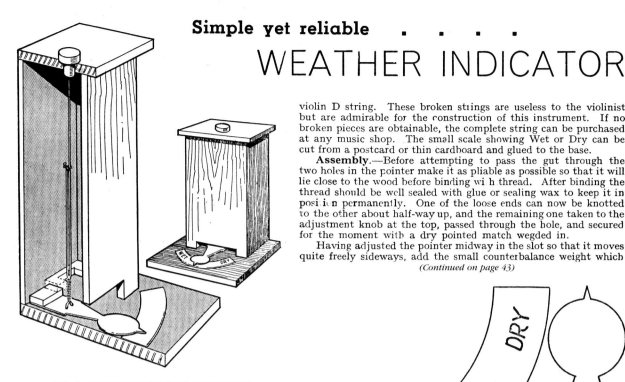

FIG. I. CUT-AWAY VIEW OF THE DEVICE
The small sketch to the right shows the appearance of the
completed indicator

HERE is a novel little instrument which, although
simple in construction, gives a reliable indication
of any change in the humidity of the air. Once
the initial adjustment has been made it may be left
severely alone and in this condition it will function
for years without attention.

Construction.—The small pieces of wood required
for the case are usually to be found in any woodworker's
box in which short ends are kept. This material may
be any hardwood such as oak, walnut, mahogany, or
even oakfaced plywood. The pieces should be cut to
finished sizes shown on the cutting list and
assembled with glue and fine nails. The back should
be left dry and pinned only in case any adjustment
may be necessary at some future time. The whole
case may be glasspapered and stained to the colour
desired.

The Internal Mechanism.—This consists of five
main parts which are, pointer, weight, gut suspension,
register through which the gut passes, and the adjustment knob at the top. It will be seen that, as the
pointer is $\frac{1}{8}$ in. thick only, a mild straight-grained
piece is necessary to eliminate warping and any ten-
tency to split when inserting the gut. The full size
shape of the pointer is given in the drawing.

One simple way of making the adjustment knob is
to obtain a small piece of $\frac{1}{2}$ in. dowel, cut square at
one end, and bore a smaller hole in the centre to take
a $\frac{1}{4}$ in. dowel. Glue the $\frac{1}{4}$ in. dowel into the $\frac{1}{2}$ in. dowel
and cut off to the required size. When this has dried
out the small hole for the gut can be bored through the
centre.

The small piece of wood for the register can be made
of any odd piece. Its function is to prevent the
suspension from swinging sideways, although giving
freedom for a central twisting action. For the suspension a piece of gut is necessary about ten inches long,
which must be of the twisted strand variety. This is
really important. In the model made as an experiment,
the writer was fortunate enough to obtain a piece of

violin D string. These broken strings are useless to the violinist
but are admirable for the construction of this instrument. If no
broken pieces are obtainable, the complete string can be purchased
at any music shop. The small scale showing Wet or Dry can be
cut from a postcard or thin cardboard and glued to the base.

Assembly.—Before attempting to pass the gut through the
two holes in the pointer make it as pliable as possible so that it will
lie close to the wood before binding with thread. After binding the
thread should be well sealed with glue or sealing wax to keep it in
position permanently. One of the loose ends can now be knotted
to the other about half-way up, and the remaining one taken to the
adjustment knob at the top, passed through the hole, and secured
for the moment with a dry pointed match wedged in.

Having adjusted the pointer midway in the slot so that it moves
quite freely sideways, add the small counterbalance weight which

(Continued on page 43)

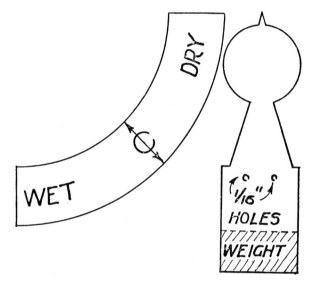

FIG. 2. FULL-SIZE DIAGRAM OF SCALE AND POINTER

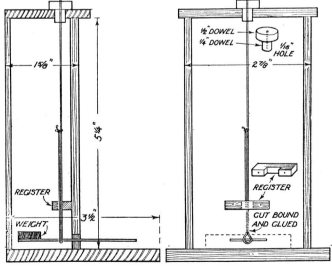

FIG. 3. SIDE AND FRONT SECTIONS WITH MAIN SIZES

DELIGHTFUL TOY-SUITABLE FOR A CHRISTMAS PRESENT
This can be made by a man with a wood-turning lathe. When painted it has a most realistic appearance

Toy . . .
STEAM
ROLLER

Children are generally pleased by a mechanical toy that bears some resemblance to the real thing, and it is more satisfactory when making such a toy to keep as far as possible to the correct proportions. Simplification must, of course, be made, but the result can be quite realistic. A description of a toy steam roller that is more or less to scale has been sent to us by a reader and we think that it will interest those readers who have a lathe. If a toy is required which is to be larger than that described, the dimensions given can be proportionately increased

IF possible, a hardwood such as beech, birch, oak or mahogany should be used for the turned parts. Plywood is satisfactory for the tender. The metal yoke which mounts the front roller can be made from half hard brass strip, but for a larger model, mild steel should be used.

Tender.—If possible, the two sides, Fig. 3, should be trued up in one length and cross-cut. The two pieces are then pinned together by veneer pins and both cut to shape and the two holes bored. Alignment of the axle holes is assured by working in this manner. The rear, front, and bottom pieces and also the piece A, Figs. 4, 5, 7, and 6, respectively, can also be prepared in one long length and cross-cut to form the individual parts. The two countersunk holes, Fig. 5, should be bored before cross-cutting, since there will then be less tendency for the wood to split.

Chimney.—Fig. 8, this is a straightforward piece of turning, but care should be taken to turn the spigot at the lower end carefully to size, since this should be a tight fit in the hole provided for its reception in the boiler.

Boiler.—If a piece of stuff of requisite size is available,

the raised front of the boiler can be initially turned completely round the boiler. It is possible, however, to economise in material by mounting the stuff out of centre, as indicated in Fig. 10. The cutting away of the front is best done with a dovetail saw, the finishing being done by paring with a chisel. In order that the boiler should seat closely against the tender, it is as well slightly to dish the end as indicated in Fig. 9.

As it is important that the chimney should be square with the axis of the boiler, it is advisable to take some care in the drilling for the chimney spigot. While the work is mounted between centres, a pencil line is run round the circumference to locate the spigot hole lengthwise of the boiler. Diametrical lines are then marked on opposite sides and their intersection with the circumferential line will give diametrically opposite points for locating the drilling. The work is now removed from the lathe and the spigot hole drilled with a $\frac{3}{8}$ in. drill held in a drill chuck, the back centre being brought up to the diametrically opposite mark to hold and feed with work whilst drilling. The shallow $\frac{11}{16}$ in. recess serves to seat the chimney and avoids the gap that would otherwise appear at the sides.

Roller, Rear Wheels, and Flywheel.—The roller is usually made in two parts in order to facilitate steering, but for a toy, a single roller will suffice, a central V groove being turned to simulate two rollers, Fig. 11. In forming the yoke

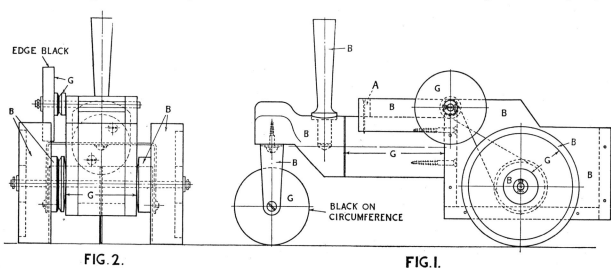

FIG. 2.

FIG. I.

LIVERY:— B = BLACK
G = GREEN

REAR ELEVATION DRAWN TO SCALE

SIDE ELEVATION WITH PARTS LETTERED FOR REFERENCE

for the roller, Fig. 12, the strip of brass or steel should be set out and shaped and the drilling completed before bending. One method of turning the rear wheels is to cut out two blanks. A blank is then screwed to the face-plate, a piece of plywood having been inserted between the blank and the face plate. The screws should be so positioned that they pass into the waste wood around the inner hub, Fig. 13. The blank is then turned to the required diameter and the face recessed $\frac{3}{16}$ in. deep to form the rim and outer hub. While the work is still mounted, the axle hole is carefully centred and drilled.

This done, the work is removed from the face-plate and mounted in a self-centring chuck for turning the inner hub. Should a chuck of this kind not be available, a piece of $\frac{3}{4}$ in. stuff can be screwed to the face-plate and recessed about $\frac{3}{8}$ in. deep and the work pressed into the recess. The frictional grip should be sufficient to enable the inner hub to be turned. It will be noted that one of the inner hubs has a V groove for

the flywheel driving belt. If a length of thin walled brass tubing $\frac{7}{32}$ in. bore can be obtained, it is a good plan to bush the axle holes. The bushes can be secured by spreading the ends slightly with a centre punch. The procedure in turning the flywheel, Fig. 14, can be the same as that employed in turning the rear wheels.

Drilling the Axles.—The rear wheels and flywheel revolve on $\frac{3}{16}$ in. bright mild steel rods and the rods are force fits in the holes in the tender. The rear wheels and also the flywheel are retained on their respective shafts by split pins and washers. The flywheel could revolve on a No. 8 round-head screw, but if this is done, the front of the tender should be taken up level with the top and should be made of thicker stuff so that the screw can pass into it without splitting the wood. The drilling for the split pins may be found difficult, but the operation can be simplified by making up a jig. This can comprise a small piece of brass in which a $\frac{3}{16}$ in. hole has been drilled and in which a diametrical hole has been bored of suitable size to take a split pin. If now the jig is slipped on the shafts in turn, the jig will position the drill for drilling the split pin holes.

Assembly.—The parts of the tender are secured together with panel pins, but the back piece should not be fixed until the $1\frac{1}{4}$ in. No. 8 screws fixing the tender to the boiler are screwed home. If the back piece is nailed in place before the tender is fixed to the boiler, difficulty may be experienced in turning the screws.

Finishing.—A realistic effect can be obtained by enamelling the parts in agreement with the usual colours of a steam roller. Alternatively water poster colours can be used. When dry two coats of clean oil varnish are applied. The livery can be as indicated in Figs. 1 and 2. If preferred, clear cellulose can be used after the poster colours. (362)

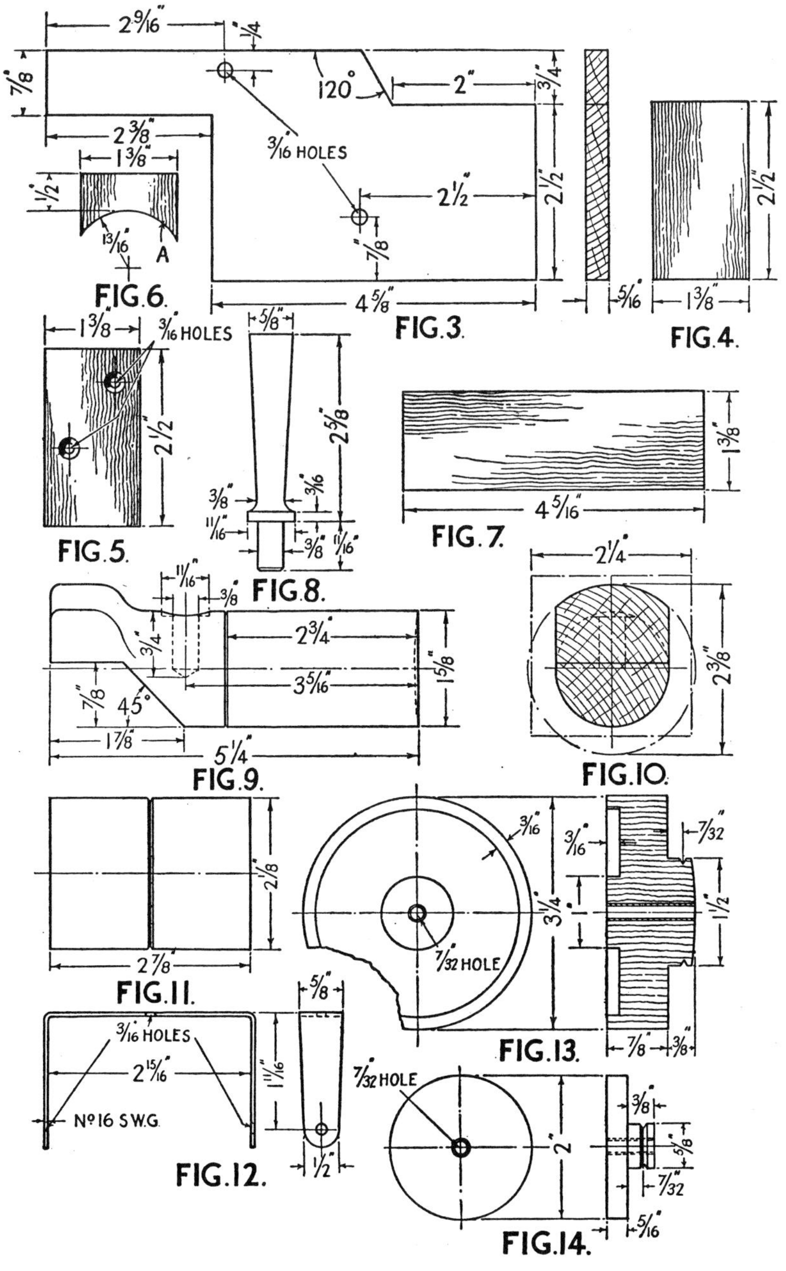

FIGS. 3-14. SIZES TO WHICH PARTS SHOULD BE CUT

Fig. 3. Side of tender. Fig. 4. Rear end of tender. Fig. 5. Front end of tender. Fig. 6. Insert "A." Fig. 7. Bottom of tender. Fig. 8. Funnel. Fig. 9. Boiler. Fig. 10. End elevation of boiler. Fig. 11. Roller. Fig. 12. Yoke. Fig. 13. Wheel. Fig. 14. Flywheel

---

WEATHER INDICATOR

(Continued from page 41)

can be made of metal or wood until it is horizontal. A little time spent on this suspension balance will amply repay itself later. When this has been done the match at the top can be glued and driven in firmly.

The Initial Adjustment.—When the knob at the top is turned in either direction the pointer should move freely with it, although the knob itself must be tight enough to remain set in any position. A glance at an ordinary barometer will give the position of the pointer and once this is set, there is no need for any further adjustment. (359)

CUTTING LIST

Finished Size			Long in.	Wide in.	Thick in.
1 Base ..	..	..	$3\frac{3}{4}$	$3\frac{1}{4}$	$\frac{1}{4}$
2 Sides	..	..	$5\frac{1}{4}$	$1\frac{5}{16}$	$\frac{3}{16}$
1 Front	..	..	$5\frac{1}{4}$	$2\frac{7}{8}$	$\frac{3}{16}$
			(Slot 2 in. × $\frac{3}{8}$ in.)		
1 Back	..	..	$5\frac{1}{4}$	$2\frac{7}{8}$	$\frac{1}{8}$
1 Top ..	..	..	$3\frac{3}{4}$	$1\frac{7}{8}$	$\frac{3}{16}$
			(With $\frac{1}{4}$ in. hole)		
1 Pointer	..	..	$2\frac{3}{4}$	$\frac{7}{8}$	$\frac{1}{16}$
			(Mild Timber)		
1 Register	..	..	1	$\frac{3}{8}$	$\frac{3}{16}$
Knob	..	..	$\frac{1}{2}$ and $\frac{1}{4}$ dowel.		

FOR THE YOUNGSTER
USEFUL DESKS

The small desks in Fig. I are suitable for a child about five years old. For older children the height of desk and stool should be increased. Also the top of the desk could be made a little larger, say 24 in. by 18 in. Hardwood, such as oak or beech, should be used for the framing. A solid flap should be clamped at each end or, alternatively, it could be from ½ in. thick chipboard. The designs are interchangeable. The splayed legs may be put on the flat top desk if desired, or the standard legs on the one with the slope. A natural waxed finish would be suitable.

FIG. I. ALTERNATIVE DESIGNS F Practically all details are interchangeable. The height desk of his own should help

T HE general construction of both desks is similar, the box being a separate unit.

Desk, Design A.—The box may be lap-dovetailed together as shown in Fig. 4, or it may be through-dovetailed or comb jointed. The bottom edges of the front and sides are rebated for the 6 mm. plywood bottom. A bevelled block (C), side elevation, Fig. 2, is glued and pinned to the back inside for the bottom (J) to be screwed to.

The front bottom edge of the back (E) is rounded. The front piece or top (G) to which the flap is hinged may have a pen groove cut in with the gouge or, alternatively, worked right through with a grooving plane. It is fixed to the box with a block screwed two ways before the bottom (J) is screwed on. The flap (H) if in solid wood should be clamped. If in chipboard the edges may be lipped.

The legs (A and B) are tapered, shouldered, and dowelled together as shown in Fig. 4. The front edges are rounded with a ⅜ in. radius, see inset, Fig. 4. Afterwards the top is cut away to fit over the box leaving a full ¾ in. thickness

for screwing, the screws to be driven in from inside the box, see inset, Fig. 4. For extra lightness and better appearance the legs may be tapered at the sides also as shown in Fig. 2, before rounding off. Finish by rounding over and smoothing the tops.

Desk, Design B.—This box without a slope is made similarly, either by dovetailing or comb-jointing. The fixed piece (R) and flap (S) should be hinged together with a pair of 2-in. brass butt hinges before fixing to the box. The bottom is screwed on as for Design (A). Cut away the box sides ⅛ in. deep for the standard legs (M). These are tenoned into the bases (K) and pegged. Fix the legs by screwing from inside the box.

Stool, Design C.—Taper the legs and connect with seat rails

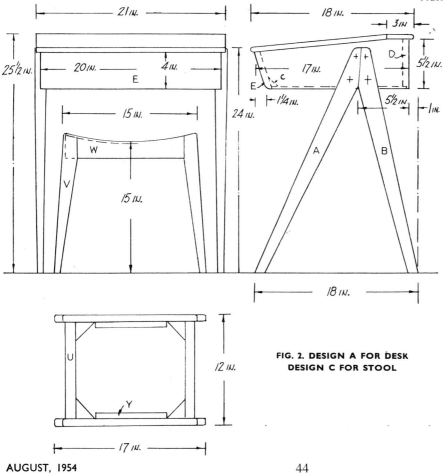

FIG. 2. DESIGN A FOR DESK DESIGN C FOR STOOL

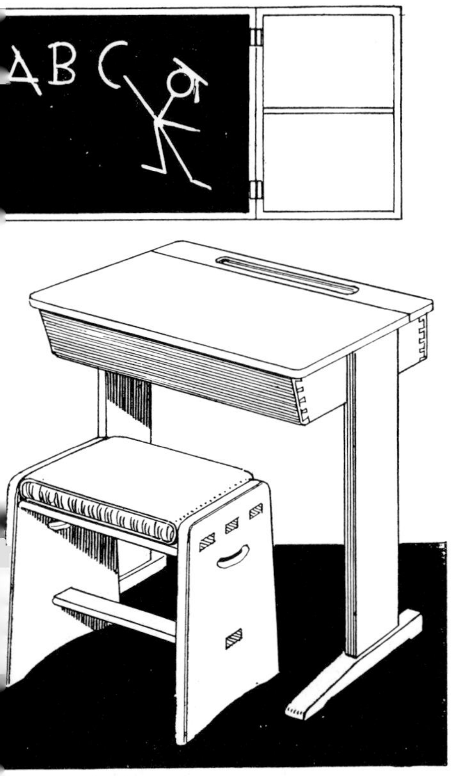

LDREN'S DESKS AND STOOLS
aried to suit the age of the child. The idea of a
ntive to doing homework

CUTTING LIST

Desk. Design A

	Long ft.	Long in.	Wide in.	Thick in.
(A) 2 Legs ..	2	4½	2½	1⅛
(B) 2 Ditto ..	2	1½	2½	1⅛
(C) 1 Block ..	1	7¼	1½	1⅛
(D) 1 Front ..	1	8½	5¾	¾
(E) 1 Back ..	1	8½	4¾	¾
(F) 2 Sides ..	1	5¼	5¾	⅝
(G) 1 Top ..	1	9½	3¼	⅝ or ½
(H) 1 Flap ..	1	9½	15½	⅝ or ½
(J) 1 Bottom ..	1	8	15¼	6mm.
1 Block ..	1	7¼	1	¾

Desk. Design B

	Long ft.	Long in.	Wide in.	Thick in.
(K) 2 Bases ..	1	5½	2	1⅜
(L) 1 Block ..	1	7¼	1⅜	1⅛
(M) 2 Legs ..	1	11¾	4¼	⅞
(N) 1 Front ..	1	8½	4¾	¾
(P) 1 Back ..	1	8½	5¼	¾
(Q) 2 Sides ..	1	5¼	4¾	⅝
(R) 1 Top ..	1	10½	3¼	⅝ or ½
(S) 1 Flap ..	1	10½	15¼	⅝ or ½
(T) 1 Bottom ..	1	8	15¼	6mm.
1 Block ..	1	7¼	1	¾

Stool. Design C

	Long ft.	Long in.	Wide in.	Thick in.
(U) 2 Rails ..		10½	2¾	1⅛
(V) 4 Legs ..	1	4	2	1
(W) 2 Rails ..	1	2½	3	1
1 For 4 braces	1	0½	2¼	⅞
(Y) 2 Blocks ..		8½	1½	⅝
1 Seat ..		10½	15¼	6mm.

Stool Design D

	Long ft.	Long in.	Wide in.	Thick in.
2 Slab ends	1	3	15¼	¾
1 Seat ..	1	5	12¼	¾
1 Stretcher ..	1	5	3¼	¾

Allowances : ½ in. on all lengths ; ¼ in. on all widths. Thicknesses net.

(Fig. 4 appears on page 46)

(W) tenoned as strongly as possible. Cut a saddle shape to the top. Dowel the end rails (U) to the legs and well brace the corners, plan, Fig. 2. Screw on blocks (Y) shaped to the line of the rails 6 mm. down to form a rebate for the bent plywood seat (see Fig. 4). This is screwed down with countersunk head brass screws.

Stool, Design D.—The slab ends are shaped and rounded as shown in Fig. 3. The seat edges are well rounded also and tenons are cut to pass through the slab ends. The stretcher rail is treated similarly and after gluing together the tenons are wedged. The whole is levelled off and all edges nicely rounded and smoothed. This stool could be in softwood. A squab cushion 13 in. by 12 in. by 2 in. thick is placed loose on top. (531)

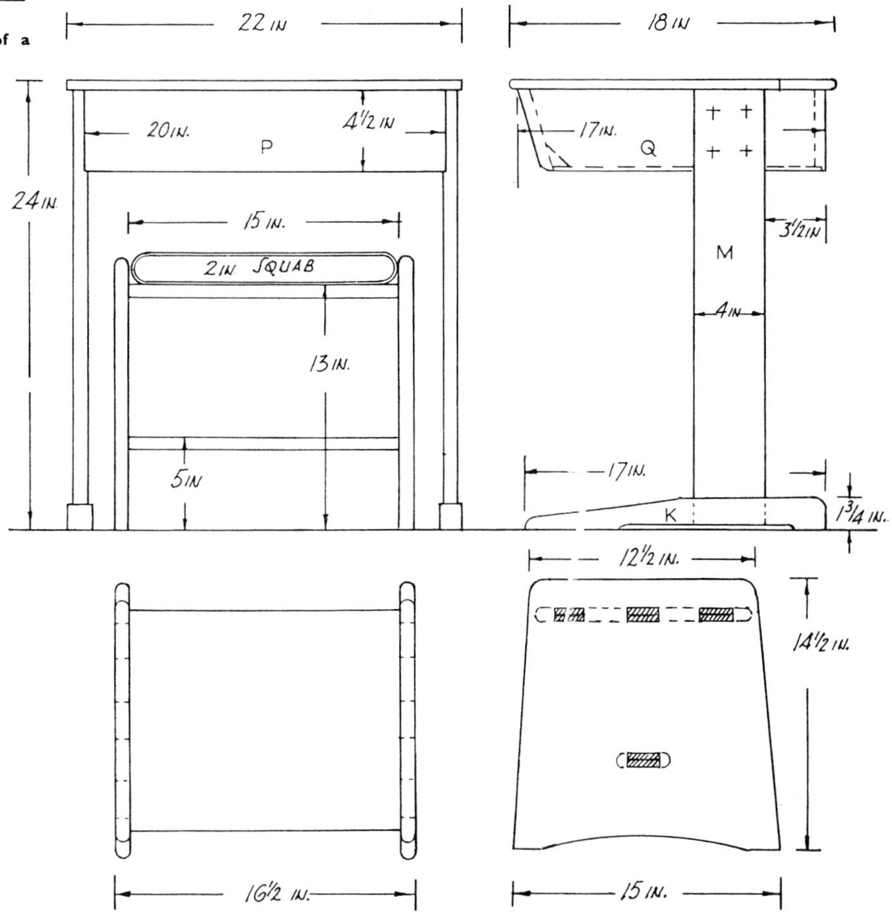

FIG. 3. DESIGN B FOR DESK, DESIGN D FOR STOOL

(Continued from page 153)

Best quality white polish is almost pure white, and this is the only kind suitable for the sort of job we have in mind. Transparent polish is unsuitable. It would leave a slight amber cast which would spoil the job. Rubbers which have been used for any other purpose are useless.

We should begin with a thin wash coat of the polish. Once across and once along the grain is sufficient. This, when hard, will protect the surface from the rubbing involved in grain filling and shield it from the oil used in or with the filler. White or transparent grain fillers are the only types suitable. Of these, white filler—such as *Alabastine*—is the most readily available. Apply it in the usual way. Clean off when hard with superfine steel wool, working along the grain only. Use a clean rag and linseed to " kill " the filler. Leave the surface as dry as possible. When this is hard polish in the usual way.

The bleaching technique is useful when a job has to be changed in colour. One reader had a gaboon cabinet which he wished to re-finish light brown. Gaboon bleaches readily. One application after stripping would turn it to a light yellowish-brown, and from this shade it could easily be stained to requirements.

Uniform colouring.—Bleaching can also be employed to give uniformity when different colours or types of wood are used in the same job. For an example, we have a buffet table with a teak top made of three boards, the middle one of which was much darker than the others. After stripping we should mask off exactly at the joints with something like Selotape and bleach the centre board. With luck we could get an exact match after one full application followed, perhaps, by another full or partial one. Most likely it would finish on the light side and could then be let down to match the others with linseed coloured with a little suitable stain.

Where a job with dark patches or streaks has to be bleached the best method is to bleach the dark areas first and, when the colour is reasonably uniform bleach the whole job. Sometimes a surface bleaches well, but contains one or two awkward dark mineral streaks which will not respond to the treatment. These may need to be painted out. This is done after bleaching and before finishing. Ordinary water colours are as good as anything for this job and can be readily mixed to shade. Sometimes dark streaks bleach partially and finish with a greenish tinge. These can be toned in to the general figure with weak naphtha stain or painted out as a last resort.

Restoring a Bleached Finish.— Where the polish only has to be replaced it must be removed without affecting the surface beneath. In this case the scraper is unsuitable as most likely it would cut through the bleached skin. Through and through veneers are sometimes used and could be scraped. Solid parts will always be surface bleached, as it is not possible to bleach through any great thickness. The safe plan is to use a good stripper and repolish when this is dry and neutralised with meth.

Precautions.—In the woodfinishing craft everything needs to be done correctly. One mistake can ruin the whole job. This applies particularly to the bleached finish. Apart from all the usual conditions and precautions which we must observe, failure can result in three main ways. We can cut through the bleached surface with papering. We must always keep in mind that this has little depth. We can undo our work with polish which contains colour. Even a trace of this, such as you find in poor white polish, will affect the job adversely. Finally, failure to neutralise the bleach will result in crinkling of the polish film. This can happen in patches if the stage has been carelessly done. Stripping is the only remedy. Neutralising needs watching on a solid job where there is no glue film to stop deeper penetration of the acid.

Readers will have concluded by this time that bleaching is a complicated operation. It is certainly not a job for the novice, but is not so difficult as we have made it sound. We have naturally stressed the dangers and difficulties. Bleached work is not suitable for the living room as it shows finger marks easily. It is most suitable for bedrooms and is becoming increasingly popular. Some people refer to it as the " blonde " finish. (523)

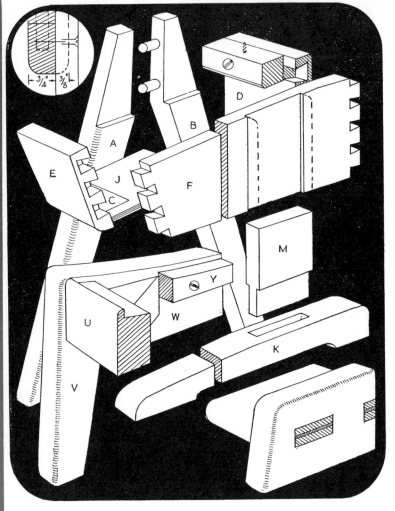

FIG. 4. CONSTRUCTION DETAILS OF DESKS AND STOOLS

(see pages 44 and 45)

ATTRACTIVE OAK

TEA TRAY

Many people regard tea trays with distrust, feeling that the handles may come off or that the bottom might give way. This tray overcomes both these prejudices. The bottom rests on a rebate within the frame and there are no handles. Carrying facilities are provided for by leaving a suitable space in the plinth for the fingers.

FIG. I. THE FINISHED TRAY
Small rubber buttons are attached to the base preventing possible damage to furniture

ALTHOUGH of simple construction, special attention should be given to the exploded view shown in Fig. 2. For the beginner this joint may present some difficulty but it is worth learning as it is often used in carcase construction.

Frame.—Having planed the pieces to size, mark out dovetails and decoration. The dovetail and bottom shoulder are cut in the usual way, a suitable bevel-edged chisel being used to remove the waste between the tail and top edge. This is carefully chopped out, working from both inner and outer face as the occasion demands. Starting at a point about $\frac{1}{16}$ in. to $\frac{1}{8}$ in. in front of the shoulder line the major part is cut away and the remainder removed by careful chiselling. The pins are made by sawing along the line on the inside face holding the saw at a slight angle. After clamping the work to the bench, waste is removed with a bevel-edged chisel. At this stage the rebate and scalloped edge are worked, the latter being made with a convex spokeshave. On completion the frame is assembled dry as a check, and any trimming which may be necessary carried out.

Finally the joints are glued together and cramps applied. Make sure the frame is square and all surplus glue removed before allowing to set.

Base.—This is trimmed to fit the rebate, and it is advisable during this operation to make a pencil mark on the underside near one edge and a similar mark on the frame. This ensures that it is placed within the framework the same way on each occasion a trial fit is made. A neat fit having been achieved a coat of polish is applied to the upper surface and when dry glued in place.

Plinth.—A chamfer is worked on the outer edge and the corners mitred. The sections are glued, placed in position, and pinned or screwed on to the frame, a space being left as shown in Figs. 1 and 2, for carrying.

CUTTING LIST

Frame.		Long	Wide	Thick
		ft. in.	in.	in.
2 Sides	..	1 6½	1¾	¾
2 Ends	..	1 0½	1¾	¾
1 Base	..	1 5¾	11¾	¼
				(ply (oak faced)
Plinth.				
2 Sides	..	1 7½	1¼	⅜
4 Ends	..	5	1¼	⅜

Allowance has been made in lengths and widths, thicknesses are net. (566)

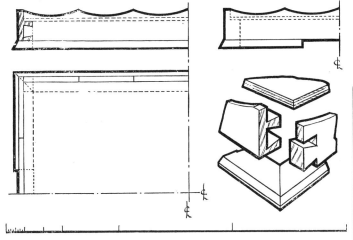

FIG. 2. SECTIONAL ELEVATIONS, PLAN, AND EXPLODED VIEW
The plinth can be pinned or screwed in place. Its purpose is to raise the frame and provide a suitable space for carrying

ATTRACTIVE

LOOSE LEAF FOLDERS

These delightful oak and mansonia folders are ideal as stamp or photograph albums, as the stiff covers keep flat such items placed within them. Coloured tape or cord serves to hold the sections together and is easily replaced when worn or soiled. The unusual decoration is simple but effective, and the method used to achieve it is given in the article

ALMOST any good quality straight-grained hardwood free from knots could be used, and the size can be altered to suit individual needs. Thickness, however, should not exceed ⅜ in. as this tends to give a rather clumsy appearance ; about ¼ in. would meet most requirements.

Oak Folder.—This, shown in Fig. 1, is made from two pieces of 12 in. by 9 in. These are planed to size and edges rounded, one piece being left slightly full in the width to allow for a saw cut and subsequent cleaning up. When prepared, one side of each piece is covered with shallow channels as in Fig. 1. This is done with a roughing, or scrub plane. If such a plane is unobtainable a good substitute can be made by reshaping an old plane iron. The blade should be ground until a curved cutting edge, similar to that shown by the dotted line in Fig. 2 (A), is formed. After removing the wire edge it is honed in the usual way, a cap iron screwed on and fitted in an ordinary jack plane. Providing the cutting edge is keen and well set good results will be achieved. No attempt should be made to keep the channels perfectly uniform as the slight deviations which occur when planing give a more interesting finish. This is clearly seen in Fig. 1. Having channelled the surfaces a strip 1 in. wide is sawn

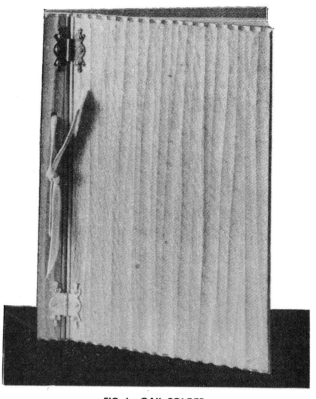

FIG. I. OAK FOLDER
The shallow grooves give the impression of an adze finish. They are made with an ordinary plane having a specially ground blade

off the wider piece, the edges cleaned up, and a bead worked on one side of each edge with a scratch stock. If not to hand a suitable scratch can be made from two pieces of hardwood about ½ in. thick and 1½ in. wide. These are shaped and screwed together as in Fig. 2 (B) with 1 in. by 8 countersunk screws. Whitworth 3/16 in. nuts and bolts make a better job, but if these are used both heads and nuts should be sunk into the wood. A fairly good cutter can be made from an old hacksaw blade filed or ground to shape shown at (C), Fig. 2. This is clamped between the two sections as indicated by the dotted lines in Fig. 2.

The pieces to be beaded are clamped to the bench and the scratch worked along the edges concerned as follows. Holding the tool at a slight angle it is pushed along, cutting a little at a time. As the work progresses the angle is altered until it reaches an upright position and no further cutting takes place. When the beads have been cut the inside surfaces of the covers are glasspapered to a fine finish working with the grain. At this

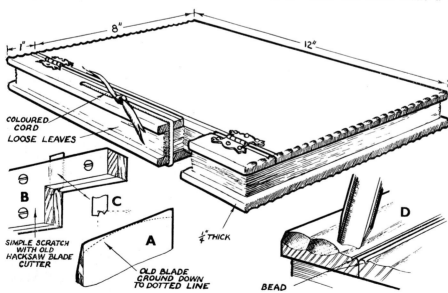

COLOURED CORD
LOOSE LEAVES
B
C
SIMPLE SCRATCH WITH OLD HACKSAW BLADE CUTTER
A
OLD BLADE GROUND DOWN TO DOTTED LINE
¼" THICK
D
BEAD

FIG. 2. PICTORIAL VIEW WITH DIMENSIONS
The advantage of this folder is that any number of leaves can be fitted

OCTOBER, 1954

48

WOODWORKER

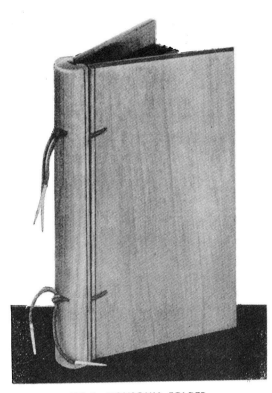

FIG. 3. MANSONIA FOLDER
An ideal folder for preserving sketches, photographic negatives, and the like

cover edges being well rounded. After preparation the parts are clamped to the bench and a bead worked on the edges indicated in Fig. 4. This is done with a scratch as previously described. If not available one can be easily made in the manner already given. The bead having been cut, a groove ½ in. wide and about ⅜ in. deep is ploughed along one face of the square section to receive the leaves and cleaned up. Cord holes are made with a ⅛ in. drill, the edges of which are slightly countersunk as in Fig. 4 (C). A narrow slot cut on the face opposite to the groove made for the leaves links the holes as in Figs. 3 and 4 (C) and serves to hold the coloured cord in place. Cord holes in the leaves are made in the manner previously given for the oak folder. At this stage the back is rounded and the sections well glasspapered.

To lace the sections together the cord is first passed through the leaves, then the covers, finishing with the back. These stages are shown in (A) and (B), Fig. 4. When assembled, the cord is pulled taut and knotted. Added interest can be given by fraying out the ends of the cord and binding with coloured cotton.   (592)

SHOOTING BOARD (*Continued from page* 196)

timber is suitable for the block, the pieces being glued and screwed together. The width of the timber need be only 4 or 5 in. It is as well to make the block longer than required, and saw it to size and shape. The bottom face is most difficult to true, and should be planed first and checked for truth with winding strips. Next plane the far end square and vertical to the base, and true the slant-face last. The piece (B) is screwed to the end of the block and, by fitting against the main stop of the shooting board, is reinforced to take the thrust of the plane. Screws fasten the block to the board as before.

The donkey's ear must be true in two directions. The 45° angle may be checked with the set square against the sole of the plane. The 90° angle, i.e. the angle between the stop and the sole of the plane, can also be checked with the set square.   (45)

stage the decorative hinges are placed in position about 1 in. from either end and fixed with round-head screws. Those shown in Fig. 1 are chromium plated, but a fine wrought-iron hinge would look well on these covers.

To ensure the cord holes being in alignment both covers are drilled in one operation. To do this they are first clamped together, smooth surfaces inside, and the holes made with a ³⁄₁₆ in. drill. Cord holes in the leaves are made by using one of the covers as a template, the paper being clamped between this and a spare piece of wood when drilling.

When making the gouge cuts a well-sharpened tool should be used. This is held at about 45 degrees and about ⅛ in. from the edge; a sharp tap with a mallet produces a good clean cut. Here again, slight deviations in angle and depth of cut add to, rather than detract from the decoration. Note that each cut should overlap the one preceding as in Fig. 2 (D). On completion, wax or clear french polish is applied, which provides a protective covering against possible finger marks. When ready the parts are bound together with a coloured cord or similar material.

Mansonia Folder.—This is produced from three pieces, comprising of two covers and a back. These are planed to size, the

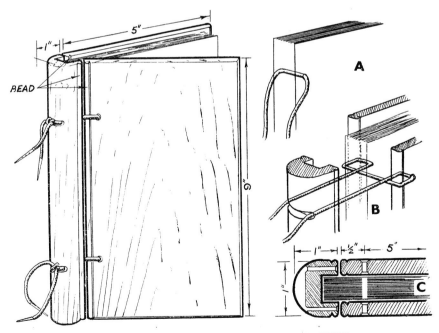

FIG. 4. LACING DETAILS AND DIMENSIONAL VIEWS
Note that both inner and outer edges of the cover are beaded. This prevents undue wear on the ends.

MAKE YOUR OWN
SALAD SERVERS

Wood servers are becoming increasingly popular. They have an attractive appearance and do their job perfectly well. From the woodworker's point of view they are excellent since they are most interesting to make. As a Christmas gift they would be most popular. A good quality hardwood should be used such as sycamore, walnut, or oak. Some prefer to leave them untreated, but a certain amount of staining is inevitable when this is done, and it is more satisfactory to go over with a clear, heat- and water-resistant varnish. In any case one should treat them with reasonable respect, and avoid dipping them right into hot, strong soda water. A wipe over with a damp cloth will clean them quite well.

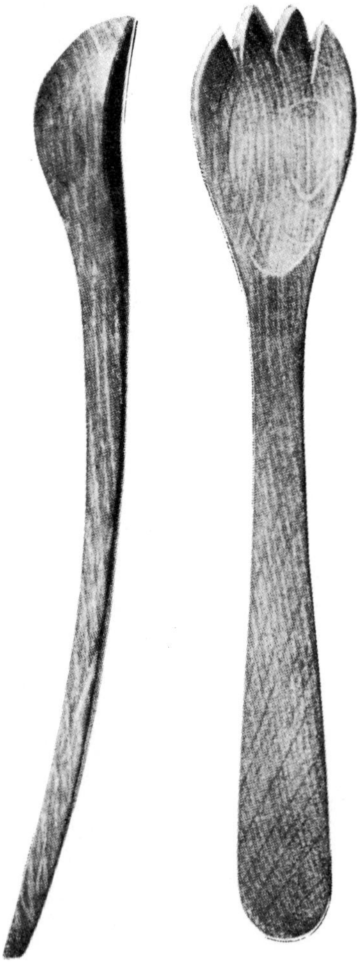

FIG. I. USEFUL SERVERS WHICH ARE INTERESTING TO MAKE

They measure about 12 in. long, and are made in hardwood

THE fork is of exactly the same shape as the spoon, except that it has the serrations at the end to form the rather blunt prongs. Each can be cut from a block of wood 12 in. by 2¼ in. by 1½ in. Prepare the two pieces of wood to this size and mark a centre line down each.

Marking Out.—Two thin cardboard templates of the shape are needed, one giving the plan and the other the elevation. These are set out by ruling in horizontal and vertical lines to form the 1 in. by ½ in. rectangles shown in Fig. 2, and plotting in the lines map fashion.

Make sure that a nice sweeping line is formed. Only one half of the plan is needed as this can be reversed to mark the other side.

Using the plan template, mark out the shape, the centre line acting as a guide for the straight edge of the template. This is shown at (A), Fig. 3. The marking of the elevation shape depends upon the facilities you have for cutting the shape. If a bandsaw is available the elevation should be marked on the wood as given at (A), because the waste parts are replaced during the cutting. The lower one acts as a support or saddle, whilst the top one gives the line to be cut.

If, however, you have only hand tools it is simpler to mark out the elevation shape on the curved surface just sawn. The card template will not stretch to the full length, but it will act as a general guide, especially if vertical lines are marked on it (as in Fig. 2) and sizes at these points marked on corresponding lines on the wood. In any case an exact shape is not essential. The chief point is to have a good sweeping line.

Having marked in one side the shape can be copied on tracing paper, and the latter used to mark the other side, and also the fork. It is, of course, much simpler to use the bandsaw.

Shaping.—Having sawn the shape by whatever method is decided on, clean up the surfaces, using spokeshave, or rasp and file. Obtain good clean shapes, taking the tool straight across so that all surfaces are square. Fig. 3 (B) shows the plan shape sawn out, and (C) the square form after the elevation has been cut.

The spoon will now have taken on its general form, but is square in section throughout. Proceed now to round over the bowl, treating each side alike so that the effect is balanced. Much waste can be chiselled away,

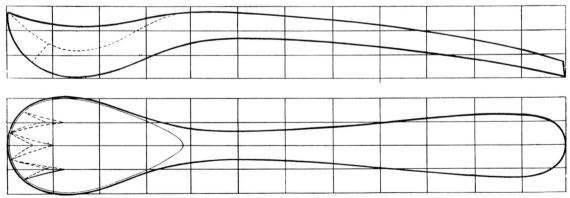

FIG. 2. ELEVATION AND PLAN SHAPES SET OUT IN LINES SPACED AT I in. and ½ in.

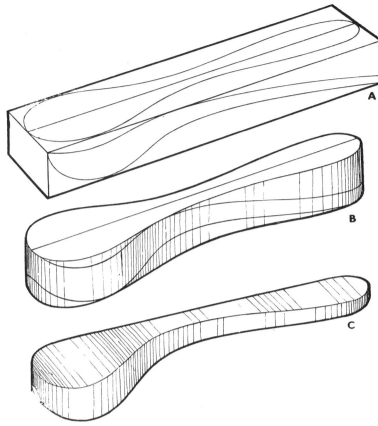

FIG. 3. STAGES IN MARKING AND SHAPING THE SERVERS

CRUET SET
(Continued from page 229)

and file. Grip the circular end of the chuck, taking care to get it correctly aligned flat with the face. Hollow out each side in turn, glasspapering before removal. Cut the joint at the bottom to fit tightly in the base, complete the rounding of the stem with a file and glasspaper.

Salt and Pepper Pots.—First turn the wood to a cylinder of 2 in. diameter, then turn the base and sides to size for about 1 in. up from base. Reverse the wood, and complete the profile of the sides and cap in one piece, allowing a distance of $\frac{1}{8}$ in. between the cap and the lower portion. Separate the two with a $\frac{1}{8}$ in. parting tool. Complete the turning of the inside of the bottom portion, glasspapering before removal, and taking great care that the top makes a good push fit in it. Remove from the lathe, put the top in the chuck, taking care to see that it is aligned, and hollow out the inside.

Both pots are made in the same manner, and are the same size. The only difference lies in the holes in the tops. The salt pot has one centre hole of $\frac{3}{32}$ in., which can be drilled in the lathe. The pepper pot has a rose of evenly spaced holes, a centre one, a ring of nine, then an outer ring of twelve $\frac{3}{64}$ in. holes. As the drill is so fine, these will probably have to be made with an electric or bench drill. The top is held on a bolt head or knob to keep it steady while drilling, and to ensure that the holes are made at right angles with the surface.

but plane, spokeshave, rasp and file are also handy. Fig. 4 shows how the handle can be held in the vice whilst the bowl is being rounded. Note the wood beneath the bowl. In parts it is more convenient to hold the wood in a handscrew, and fix the latter in the vice.

When a good balanced shape has been formed take out the tool marks with the file, and follow with the scraper to remove file marks. The rounding is continued a short way along the handle, but the latter is rectangular towards its end.

Hollowing the Bowl.—A fairly quick gouge is used for this. For the bulk of the work a $\frac{1}{2}$ in. half-round carving tool is invaluable. If, however, you have a really large gouge, say $1\frac{1}{2}$ in., you will find this extremely useful for finishing off. It will take out the smaller gouge marks and enable a good balanced hollow to be formed. A shaped scraper is also handy for finishing. Finally wrap some medium or coarse glasspaper around a rounded block and use this to clean up. This is followed by fine glasspaper, and in fact the whole thing can be finally glasspapered at this stage. Incidentally a sandbag is invaluable when hollowing out, the spoon being cramped down upon it. It gives exactly to the shape needed and makes a firm base.

Fork Prongs.—Mark these in by stepping equally each side of a centre line. Both front and back should be marked. With a fine saw cut down at each side, taking care not to pass beyond the line. The best plan is to stop each line at least $\frac{1}{8}$ in. short, and then finally saw down to the bottom, glancing at both sides to see that the saw does not cut in too far. Finally clean up with a tapered file, examining both sides to ensure a balanced effect. (659)

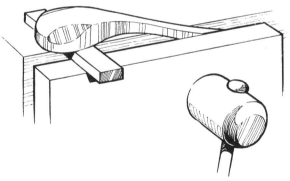

FIG. 4. HOW THE WOOD CAN BE SUPPORTED

Mustard Cellar.—This is started in a similar manner. First turn a 2 in. diameter cylinder, then form the base and as much of the sides as you can reach. Reverse the wood in the chuck, complete the side, and hollow out the middle. Glasspaper before removing.

The base of the inside container is started first. It is then reversed and the rest of the side, the rim, and finally the inside turned.

The handle is glued to the base, and fastened right through the joint with a thick panel pin, the place for which is first drilled with a fine drill.

All the wooden parts are polished with thinned french polish. It is better to polish the inside of the pots as it will keep the salt from getting damp. (660)

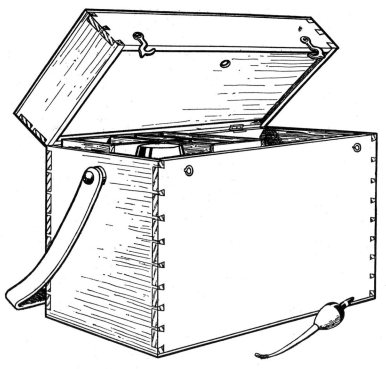

FIG. I. THE BOX ON COMPLETION

Its sturdy construction should give many years of useful life. If preferred attache case clips can be fitted instead of side-hooks

FISHING TACKLE — 2.

THE FISHERMAN'S BOX

This article in the series on fishing equipment provides the information for making what must be one of the most important requirements of the serious angler. The average woodworker will find no difficulty in making this job, as no unusual joints or construction techniques are involved in its design

compartment below and exposing the bait and spare reel chamber. No cover is provided since, when the box is closed, the inner lid, which is hinged to the lid proper, bears on to the tray top, preventing small items from spilling out.

Lid.—This is intended to be used as a storage compartment for a folding landing net and a rod rest or two. If needed, spring clips could be screwed in to suit individual pieces of equipment.

Construction, Carcase.—The box body and lid are jointed up as one piece, the third pin down from the top being made much bigger than the others to

THIS box has been designed to carry the usual small tackle required by an angler together with his refreshments, and can be used as a seat when fishing.

Main Carcase.— The body of the box contains two main compartments, one to hold baits and tackle, the other food and drink. The latter compartment is equipped with a plywood bracket made to hold a vacuum flask, but could easily be adapted to hold other shaped receptacles such as beer or milk bottles. Above these compartments is a loose tray which can be slid the length of the box or lifted out.

Tray.—This has five compartments, the sixth being omitted to allow it to slide right to the end of the box, thus completely covering the refreshment

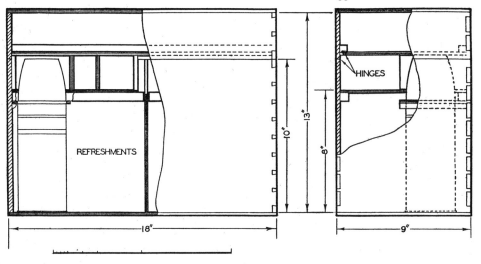

REFRESHMENTS

HINGES

13″

10″

8″

18″

9″

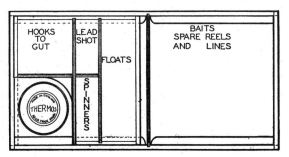

HOOKS TO GUT

LEAD SHOT

FLOATS

SPINNERS

THERMOS

BAITS SPARE REELS AND LINES

FIG. 2. SECTIONAL ELEVATIONS AND PLAN

Adequate space is provided for refreshments which, being contained within the box, can be kept in good condition in the severest of weather

allow the lid to be sawn away after assembly as indicated in Fig. 2.

Prepare all timber to size, and mark out dovetails as shown in Fig. 2. Cut and fit the joints together dry as a check, and mark out housings for central partition in body cheeks, but do not cut them. Glue up the carcase and glue and screw plywood top in place.

When set, saw round the carcase through the third pin to separate the lid from the body, and cut the housings for the central partition. Glue and screw the plywood base to the body and clean up.

If the central partition is required to be a permanent fixture it should be glued and pinned in place before fixing the tray runners. In this case the runners may be in continuous lengths along the cheeks of the body. However, if it is desired to have this central partition removable, the runners should be cut away above the housings as in Fig. 3. Having housed the centre panel, the position of the runners are marked out, glued, and pinned in place. The circular hole for the vacuum flask bracket is cut with a fly cutter or trepanning tool, but if not to hand a fret or coping saw will serve quite well. When prepared, it is fitted below the front tray runner and glued and pinned to it (see Fig. 3). A small fillet is glued beneath the adjacent edge to support the bracket at the side. Additional security for the flask can be

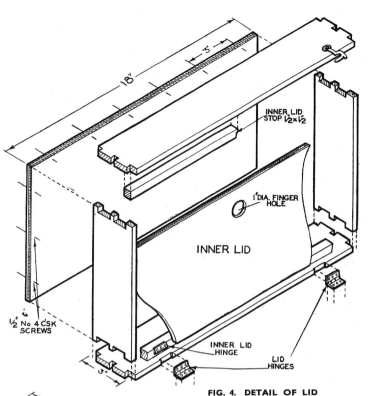

FIG. 4. DETAIL OF LID
This is in effect a small box which is intended to house a folding landing net and rod rest

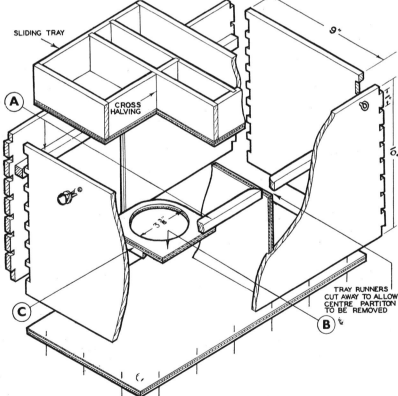

FIG. 3. MAIN CARCASE AND TRAY
All joints are assembled with resin glue and additional strength is given to butt joints by dovetail pinning. The letters (A), (B), and (C) indicate the following : (A) tray runner, (B) vacuum Bask bracket, (C) bracket support fillet

obtained by gluing to the base of the box body directly beneath the upper bracket a similar holder. This is not shown in the illustration, since it is not really necessary as the inner lid of the box top bears down flush on to the flask, when closed, making it comparatively stable.

Sliding Tray.—This is made entirely in $\frac{1}{4}$ in. ply, or a $\frac{1}{4}$ in. fine grain lightweight hardwood such as obeche can be used for the surround and partitions. The construction is shown in Fig. 3. The cross halving joint should be carefully and accurately made first, the remaining sections shaped and fitted accordingly. Finally, the plywood base is cut and the whole assembled. All the joints are glued and pinned together dovetail fashion.

Lid.—When sawn away from the main body the rough edges are cleaned up and the inner lid hinge bearer and lid stop cut to length. The hinges must be set forward sufficiently to allow the inner lid to open. Care should be taken therefore when cutting the housings to allow for this. When prepared, the hinge bearer and stop bar are glued and pinned in position. The inner lid is cut slightly full, about $\frac{1}{16}$ in. being added to length and width,

FISHING TACKLE

a finger hole made as shown in Fig. 4, and the hinges screwed in place. This, being only $\frac{1}{4}$ in. thick, will allow the screws to project through the wood. These projections should be filed down to within $\frac{1}{16}$ in. of the lid and riveted over. The inner lid may now be fitted and, when lowered, should not close down. The edges should now be planed down until the lid is a tight fit. If this is done well, no fastenings will be necessary.

The two sections are now hinged together and the hook and eye fastenings screwed in place or, if preferred, a box lock may be fitted. Holes for the domed bifurcated rivets which hold the leater strap are drilled, but it is advisable not to rivet them until the varnish is dry.

Finish.—This box looks and stands up well to wet and damp conditions if stained with *Colron* wood dye and given two coats of best copal varnish.

CUTTING LIST

				Long ft. in.	Wide in.	Thick in.
Carcase						
2 Cheeks	..	..	..	1 $6\frac{1}{2}$	$13\frac{1}{4}$	$\frac{1}{4}$
2 Ends	..	..	..	$9\frac{1}{2}$	$13\frac{1}{4}$	$\frac{1}{4}$
Tray						
1 Surround and partitions			3 6	$2\frac{1}{2}$	$\frac{1}{4}$
1 Base	..	..	..	9	9	$\frac{1}{4}$ ply
Body						
1 Partition	..	..	..	$9\frac{1}{4}$	$7\frac{1}{4}$	$\frac{1}{4}$ ply
4 Runners	..	..	..	$9\frac{1}{2}$	—	$\frac{1}{2}$ sq.
1 Bracket	..	..	..	$4\frac{3}{4}$	$4\frac{1}{4}$	$\frac{1}{4}$ ply
1 Base	..	..	..	1 $6\frac{1}{2}$	$9\frac{1}{4}$	$\frac{1}{4}$ ply
1 Fillet	..	..	..	5	—	$\frac{1}{4}$ sq.
Lid						
1 Top	..	..	..	1 $6\frac{1}{2}$	$9\frac{1}{4}$	$\frac{1}{4}$ ply
1 Inner lid	..	..	..	1 6	$8\frac{1}{2}$	$\frac{1}{4}$ ply
1 Hinge bearer	..	..	1 6	—	$\frac{1}{2}$ sq.
1 Stop bar	..	..	..	1 6	—	$\frac{1}{2}$ sq.

Allowance has been made in lengths and widths, thicknesses are net. (725)

MAKING A GUITAR
(Continued from page 35)

acoustic results. This shows the section and elevation as used for all the transverse bars of the guitar, except the top one on the front.

The back is placed in its correct position on the ribs and the location of the back bars are marked on to the linings. The bars are cut off to $\frac{1}{16}$ in. short of the outline marks on the back, and recesses cut in the linings, but *not* in the ribs. The bars should then fit into the recesses of the linings inside the ribs. A little chalk marked on to the ends of the bars as they are being fitted will show any discrepancy. If this part of the work is done properly the back will hold the ribs in the correct position and the assembly of the instrument will be without strain. The tone of such an instrument will be much more satisfactory than one which has to be forced together.

The front is made from spruce cut on the quarter in the traditional manner always used when this wood forms the soundboard of any instrument. This is best made in two pieces, as suggested for the back. The wood is jointed with the narrowest grain in the centre, which means that the heart wood should be on the outside of the front, the edges nearest the bark being jointed. The finished thickness should be an even 2 mm. all over when using wood of average density. The outline of the front is marked and cut out in the same way as the back, but the button is not included.

At a point $6\frac{1}{8}$ in. from the top of the marked outline, and exactly on the centre line, put a pencil dot on the front. Open a pair of compasses or dividers to $1\frac{11}{16}$ in. and scribe a circle $3\frac{3}{8}$ in. in diameter with the centre exactly on the pencil dot. This is the finished size of the soundhole. Cut this to a perfect circle. Mark the least perfect side of the wood to be kept as the inside of the front. The pattern of inlay is now inserted round the soundhole. To do this use a small cutting gauge and, working from the inside of the soundhole, shallow cuts are made and the wood removed to allow for the insertion of the pattern of inlay to be decided by the maker. Purfling, of the same type as used around the margins of violins, can be used, but the number of bands inserted must be left to individual tastes. A width of about 2 in. at the top of the soundhole will be covered by the fingerboard, so it is not necessary to insert the inlay all round the hole. (723)

WOOD TURNING *(Continued from page 33)*

the dinner table just draw in ink on the tablecloth a few simple designs, then grip, say, a knife and pretend that the edge of the table is the rest. (With the choirboy in mind, however, perhaps it would be better not to use ink for hygienic reasons). Your left hand can hold the blade with the thumb underneath (which I find most natural), and with your right hand just move the handle about to follow the design. What I want you to discover is how you can push the blade forward, compressing the parts of your left hand against table edge. You will find for larger curves it is better to grip between the fingers, but let part of the hand near the wrist-watch touch the table edge. It is a controlled movement that we are trying to get, and this action of one hand against the rest, while the other moves the tool about is ideal for this sort of face turning.

The pair of rosewood candlesticks (Fig. 4) were done in this way circa A.D., 1908 but carved by the boy next door. They are not given as an example of good design, but I'm proud of them as I was younger then. The central part is a copy of a silver cup you can win by sailing your yacht round the Isle of Wight. It is a good thing to keep your eyes open for nice combinations of curves, and it will surprise you in the way it will broaden your outlook on what to turn. When in business I always looked in antique shops, some of which had old stuff in them, and in those days people introduced such work into the job, whereas modern stuff is made because it can easily be sanded smooth in a machine.

Those who have to turn large diameter work will find scraping tools a help—I'm thinking of pattern makers in particular. Their trouble is that the shape must be true to a template, and it is often built up with wood which has the grain in various directions.

Scraping Tools.—Some people like to buy readymade tools. I've a set myself made specially for brass finishers. Files are quite all right, however, or, for very small work, pieces of band-saw blade. You certainly will find yourself using just two or three and find the movement of the hands provide all the curves you need. Should your aspirations rise to making a set of chessmen, I do suggest that you grind tools to suit the main curves, and just push them in. Then all will be alike. (657)

PROPAGATOR
or MINIATURE
GREENHOUSE

The amateur gardener will appreciate the advantages of a propagator since it enables seeds to be germinated under the most favourable conditions. Further, it is useful for striking cuttings and for forcing purposes. A feature of the propagator to be described is that it is heated by an ordinary electric lamp enclosed in a metal cylinder so that no moisture can reach the electrical connection of the lamp. Thus, the risk of electric shock is practically eliminated

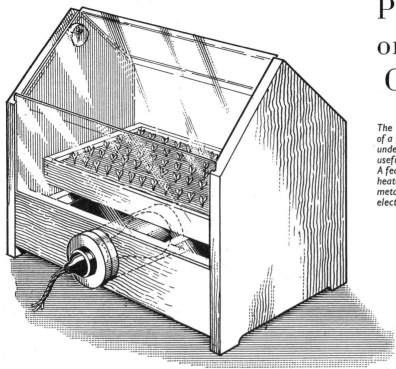

AN ITEM WHICH WILL APPEAL TO THE HOME GARDENER
In addition to the electric bulb heater, a cam arrangement is fitted at the top to enable the glass to be raised, and so vary the ventilation

A USEFUL size for the propagator is 18 in. by 12 in. and 17 in. to the apices of the gable ends (*a*), since a propagator of this size will accommodate a standard 15 in. by 9 in. seed box. The drawings give dimensions for solid stuff, but a satisfactory material is 9 mm. plywood, providing that the propagator is well painted before being put to use. If plywood is used, it is advisable to cut the stuff for the ends (*a*) so that the grain of the outer laminae runs vertically. This will result in cleaner plough grooves for the glass and there will be less tendency for the laminae at (*b*) to break away.

Construction.—The two gable ends (*a*) are best prepared in one long length to facilitate ploughing. The plough grooves can extend along the entire length of the stuff since, in an article of this description, it will not matter if the grooves show below the rails (*c*). After ploughing, the opposite ends of the length are cut at 45 degrees to form the gables. When this has been done, the length can be cross cut and shaped to form the feet. As the top panes of glass rest at an angle of 45 degrees, it will suffice to support them on ¼ in. by ¼ in. fillets fixed to the gable ends by ½ in. panel pins. The rails (*c*) can be secured by bare face tenons as shown in Fig. 1 or by dovetail halving as indicated in Fig. 2.

Lamp.—A 40 watt lamp will be found to give adequate heat for most purposes, and a lamp of this size is easily accommodated in a ½ lb. cocoa tin, the bottom of which has been removed. A hole will therefore have to be cut in one of the rails (*c*) to take the tin which should be a tight fit in the hole. The tin can be fixed in position, by drilling a small hole in the wall of the tin to take a gimp pin. The pin is driven into the rail from the inside using a large half-round file to drive the pin. If the lid of

the tin is removed, this operation should not be difficult.

The lampholder is mounted on the lid of the tin, therefore by removing the lid, the lamp can be withdrawn, if required, and replaced by another lamp of different wattage. The lampholder will require a 1¼ in. diameter hole in the lid and this can be done by pinning the lid to a block of wood and boring the hole with a centre bit.

Referring to Fig. 1, it will be seen that the seed box rests on two rails (*d*) and that these are stubbed into the rails (*c*) in order to give adequate support to the seed box when filled with soil.

Assembling.—The parts are put together with a thick varnish paint in the joints. If these are well made, the paint may suffice to hold them together, but it is as well to pin them, using 1 in. panel pins.

The bottom (*e*) is cut out a little full so that the edges can be shot to obtain a close fit. The holes at one end of the bottom are for the purpose of allowing any water, collecting on the bottom, to run away. Instead of holes, the bottom may be made a little short in its length, say 3/16 in., so that a gap is formed at one end. To enable the water to run freely, the bottom should be inclined slightly towards the holes or the gap.

Ventilation.—If good results are to be obtained with a propagator, careful attention must be given to ventilation. In order to adjust the amount of ventilation it is suggested that a wooden disc or cam (*f*) about 1½ in. diameter be eccentrically mounted on one of the gable ends as shown in Fig. 3. The disc is secured by a round-head screw having a washer under the head. The screw should be sufficiently tight to assure that the disc does not move from an adjusted position, but it should not be so tight that the disc cannot be turned by the fingers.

It is advised that the lampholder be wired to a three-pin plug using three-core flex. The earth wire should be soldered to the lid of the tin or secured by a small screw and nuts. By taking this precaution, the possibility of electric shock is remote.

If the propagator is painted inside and outside, it is advisable to wait for the smell of the paint to disappear before putting the propagator to use.   (756)

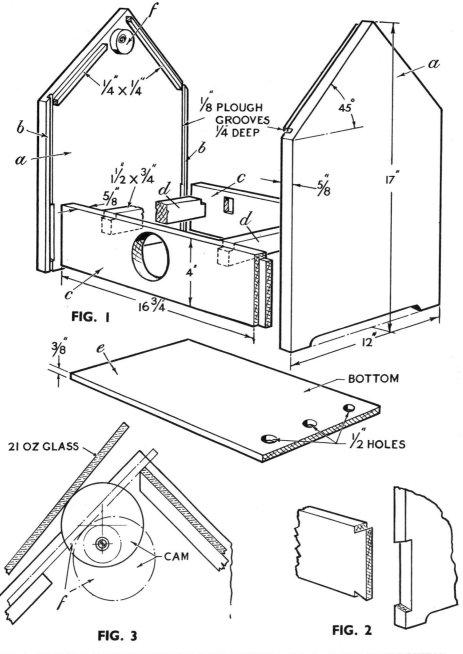

FIG. I. HOW THE MAIN STRUCTURE IS PUT TOGETHER.   FIG. 2. ALTERNATIVE DOVETAIL
JOINT FOR THE RAILS.   FIG. 3. DETAILS OF VENTILATOR CAM

if the marking has been accurate. Finally, mark the 45 deg. lines at the edges, and join these down the far surface.

Cutting.—The corners can now be sawn away and trimmed with the plane. To mark the sides of the fingers, divide the width into five (or whatever odd number is chosen) and, setting the gauge to each mark in turn, mark both pieces with the fence of the gauge bearing against the face edge in every case.

The cuts are made immediately to the waste side of the line. Slight trimming with the file may be necessary later after the waste has been removed, but such work should be a minimum only. Remove the waste by boring holes near the shoulder line, and finishing with the chisel. Start the joint together to test the fit, then cover the bearing surfaces with candle-grease.

The general cutting and boring for the centre pin is similar to that for the knuckle joint. Cramp the parts together (they should have a moderately tight fit, as over-tightness may cause splitting) and fix a straight-edge along one side so that they are in alignment. Bore about half-way in from each edge using a $\frac{1}{8}$ in. bit. Either a spoon bit or an engineer's morse drill can be used. In both cases it is advisable to start the hole with a smaller-pointed bit. If this is not available, pop the hole with a centre punch and use a small drill or spoon bit first.   (494)

FINGER JOINT (*continued from page* 48)

to exactly half the thickness of the wood, and mark the end and top edges (see centre line), using the gauge from the face side in every case. With the same setting mark lines on both sides, working the gauge from the end (see X). Re-set the gauge to the exact thickness of the wood, and mark the two edges in from the end.; The intersection with the centre line gives the pin position. Once more re-set the gauge and mark line (Y) so that its distance from (X) is equal to the thickness. The line of the pin will automatically be centred between them

Please ask your newsagent to reserve a copy of WOODWORKER regularly. It is the only way of ensuring that you receive your copy.

An old saying often heard in workshops and worth remembering is " measure twice and cut once."

Vol. 60 No. 757

WOODWORKER

DECEMBER, 1956

—TABLE—

NAPKIN HOLDERS

Some of the many novel forms that table napkin rings can take can be judged by the examples in Fig. 1. At this time of the year small items of this kind which do not take long to make make more attractive gifts than similar shop bought items

**FIG. I
USEFUL
CHRISTMAS
GIFTS**

**A NOVEL AND
ATTRACTIVE
USE OF
LAMINATED
WOOD**

THE octagonal oak ring with chamfered edges (Fig. 1), relies for its attractiveness upon the subtle changes of tones caused by the light falling on the various facets. To make a set of these, usually half a dozen, prepare a length of straight-grained oak, free from knots or blemishes, about 2 ft. 4 in. long, 2¼ in. wide and ⅞ in. thick. Allowing about ¼ in. of waste between each block, mark off six squares. Draw diagonals (D) Fig. 2, and with a pair of compasses take the distance where the lines cross at the centre to one of the corners. From each corner on each square now mark a point on the sides of the square (½D) as in Fig. 2. Join these points across the corner so producing a true octagon.

For most purposes a hole of about 1½ in. diameter is suitable for the normal-sized serviette, but if in doubt a check should be made by rolling a napkin to ascertain its size. If a lathe is not to hand, the hole is easily made by boring a series of smaller holes close together, the outer edges of which just clear the larger circle,

Fig. 3 (B), and paring back to the line with a paring gouge. Complete all the holes before separating the blocks.

Carefully saw off the corners and clean up with glasspaper before cutting the chamfers. This method ensures a crisp, finished appearance.

Give each ring one or two coats of clear french polish to seal the pores and prevent the accumulation of dirt. Alternatively a clear varnish or cellulose can be used.

Laminated Holders.—The remaining holders rely, apart from the novel fish shape, on contrasting wood for their effect. At first sight it seems that to make these would be a fairly long and tedious business, but it is in fact quite simple. The laminated pieces are glued together in the length before marking out and cutting the shapes. For holders of this kind it is advisable to use contrasting woods such as mansonia and sycamore.

Each of the thin strips is about ¼ in. thick and ⅞ in. wide, and the outer pieces 1 in. wide. The length is dependent upon which shape to be cut. In Fig. 3 (A),

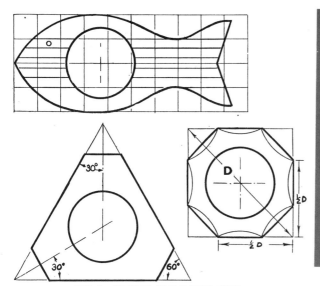

FIG. 2. SHAPES (HALF FULL-SIZE)
The fish shape is set out on a ½ in. squared graph which can also be used as a scale

TABLE PLATTERS AND TRAY

(Continued from page 237)

small oddments of wood can be used for them, or all can be cut from a single piece, the cuts being made on the bandsaw if this is available, or with the bow saw. Plane the edges so that all five make a fairly loose fit in the tray and with each other. With pencil mark lines around the edges to indicate where the wood has to be cut away as at (A), Fig. 4.

With a fairly quick gouge hollow out the centre as far as possible. It will be found easier to work across the grain where practicable. This is shown to the left at (B), Fig. 4. Chop down with chisel along the line marking the inner side of the hollow, and complete the hollowing with the router (B). Using a gouge of suitable curvature work the hollow up to the pencil line as at (C). Finish into the flat bottom as cleanly as possible.

The flat surface can either be finished by scraping followed by glasspaper, or it can be as at (D), Fig. 4, in

spaces for three of the shapes are shown set one behind the other, and it is as well to note that it is the triangular one which determines the over-all width.

Having found the over-all length required, prepare the pieces and glue together to form continuous strips. When set, mark out the shapes. Bore the centre holes, glasspaper to a fair finish, and cut out. If a curved shape, such as the fish, is used this is best set out on a piece of stiff card, cut out, and used as a template. Fig. 2 shows the various shapes, apart from the square, set out to the same scale, the ½ in. squared graph upon which the fish is drawn being the key. This is shown half full size.

On completion it is advisable to coat all the pieces with french polish to make cleaning easy. (479)

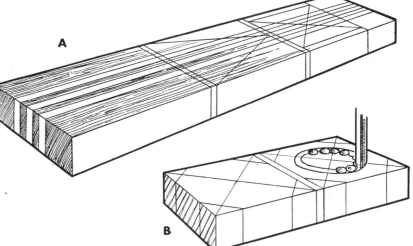

FIG. 3. METHOD OF SETTING OUT THE SHAPES AND CUTTING THE HOLE

CITY AND GUILDS OF LONDON INSTITUTE

We have received the following publications :

General Regulations, comprising general Regulations, Calendar 1956-57, and Timetable and Fees for the examinations of 1957. Gratis.

Regulations and Syllabuses, *E,* Building Subjects, 1956-57. Amongst others these include Carpentry and Joinery, Wood-cutting, Machinists' Work, Painters' and Decorators' Work, Hand Railing and Stair Construction, Furniture Industry (including cabinet making, chair making, upholstery, hand and spray polishing, also advanced course in machines, tools, and processes). Price 4s. or 4s. 6d. post free.

Regulations and Syllabuses, *J,* 1956-57, including Teacher's Certificate in Handicraft, Technical Teacher's Certificate, Domestic Subjects (Further Education), Teacher's Certificate. Price 2s. or 2s. 3d. post free.

Seventy-Sixth Annual Report, 1954-1955. This describes broadly the activities of the Institute and the subjects it covers, the work of the Art School and College, and the function of the Associated Examining Board. Price 2s. or 2s. 3d. post free.

which the whole thing is finished with a flat gouge, the marks being left to show. The latter is probably the simpler, and looks most effective.

Finish.—As foodstuffs have to be placed on the platter a waxed finish is scarcely suitable unless it is applied sparingly and rubbed really well in. Either french polish (use white for the light platters), or a clear cellulose can be used. An alternative is a clear varnish such as *Valspar,* though a certain amount of darkening is unavoidable when this is used.

CUTTING LIST

			Long ft. in.	Wide in.	Thick in.
Tray					
1 Panel	..	..	..1 2	7¾	¼
2 Mouldings	..	..	..1 3½	1¾	1
2 Mouldings	..	..	.. 9½	1¾	1
Platters					
1 Piece	..	..	.. 10½	5¾	⅞
4 Pieces	..	..	.. 7	4	⅞

(453)

TWO-SEATER TOBOGGAN

Although in this country we do not get a lot of snow, at any rate in the South, most people enjoy a run on a toboggan. It is well worth making one so that it is ready for when there is a fall. That shown in Fig. I measures just over 5 ft. long and will hold two adults or three children at a pinch

A S the main runners are bent to give the curvature they should be made in a suitable hardwood such as beech which bends well. Alternatively ash or birch could be used. The nose piece to which they are fixed should be in a hardwood which is not liable to split. Elm is excellent in this respect, though other hardwoods could be used. Sides and seat slats could be in softwood.

The whole thing is painted to protect it from damp, but it is inevitable that the runners will become exposed with friction, even when metal facings are added. It is advisable to wipe them dry and keep the toboggan under cover when not in use.

Runners.—Fig. 3 shows how each pair of runners fits into notches cut in the nose-piece. They are screwed in, but it is also advisable to use a water-resistant glue such as resin. They are screwed to the sides. Cut the last-named to size, and prepare the two nose-pieces from $\frac{7}{8}$ in. stuff. Note that the runners, which are $1\frac{1}{4}$ in. wide, are thinned down at one side only towards the front so that they finish flush with the nose-piece, whereas they overhang the sides. They can be made straight and trimmed flush after fixing.

The simplest plan is to cut out one nose-piece to a fair curve (see Fig. 3) and mark the other from it. The notches are cut with saw and chisel. Note how the end is cut at an angle so that it resists any tendency for the runner to fly out.

In the case of the bottom runner the notch is slightly curved, but do not attempt much curvature because the strain on the holding screws would be too great unless the runner were steamed first. It is better to give a *slight* curve and rely upon a certain amount of shaping after fixing. This necessitates the screws being well countersunk.

At this stage the runners point outwards and are straight. The problem is to fix them to the sides, and a certain amount of improvising is necessary in arranging methods of holding the work. The fixing is greatly simplified if a steaming chamber is available. The wood should be left in for about an hour and bent around pegs or held with cramps. An exact curve is not necessary. If steaming is not possible the bending can be helped by pouring a kettle of boiling water over the wood beforehand. In both cases no glue must be applied over the damp wood. The simplest way is to steam (or damp), screw the runners to the nose-piece and side, and leave to dry. The whole is then taken to pieces, glued, and assembled afresh.

Assembling.—Various methods can be used. One is to screw both runners to the nose-piece and fix the side to the lower one. The top one will lie loosely across the side, probably as in Fig. 4 (it depends on the degree bending already given). Put a block beneath the nose and fix two cramps to hold the lower runner to the bench as shown. It is then a matter of adjustment, pushing the block inwards and cramping down the top runner until the degree of rise is correct. The latter is not critical, but both sides must be alike. It may be necessary to pull the top runner outwards as shown by the arrow. When correct the fixing screws can be driven in.

The seat slats can now be fixed. They should be chamfered around the top edges, and the screws should be well countersunk. Note that the second slat from the front projects so as to form a foot rest for the rear passenger (see Fig. 2). The front and rear slats are wider than the others, and if these have two screws each there is no risk of the whole working out of truth.

If metal runners are used the fixing screws must be countersunk.

FIG. I. YOU CAN HAVE A REALLY GOOD RUN ON THIS

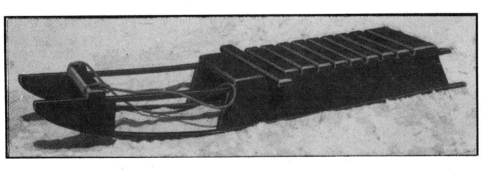

FIG. 2. COMPLETED TOBOGGAN. BOTH HARDWOOD AND SOFTWOOD ARE USED
Over-all length is just over 5 ft., though this could be adapted within a little

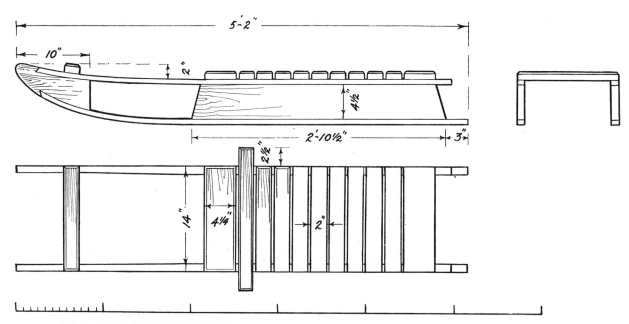

FIG. 3. SCALE ELEVATIONS AND PLAN WITH MAIN SIZES. THE RUNNERS MUST BE OF HARDWOOD

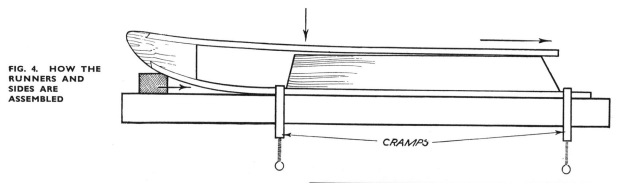

FIG. 4. HOW THE RUNNERS AND SIDES ARE ASSEMBLED

CRAMPS

They should extend up to the nose and be bent around to the top edge. A thickness of about $\frac{1}{16}$ in. is suitable. Brass is free from rusting but is expensive. Iron is cheaper, but needs to be wiped dry after use and given a wipe over with oil. (466)

CUTTING LIST

				Long ft. in.		Wide in.	Thick in.
2 Runners..	..	..	..	4	10	$1\frac{3}{8}$	$\frac{3}{4}$
2 Runners..	..	..	..	5	1	$1\frac{3}{8}$	$\frac{3}{4}$
2 Nose-pieces	••	..	..		$10\frac{1}{2}$	$5\frac{1}{2}$	$\frac{7}{8}$
2 Sides	..	..	..	2	$11\frac{1}{2}$	$4\frac{3}{4}$	$\frac{7}{8}$
2 Slats	..	..	..	1	$2\frac{1}{2}$	$4\frac{1}{2}$	$\frac{7}{8}$
9 Slats	..	..	..	1	$2\frac{1}{2}$	$2\frac{1}{4}$	$\frac{7}{8}$
1 Slat	..	..	..	1	$7\frac{1}{2}$	$2\frac{1}{4}$	$\frac{7}{8}$

TABLE LAMP
(*Continued from page 235*)

using a hot caul having an intervening piece of paper to prevent adhesion. Complete all four sides. When set wash off the gummed paper with clean cold water and allow to dry.

With a cutting gauge set $\frac{1}{16}$ in. bare cut the grooves for the line. This is glued in and held till set with strips of gummed paper. Trim the ends, wash off the paper and when dry scrape and glasspaper.

Top.—Prepare to size, bore a hole through the centre for the flex, glue and pin in place, and cover the pin heads with a suitable filler.

If it has to be veneered, complete the edges, and glue and pin in place, driving the pins just below the surface. Glue on the surface veneer and when set bore the centre hole and trim the edges.

Base.—This is built from two pieces as shown in Fig. 2. If the wood is the same as that used for the inlay they can be shaped and screwed on direct. If not, veneer the exposed surfaces before fixing. Bore a hole at the base of the stem in the centre of one of the panels, thread the flex, and screw on the base.

Finish.—An item of this kind relies for its effect upon the natural colours of the wood; if stained too much a great deal of contrast is lost. For this reason it is suggested that two or three coats of clear french polish be used followed by a thin coat of wax. A piece of felt or similar material glued to the base will prevent damage to other articles upon which the lamp may be placed.

Please ask your newsagent to reserve the WOODWORKER for you each month.

TRUG ——

—— BASKETS |

These baskets make useful additions to the garden equipment and schemes of work particularly in rural areas. Being simple and straightforward to make boys not capable of more advanced construction can accomplish them successfully. Of the two designs shown that with the rounded ends is a little more difficult to execute

Designed by
W. E. BAGGALEY,
The Wishing Tree School,
St. Leonards-on-Sea Sussex

In order to make the series interesting, varied, and useful to all handicraft teachers we invite teachers to send in designs which they have found successful in their work. A fee of 2 guineas will be paid for any original design published. Dimensioned pencil sketches with notes describing construction should be sent. A photograph, if available, would be of added help. All photographs will be returned. Designs should be in contemporary style—simple and clean in line and suitable for the average boy to make. The name of successful entrants can be published with the designs if desired

FIG. I. ROBUST AND USEFUL BASKETS

P REPARE from any suitable softwood the two side boards each to measure $13\frac{5}{8}$ in. by 4 in. by $\frac{1}{2}$ in. Shape two of the corners of each board to suit one of the designs given in the elevation in Fig. 3. The rounded end is a quadrant of 4 in. radius and can be cut with bow or coping saw and smoothed with spokeshave. The bevelled end is at an angle of 45 degrees to the edge and is $2\frac{1}{4}$ in. long on the square. These bevels can be cut with tenon saw and finished with the smoothing plane. Make sure that the shaped edges are square with the face side in order that the laths will rest flat on them.

Handle.—Make up the two carriers for the handle to the shape shown in Figs. 2 and 3. These are best made from a hardwood such as beech and each should measure 8 in. by $1\frac{1}{2}$ in. by $\frac{5}{8}$ in. A lap $4\frac{3}{16}$ in. long by $\frac{1}{4}$ in. deep is cut out of each to fit over the sides. This makes a good sawing exercise preliminary to cutting tenons and should be marked out accurately with knife and square for the shoulder and with a gauge along the grain. Mark out the semi-circular end shapes on the top end of each carrier and pare off the waste with the chisel. Finish with the spokeshave.

The $\frac{3}{4}$ in. diameter holes to contain the handle should now be bored on the centres used to describe the semi-circles, and should be cut to a depth of $\frac{3}{8}$ in. Before boring test your bit on a waste piece of wood to make sure that the beech or birch dowel rod used for the handle will be a tight fit in the holes. Often it is advisable to use an $\frac{11}{16}$ in. bit and to ease the dowel ends with a file to fit tightly into the holes as dowelling is often made a fraction under the stated size. Cut the dowel handle to a length of 9 in.

Mark out the correct positions for the carriers in the centre of the sides and drill two holes in each side as

shown in the section Figs. 2 and 3 to take $\frac{3}{4}$ in. No. 6 countersunk brass screws. The carriers can now be glued and screwed to the sides. One of the modern waterproof resin glues should be used for this purpose as the baskets are used mainly out-of-doors.

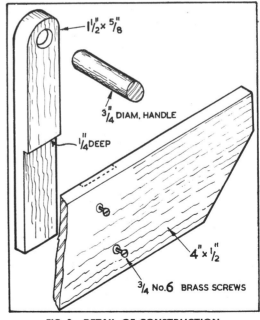

FIG. 2. DETAIL OF CONSTRUCTION
Use a resin adhesive or one not likely to be affected by moisture

Laths.—Cut off a sufficient number of pieces of builders' lath each to measure $8\frac{3}{4}$ in. long. It might be worth making up a simple jig for this purpose composed of a square cut in a mitre block with a stopped end $8\frac{3}{4}$ in. away from the cut. Skim over all the laths with a smoothing plane sufficient to remove the saw marks. Calculate the width of spacing between the laths and make up a spacing strip as shown in the inset in Fig. 3.

Assemble.—Use resin glue to fix the handle into the carriers. A small nail may also be driven through the side of each carrier to retain the handle in position in the manner used when making deck chairs.

Glue and nail the laths along the bottom edges of the sides using the spacing strip to keep them an even distance apart. Two panel pins driven into each end of each lath in dovetail fashion together with resin glue will make a firm job. Finally attach the laths to the bevelled or rounded ends.

Finish.—The baskets can be left in the natural wood or given two coats of clear copal varnish.

CUTTING LIST

	Long ft. in.	Wide in.	Thick in.
2 Sides	1 $2\frac{1}{4}$	$4\frac{1}{4}$	$\frac{1}{2}$
2 Carriers	$8\frac{1}{2}$	$1\frac{3}{4}$	$\frac{5}{8}$
1 handle	$9\frac{1}{2}$		$\frac{3}{4}$ dia.
21 Laths	$9\frac{1}{4}$	$\frac{7}{8}$	$\frac{3}{16}$
4 Brass C/S Screws ..	$\frac{3}{4}$ No. 6 g.		
Panel Pins	$\frac{3}{8}$ No. 17 g.		

Allowances are made in lengths and widths. Thicknesses are net. (534)

TECHNIQUE OF BLEACHING

(*Continued from page* 33)

How would you fake defects ? Ivory-coloured hard stopping made as we described earlier is the thing for small holes or chips. A little polish pigmented with Chinese white and if necessary a touch of another colour is suitable for painting out mineral streaks or other surface faults in the timber.

Can the bleached finish be imitated without going to the trouble of bleaching ? A fair imitation which would not deceive anyone who knew better is possible on wood which is itself fairly light in colour. This should be wiped with a 50/50 mixture of flat white paint and turps or white spirit so that the grain still shows. When hard, the surfaces are polished in the usual way.

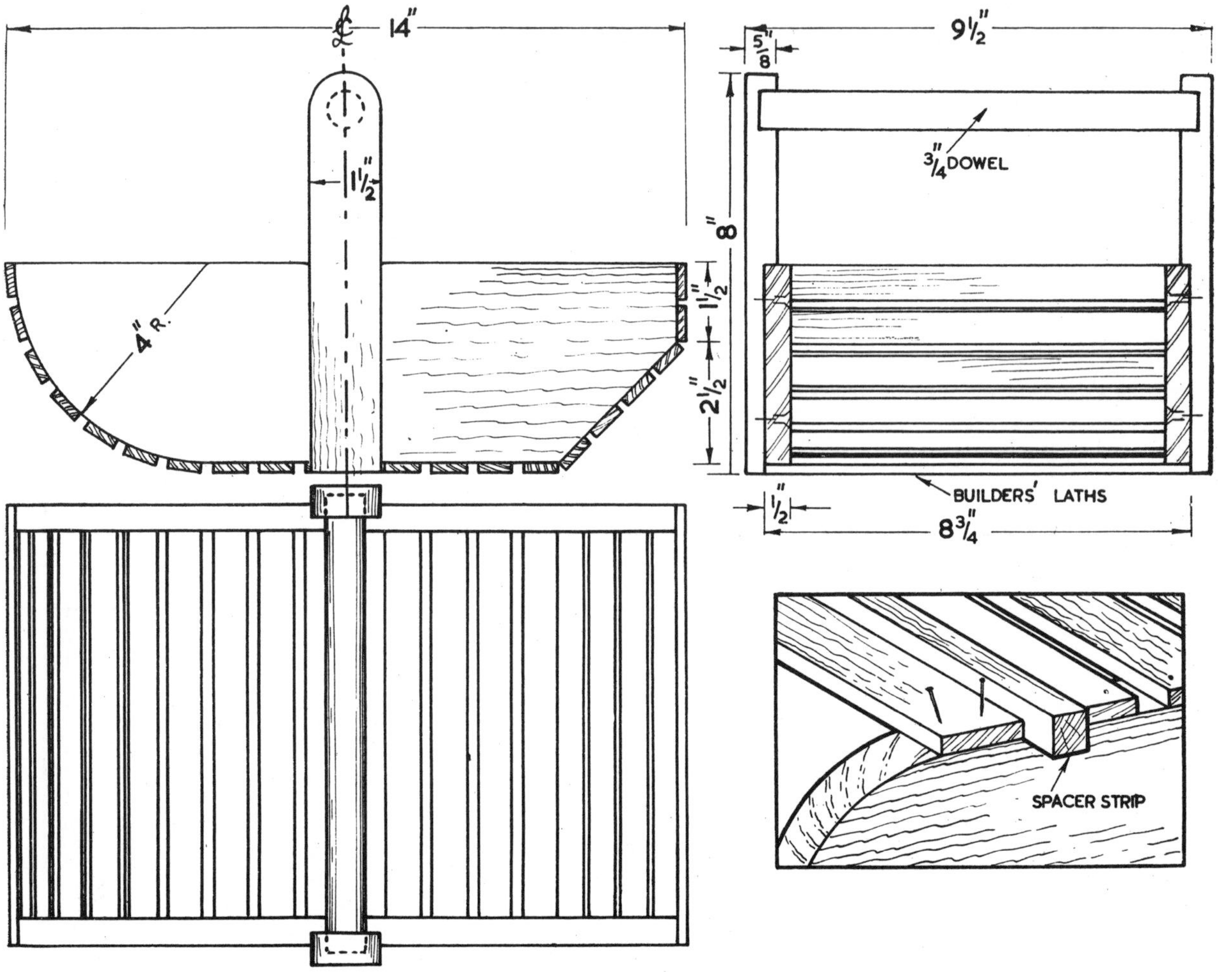

FIG. 3. PLAN AND ELEVATIONS WITH MAIN SIZES, AND DETAIL SKETCH
Note that the front elevation shows one end of each design. Inset : Using the spacer strip

In order to make the series interesting, varied, and useful to all handicraft teachers we invite teachers to send in designs which they have found successful in their work. A fee of 2 guineas will be paid for any original design published. Dimensioned pencil sketches with notes describing construction should be sent. A photograph, if available, would be of added help. All photographs will be returned. Designs should be in contemporary style—simple and clean in line and suitable for the average boy to make. The name of successful entrants can be published with the designs if desired.

Shoe Cleaning Box With Footpad

Designed by A. BEEVERS,
Heath County Boys' School

This piece of work was specially designed to give boys, during the earlier stages of their instruction, a job which is both interesting and useful and yet incorporates only the simplest forms of jointing. It gives boys the satisfaction of making something worth-while without encountering operations which might prove too difficult.

A S will be seen from Fig. 1 the box contains two compartments—one for polish tins and one for brushes—and a handle in the form of a footpad for resting the shoe on while cleaning.

Construction.—The ends are housed into the sides and the partition is stopped housed into the ends. The vertical posts are fitted to the ends with bridle joints.

FIG. 1. A ROBUST JOB OF PRACTICAL USE IN THE HOME
The construction is extremely simple, calling only for elementary housing and bridle joints

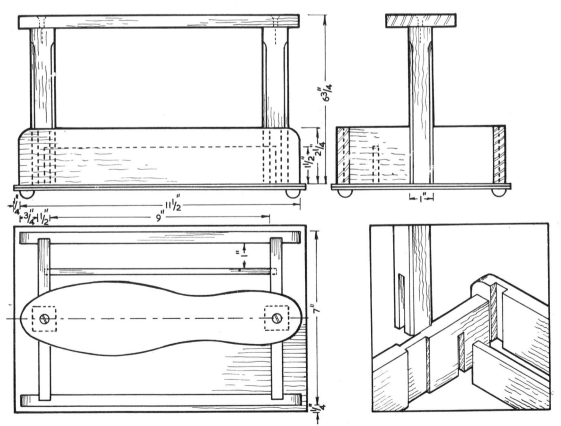

FIG. 2. PLAN AND ELEVATIONS IN PART SECTION AND DETAILS OF CONSTRUCTION

The footpad and plywood base are held in position with screws. The details of the joints can be seen in the inset sketch in Fig. 2.

Notice that the screws holding the footpad to the posts are held in the end grain of the posts. This is not always satisfactory for gripping especially when the wood is soft and open grained. Two useful tips to overcome this difficulty are illustrated in Fig. 3. At (A) a rawlplug is inserted into a hole of suitable size. If the outside of this plug is glued when inserted it will hold the screw much better than the end grain would alone. The method shown at Fig. 3 (B) is to bore a ⅜-in. diameter hole through the post and to glue in a piece of dowel rod. The screw will then pass through the dowel rod, gripping firmly in its cross grain.

Procedure.—Prepare wood for the two sides and two ends of the box to 2¼ in. by ½ in. in section and 11½ in. and 6½ in. long respectively. Cut the housings on the sides to half the depth of the wood, setting them in ¾ in. from the ends as shown in Fig. 2. Cut a ½ in. rounded corner at each end of the sides.

Make up the partition to 9½ in. long by 1½ in. by ¼ in. and fit it into stopped housings cut into the ends. The width of the compartment for the polish tins should be 1 in., which means that 1¼ in. must be allowed from the end of the wood when marking out the housings.

Each post should be planed to measure 6¼ in. by 1 in. by 1 in. and the bridle joints marked out and cut. Make the bridle slot ¼ in. wide which will allow for ¼ in. deep grooves on either side of the end pieces to accommodate the posts. Make sure that the top ends of the posts are square and flat. The ⅛ in. by ⅛ in. stopped chamfers may now be cut along the posts.

Assembling.—Clean up the parts and glue the partition into the stopped housings in the ends, fixing with panel pins. Glue the housings in the sides and attach to the ends, again using panel pins. Set the frame square until the glue sets.

Plane up a piece of ¼ in. plywood for the base to 12 in. by 7½ in. This can be attached to the box with ¾ in. No. 4 screws. The posts may now be glued to the ends and, for added security, a nail may be driven through each to pass through the joints. Finally, four hard rubber feet should be screwed under the corners of the base.

Making the footpad.—The outline shape of the foot-pad handle is given in Fig. 3 (C). Use a paper template folded in half to transfer the half pattern from the square net. When the outline is cut and the paper opened out you will obtain the full pattern. Alternatively the outside halves of a pair of shoes may be used to obtain the shape. The pad is made from ½ in. plywood. A piece measuring 12 in. by 3¼ in. is required. Cut out the shape with a bow or coping saw and clean up the edge with a

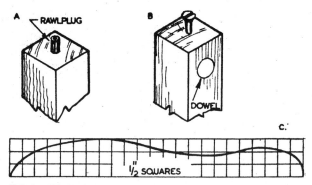

FIG. 3. (A) AND (B)., ALTERNATIVE METHODS FOR FIXING THE FOOT-PAD. (C), HALF THE OUTLINE OF THE FOOT-PAD SHAPE PLOTTED ON A ½ IN. SQUARED GRAPH

spokeshave. The pad may now be screwed to the posts. It is a good idea to glue a piece of thin sheet cork to the top of the pad to prevent the foot slipping off when in use.

Finishing.—It is suggested that the box be given a coat of button polish and, after glasspapering down, rubbed over with a mixture of equal parts of turpentine and raw linseed oil.   (574)

READER'S COT MATTRESS

" I have recently made the baby's cot which you gave in one of your issues a few months ago, but was stumped for a good spring. Webbing and strip plastic did not appeal to me and is rather expensive. I had the idea of using spring curtain wire, and the total cost was about 7s. 6d. The drawing I think will explain my idea. I have not put dimensions as these will vary, but in my cot the springs are about 2 in. apart, and there are 3 springs lengthwise, these being interwoven with the cross-wise springs. The method of fixing the ends is, I think, rather neat as nothing shows. Holes are drilled in the sides and ends so that the wire just goes through. Then a saw - cut is run through the holes. I did mine on a circular saw, but a plough plane or even a tenon saw could be used. The wire was cut about 2 in. short to allow for springing and one end passed through the side. Screw on the eye (not hooks) and when the spring is pulled the eye sits nicely in the saw-cut. Put the other end through the opposite hole and screw on the eye, and the job is done. A reliable hardwood such as oak or beech is needed for the frame to take the pull imposed by the springs."   (609)

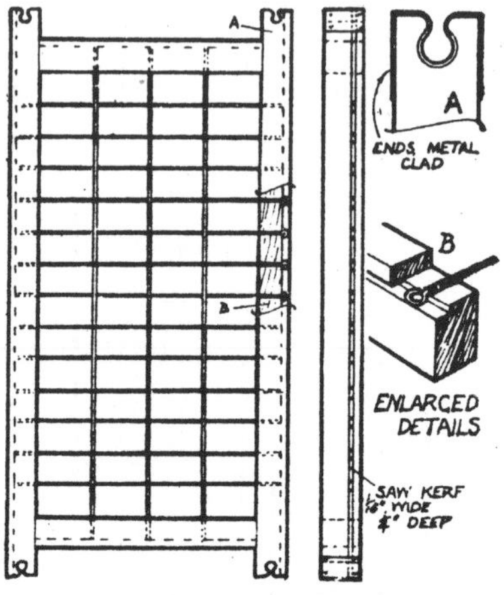

DETAILS OF MATTRESS
(A) shows end detail, and (B) method of fixing wire

CUTTING LIST

				Long		Wide	Thick	
				ft.	in.	in.	in.	
2 Sides	..	..	..	1	0	2½	½	
2 Ends	..	..	..		7	2½	½	
1 Partition	..	..	..		10	1¾	¼	
2 Posts	..	..	..		6¾	1¼	1	
1 Pad	..	..	..	1	0	3¼	½	(ply)
1 Base	..	..	..	1	0½	7¾	¼	(ply)

2 Screws 1¼ in., No. 8 gauge
10 Screws ¾ in., No. 4 gauge

Allowances have been made in lengths and widths. Thicknesses are net.

A SIMPLE TOWEL HOLDER

designed by G. TUCKER

ALTHOUGH THE IDEA of this form of towel holder is not new, many handicraft teachers will not know of it and it makes a very useful exercise in a first year course. The device for holding a tea cloth or hand towel is quite simple, but its grip is strong and positive. As will be seen from the sectional view in Fig. 2, a ⅝ in. diameter glass marble is trapped between front and back boards in such a way that it can roll up and down a sloping groove in the back board. When a tea cloth is inserted upwards the marble lifts to enable the edge of the cloth to pass it and then falls back. trapping the cloth in the process. The cloth is withdrawn from the holder by pulling it sideways.

Construction

This is very simple. The middle piece of wood is housed and glued into the back piece, while the front piece is glued and screwed to the middle piece.

The complete holder is made from one piece of timber about 13 in. long and planed to 1¾ in. by ½ in. From this, three pieces should be cut and squared up to 6 in., 4¼ in., and 1¾ in. long respectively. The smallest piece should be housed into the largest piece to a depth of ⅛ in. in the position shown in Fig. 2 and the sloping groove should be cut into the back board to the dimensions given on the same drawing.

Before assembly the corners and edges of the pieces should be shaped as shown and holes drilled and countersunk to receive screws for attaching the front piece to the middle block and for the wall fixing screws in the back board.

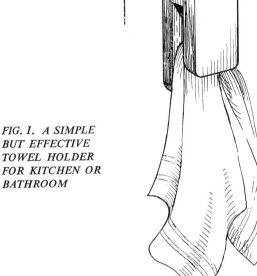

FIG. 1. A SIMPLE BUT EFFECTIVE TOWEL HOLDER FOR KITCHEN OR BATHROOM

It is also a good idea to paint the parts before assembly. When gluing the parts together do not forget to insert the marble during the process.

Material required

1 piece of timber 13 in. by 2 in. by ½ in.
2 1¼ in. No. 8 screws.
1 ⅝ in. diameter glass marble.

(615-300)

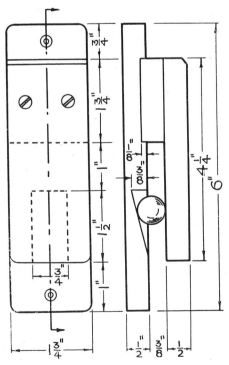

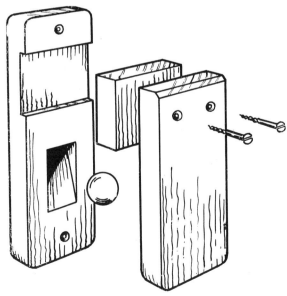

FIG. 2. DIMENSIONS AND EXPLODED VIEW OF CONSTRUCTION

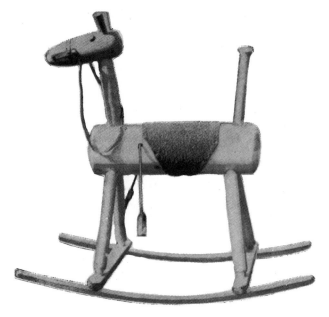

ROCKING HORSE

designed by T. E. JONES, D.L.C.(Hons).

FIG. 1. UP-TO-DATE ROCKING HORSE
Still a delightful toy.

THE SOMEWHAT WHIMSICAL animal illustrated in the photograph in Fig. 1, is a modern version of the traditional rocking horse, a toy which still offers an un-ending source of pleasure to very young children.

For the handicraft teacher the job gives an opportunity for group work with the added incentive of a little social work if the toy is made with a view to presenting it to the local nursery school. Most of the work involves elementary turning between centres, and twelve boys could gain useful experience if they each turned one part.

The horse is generally quite straightforward to make, except great care must be exercised in drilling the holes at the correct angles to receive the legs: it might be advisable to devise jigs for this purpose.

The Body

This is part A in Fig. 3, and because of its size will need to be built up by gluing together a number of pieces of softwood to form a square section not less than 5½ in. by 5½ in. This should be planed down by hand to a rough circular shape before fitting it in the lathe.

The turning of this is quite straightforward and it should be finished by glasspapering it very smooth. The hollowing on the top surface for the seat is carried out with a spoke-shave. To form the seat plastic foam is fitted into this recess and glued into place. This is then covered with suitable material and tacked into position as shown.

Other turned work

The legs, tail, neck, head, ears, eyes and nostrils are all shown fully dimensioned in Fig. 3, so little need be said about the turning of these except that, apart from the head, they are best made in hardwood such as beech or ash. It is a good idea to make the eyes and nostrils from a con-trasting wood such as rosewood.

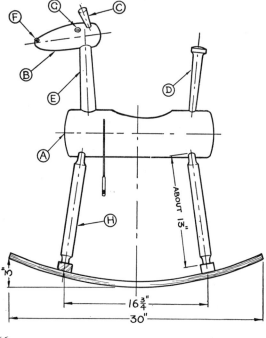

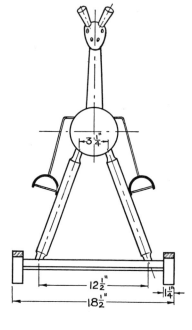

FIG. 2. FRONT AND SIDE ELEVATIONS *Dimensions of the lettered parts are given in Fig. 3.*

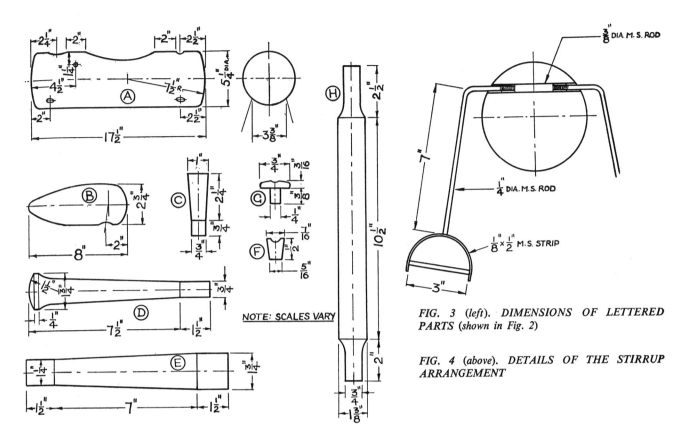

NOTE: SCALES VARY

FIG. 3 (*left*). *DIMENSIONS OF LETTERED PARTS* (*shown in Fig. 2*)

FIG. 4 (*above*). *DETAILS OF THE STIRRUP ARRANGEMENT*

When all the turning is done the holes can be very carefully drilled to receive the various members and the parts of the horse can be temporarily assembled to check the accuracy of the drilling. The holes for the neck in the head and body will have to be drilled with an expansive bit.

The rockers

These, as will be seen from Fig. 2, are 30 in. long by 1¼ in. by ¾ in. in section.

They can be made either by steam bending or by laminating. Those shown in the photograph were steam bent from a piece of 3 in. by ¾ in. elm and sawn down the middle after the shape had set.

Alternatively, a former can be prepared to the inside curvature and four pieces of 3/16 in. by 1½ in. ash can be glued and cramped to the former until the glue has set, to make each rocker.

Cross-members

The two cross-members which hold the lower ends of the legs are made 18½ in. long by 1½ in. wide by ⅞ in. thick. They are held to the rockers by screws driven in through the latter from the underneath side.

If the legs are fixed into the body and the whole stood on the cross-members the positions and angle for the holes in the latter will be obtained. Drill the holes and attach the cross-members to the legs before screwing the rockers.

Polishing

All parts should be polished or lacquered before assembly and it is suggested that clear brushing cellulose, rubbed down with steel wool and wax gives a good finish.

The stirrups

The details of these are shown in Fig. 4. A ⅜ in. diam. hole is first drilled horizontally through the body of the horse in the position shown in the elevation in Fig. 2. A 3½ in. length of mild steel rod ⅜ in. in diameter is then drilled and tapped ½ in. deep for a ¼ in. thread at each end. This is then driven into the hole in the wooden body as shown in Fig. 4.

The two stirrup irons, of ¼ in. diam. mild steel rod, are each threaded along one end to engage in the tapped holes in the ⅜ in. bar.

The stirrups are made from ⅛ in. by ½ in. strip bent into semicircular form and connected by a foot bar of ¼ in. diam. mild steel. The stirrup irons are also attached to the stirrups at the centre of the curve. These rods can be connected to the curved strip by either drilling and riveting, or by drilling and brazing them in place.

Next the stirrup irons need bending as shown in Fig. 4, and the stirrups can be screwed into the body loosely to give them some degree of to and fro movement.

Finally, to complete the job, reins can be made from plastic strip and attached to the head.

Cutting List				Long ft. in.	Wide in.	Thick in.
1 Body. A	..	..	..	1 8	5½	5½
1 Head. B	..	..	..	10	3	3
2 Ears. C ..	..	..	..	4	1¼	1¼
1 Tail. D ..	..	..	..	11	2	2
1 Neck. E	..	..	..	1 0	2	2
2 Nostrils. F	..	..	..	2	⅝	⅝
2 Eyes. G ..	..	..	..	3½	1	1
4 Legs. H	..	..	..	1 5	1½	1½
2 Cross-members	..	..	..	1 7	1¾	⅞
1 piece for rockers	..	..	2 8	3	¾

Allowances have been made for waste in turning.

Ski-bike

by P. A. Lee, D.L.C.

Before commencing you would be well-advised to make a full-size drawing of the ski-bike. To make this easy the elevation is suitably drawn on a numbered grid, page 17.

The first job is to make the seat member and the bottom member. Both have canted ends scarf jointed to them. These scarfed joints are eventually strengthened by the mortice and tenon joints passing through them. Bore the canted ends to receive the steering column and use beech or a similar hardwood to prevent wear. The bores are $1\frac{1}{4}$ in. dia.

The three connecting members are mortice and tenoned into the seat member with through tenons, wedged in saw cuts. Use the same joints at the bottom, with the exception of the back member which you should make as a bridle joint over the back runner. Cut the bottom member down to the same width as the back runner so that you can bridle-joint it to the back upright.

Again, the steering column is bridled over the front runner. Before jointing the column, turn it down as shown to $1\frac{1}{4}$ in. dia. to give the necessary steering movement to the front member and ski. Screw the foot rest to the bottom member so that it rests against the front upright.

The handlebar is through-mortice and tenoned into the steering column and wedged in saw cuts. Shape it by bow-sawing or bandsawing to the outline and then spokeshave to shape to give round handlegrips. Before you assemble the steering column and handlebar, make a beech distance piece, $2\frac{1}{2}$ in. dia., 1 in. thick, and bore it to $1\frac{1}{4}$ in. dia. Glue and screw this to the steering column in the position shown.

Trace the runners from the full-size drawing and marked on to 6 in. by 1 in. board, and cut them out with a bow saw or bandsaw. The actual skis, which are screwed to the runners, are laminated with four strips of beech or ash, $\frac{1}{8}$ in. thick, giving a total thickness of $\frac{1}{2}$ in. When you are making these, you'll find it a great help to have one half of the mould screwed to a baseboard. It will assist in keeping the laminae flat and in line edgewise. Allow the adhesive holding the laminae plenty of time to set, and trim off with a shaper tool to remove any surplus. Then glasspaper the edges and shape the ends as shown in the plan view. When these have been screwed to the runners, screw the back runner to the bottom member.

Use rust-proof screws–cadmium plated, galvanised, or brass.

Inspired by ideas and photographs supplied by the Swiss National Tourist Office. Photograph by M. V. Handscombe Langford.

The Ski-bike can be used by the young and not so young whenever weather conditions allow, and forms an interesting new form of winter snow travel. The latest rage at Winter Sports resorts, it is much easier to ride than conventional skis.

All that now remains is to bore the holes for the bolts at the front and back. The back bolt merely secures the back runner to the bottom member. The front bolt serves the same function, but should also allow some rotation of the front runner about the bolt centre. The amount of movement should be small—about $1\frac{1}{2}$ in. at the greatest point of movement. The idea of this pivot effect at the front is to enable the ski-bike to negotiate bumps and undulations more easily.

When complete, paint or coat the ski-bike with clear polyurethane or a similar finish. It is essential to coat the article in some way as it is sure to be subjected to severe wetting in use, and any swelling, particularly of the steering mechanism, would adversely affect this part of the ski-bike.

Cutting List

	Long ft.	*Long* in.	*Wide* in.	*Thick* in.
1 Footrest		$9\frac{1}{2}$	$1\frac{3}{4}$	$1\frac{1}{2}$
1 Seat member	2	1	$6\frac{1}{4}$	1
1 Bottom member	2	8	$3\frac{1}{4}$	1
1 Front upright	1	$2\frac{1}{2}$	$1\frac{3}{4}$	$1\frac{1}{2}$
1 Back upright	1	5	$2\frac{1}{4}$	2
1 Centre diagonal upright	1	5	$1\frac{3}{4}$	$1\frac{1}{2}$
1 Front runner	1	$7\frac{1}{2}$	$6\frac{1}{4}$	1
1 Back runner	2	1	$6\frac{1}{4}$	1
1 Handlebar	1	$6\frac{1}{2}$	$2\frac{3}{4}$	$1\frac{1}{2}$
1 Steering column	2	$3\frac{1}{2}$	$2\frac{1}{4}$	2
1 Part (A)		3	$2\frac{3}{4}$	1
1 Part (B)		$5\frac{1}{2}$	$3\frac{1}{4}$	1
1 Part (C)		$5\frac{1}{2}$	$3\frac{1}{4}$	1
4 Laminae for front ski, each	1	8	$3\frac{1}{4}$	$\frac{1}{8}$
4 Laminae for back ski, each	2	$3\frac{1}{2}$	$3\frac{1}{4}$	$\frac{1}{8}$

Allowances have been made to lengths and widths; thicknesses are net. It is recommended that redwood or a similar softwood be used for the first ten items, provided it is strong, free of large knots, and straight-grained: beech, ash, or a similar hardwood should be used for the remainder.

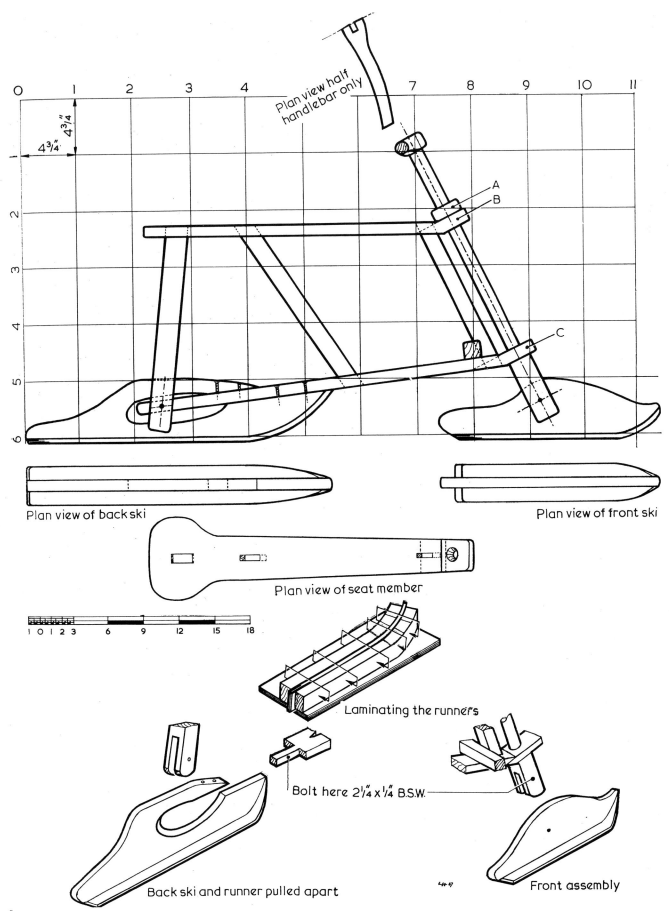

Plan view half handlebar only

4¾" 4¾"

A
B
C

Plan view of back ski

Plan view of front ski

Plan view of seat member

1 0 1 2 3   6   9   12   15   18

Laminating the runners

Bolt here 2¼″ x ¼″ B.S.W.

Back ski and runner pulled apart

Front assembly

Squared off elevation, plans and details.

'Single Handy' tray

F. Barnes

This is an easy-to-make and inexpensive tray for elderly or partially disabled people. It enables them to carry cups, saucers, tumblers, etc., using one hand, leaving the other hand free to open doors, grip the handrail on the stairs, and so on.

The two ends are cut from $\frac{3}{8}$ in. ply, or some similar material, and sawn to the outline shown in the illustration. Cut the small notch at the base with tenon saw and chisel, making it $1\frac{1}{2}$ in. long by $\frac{3}{8}$ in. deep to accept the tongue on each end of the bottom.

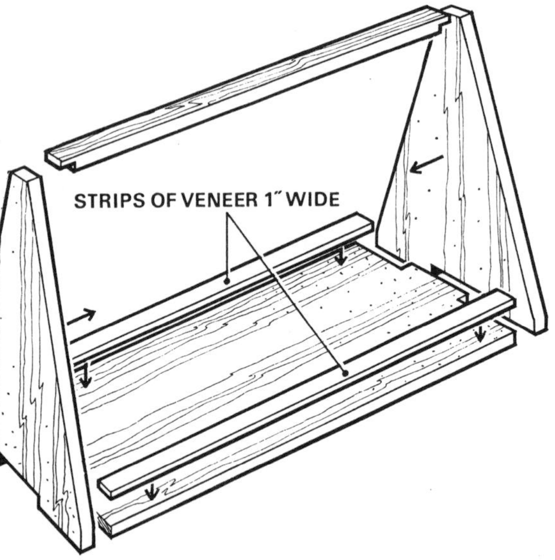

STRIPS OF VENEER 1" WIDE

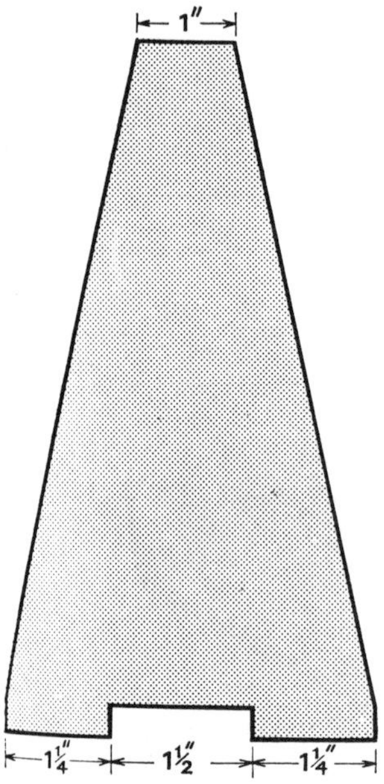

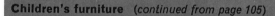

1"
1¼"
1½"
1¼"

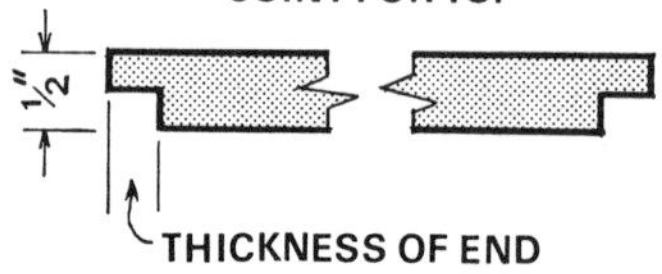

JOINT FOR TOP
½"
THICKNESS OF END

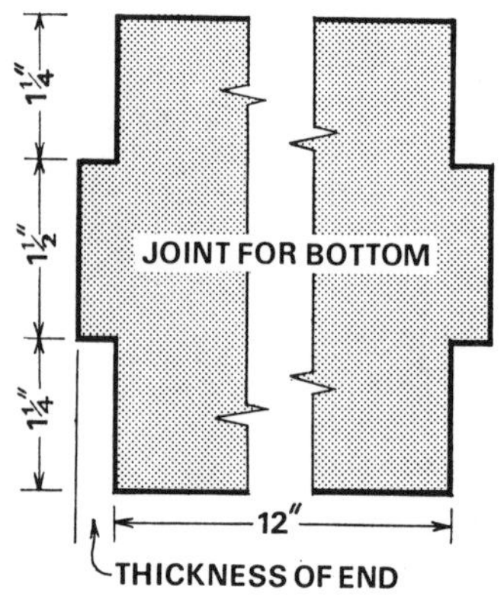

1¼"
1½"
1¼"
JOINT FOR BOTTOM
12"
THICKNESS OF END

A piece of ply or similar stuff, $\frac{3}{8}$ in. thick, is used also for the bottom, and should be cut to size, 12 in. long by 4 in. wide. Then strips of thick veneer, or thin ply, are glued to the long edges to make a rim to stop cups, saucers, and the like from sliding off.

Use 1 in. by $\frac{1}{2}$ in. softwood for the top, which is, of course, the handle, and this piece is lapped over the ends, as illustrated. Alternatively all joints could be dovetailed but for security it is emphasized that these simple joints are made to permit screwing or pinning both ways.

Joints can be screwed and glued, and after a thorough glasspapering, the tray could be painted with an enamel such as *Valspar* which is highly resistant to hot tea cups and spilt liquids.

Children's furniture (*continued from page 105*)

Assembly consists of bolting (or screwing) the aluminium brackets loosely both to the stretcher and the ends. Then glue the lippings to the top, and once the adhesive has set, you can position the top in the housings and glue up, finally tightening up the bolts or screws.

Finally, give the whole job a thorough glasspapering, and apply paint to your personal choice.

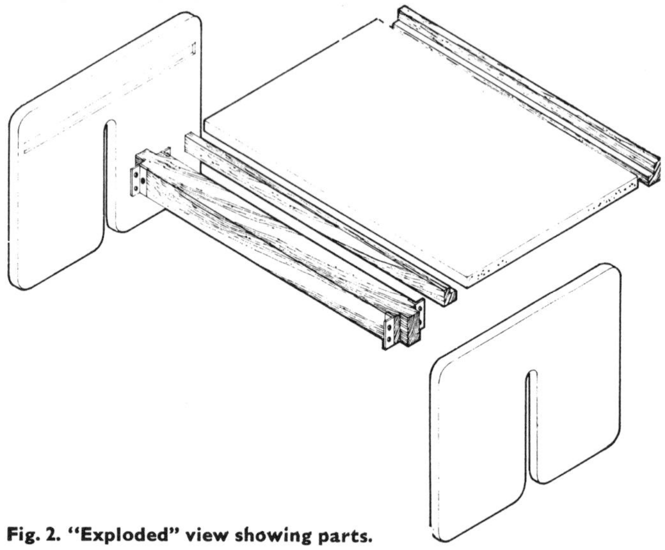

Fig. 2. "Exploded" view showing parts.

Cutting List

	Long ft. in.	Wide in.	Thick in.
2 Ends	1 4½	13¼	¾
1 Top	1 11½	15¾	¾
2 Lippings	1 11	1½	1
1 Stretcher	2 0½	2¼	2

Allowances have been made to lengths and widths, thicknesses are net. ■

TRINKET BOWL
by David Fisher

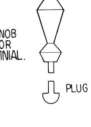

The bowl shown was made from one piece of utile, which was an end piece trimmed off a wide plank, containing a deep shake. This piece cut in half, with the shake, gave me two pieces suitable for a lid and bowl of the same texture. All that was necessary additionally was an odd piece of the same material, to use for the knob at the top. No overall sizes are quoted as this design will suit any small blocks of wood available.

The bowl is turned first, and I usually mount the block straight on to the large face plate, with access for shaping the bottom and sides first.

Turn the required shape and cut a recess in the bottom to receive the three inch face plate, or if one of these is not available, turn a block of

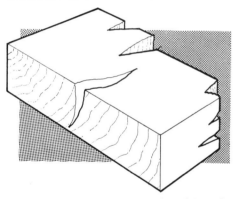

Fig. 1. This is a pretty fair indication of the end piece of utile that I used. As it is unlikely you will have an identical piece, it will be a question of using odd pieces of scrapwood.

Fig. 2. Illustrating the hollowing out of the body and the lid.

scrap hardwood to this diameter, and use it in the same way. This recess will need to fit perfectly as any discrepancy will cause the bowl to run out of true when remounted. Finish the bottom of the bowl in readiness for the desired finish at this stage.

Remove the bowl from the lathe and remount on to the smaller face plate as before, removing the larger one at the same time. Remount the bowl on to the lathe and turn out the inside of the bowl and cut in the sides to the top edge to fit the design. It is wise to taper in at the top edge of the job as the width of the wood for the lid was the same diameter as the bowl. Finish off the bowl in the usual way and prepare for the

finish. Remove the complete unit from the lathe and start on the lid.

The lid material is mounted on to the face plate in the same way. The outside or top is turned first; and where the lid meets the bowl the diameter is left oversize. Cut a hole through the centre to take a $\frac{1}{4}$in diameter bolt and finish off the top ready for polishing.

Remove from the lathe and prepare a suitable scrap block to the diagram shown, and bolt the lid into this jig and remount on to the face plate in the usual way. Turn out the inside of the lid and be careful not to cut too much wood away from the bolt.

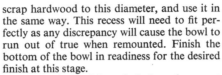

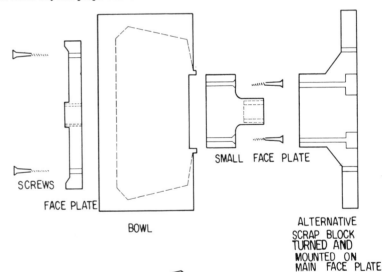

SCREWS

FACE PLATE

BOWL

SMALL FACE PLATE

ALTERNATIVE SCRAP BLOCK TURNED AND MOUNTED ON MAIN FACE PLATE

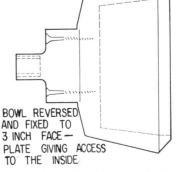

BOWL REVERSED AND FIXED TO 3 INCH FACE PLATE GIVING ACCESS TO THE INSIDE

KNOB OR FINIAL.

PLUG

Fig. 3. Method of turning up the bowl.

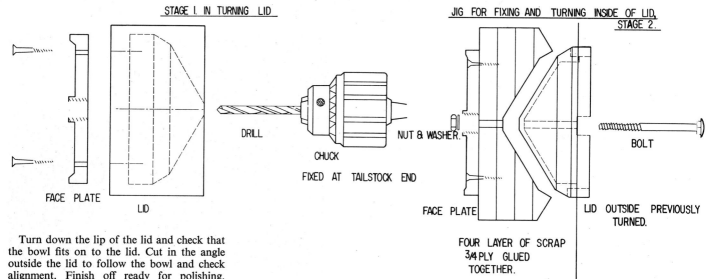

STAGE 1. IN TURNING LID

JIG FOR FIXING AND TURNING INSIDE OF LID,
STAGE 2.

DRILL

NUT & WASHER.

CHUCK

FIXED AT TAILSTOCK END

FACE PLATE

LID

FACE PLATE

FOUR LAYER OF SCRAP
3/4 PLY GLUED
TOGETHER.

FINAL PARTING LINE.

BOLT

LID OUTSIDE PREVIOUSLY
TURNED.

Fig. 4. Stages in making the lid.

Turn down the lip of the lid and check that the bowl fits on to the lid. Cut in the angle outside the lid to follow the bowl and check alignment. Finish off ready for polishing. Remove from the lathe and dismantle the bolt. Cut away the centre tube of wood by hand, and leave it ready to receive the knob and plug.

The knob is turned between centres, and the diameter of the stem is made to fit nicely into the hole. A plug is similarly turned, and both are glued into place.

You can now apply the finish, and I usually use french polish for this in the time-honoured tradition; by hand, out of the lathe. As my workshop is not warm enough during the winter months when most of my turning is done, I find it necessary to take my projects into the house, where conditions are right and a good finish can be achieved. However, any of the usual finishes will be suitable, and if a finish is required whilst on the lathe, this can be carried during the turning operation.

A "TRIKE" FOR THE KIDS

By T. Diss

Here is a design for a small "three wheeler" for children in the age range 1½ to 3 years. Most factory-built trikes are quite expensive these days, but the woodworking enthusiast will have most of the timber tucked away in the corner of the workshop and will only have three plastic wheels to buy.

The main body is made from any suitable hardwood such as rauli, beech, or oak and a close grained, good turning wood is preferred for the steering column, as all of this is made on the lathe.

The design incorporates two useful features. Firstly, the steering column has nylon or plastic bearings to reduce wear on the column, and secondly, the rear wheels are widely spaced to give stability and, therefore, just one front wheel gives the control for easy steering.

SEAT

Tackle the seat first. This is specially important because the steering hole can be drilled with a twist or expanding bit and the lathed column can be made to fit this hole. Another useful tip is to leave the cutting of the housed joints, top and bottom of the seat, until the parts to fit in these are ready.

After marking out the detail on the rectangular piece of wood, cut the outside shape oversize with a coping saw or jig-saw. Finish the edge with a spokeshave and mark out the chamfer lines with a pencil on the top and bottom, with a home-made thumb gauge. Spokeshave the chamfer and finish with glasspaper. Carefully drill all five holes and in the centre pattern remove the thin ⅛in strips joining all four holes with a coping saw. Glasspaper these with paper wrapped around a thin file.

STEERING COLUMN

The whole of the column comprises three separate parts. All these are made on a lathe.
1. Firstly, the wheel forks. Prepare the square block for holding on centres in the lathe and plane off all four corners to make it octagonal in shape. Round it all off to 2⅜in dia, and with a parting off tool cut the shoulder in the correct position.

Latheing down the top section needs special care as this part must fit exactly into the steering hole drilled in the seat. It is not normal to remove centred-up work in the lathe but this is an exception to the rule. Carefully check the work in the hole and try to get a good running fit: there should be no slackness at all. Return the job to the lathe and finish with glasspaper.

When completed, pencil in the lines for cutting out the middle section of the forks. This is best done with a rip saw, and a coping saw frees the waste. Smooth up the rather large inner surfaces that have come against the saw. Some readers might like to drill the front axle hole first and care be taken to drill this through squarely. The last job to be done on this part is the drilling of the other end to take the crossbar head.

2. Steering collar. The one important dimension on this part is the internal hole diameter, and this must be the same as the top of part C. Some notice must be taken of the way of the grain for this collar. It was found best to part-off a piece from a larger block made round in the lathe. One could make this from a square of wood held on to the lathe with a small faceplate but this is not advised, as trouble could arise from splitting along the short grain.

3. Crossbar head. This is turned between centres and care is taken over the size of the circular tenon, as this must fit snugly into the hole in part C. After finishing off, remove from lathe and drill the hole squarely to take the handlebars.

Nylon bearings can be cut from thin ⅟₁₆in sheet nylon but this can be expensive and may be difficult to obtain. A good suggestion is to use the tough plastic side of a half gallon orange squash container. This cuts very easily with a *Stanley* knife and can be made to measure.

BACK WHEEL HOLDER (n.b. Grain of wood must run vertically)

After planing to width and thickness, the shape can be pencilled on the face side and cut with a coping or jigsaw. Next, mark out the position of the decorative hole and drill this. With the marking gauge mark the positions on both edges for the axle hole. This is a tricky operation and needs special care in drilling. Drill halfway or just over from both ends and try to meet in the middle. This is best done with a colleague who can check the uprightness of the brace. Should the holes not meet, a tapered round file will help to get a hole just big enough to take the axle rod. Care is needed to see that the hole is

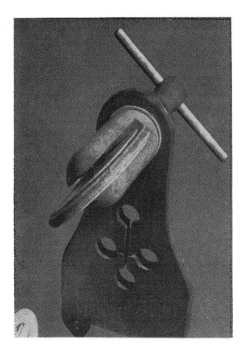

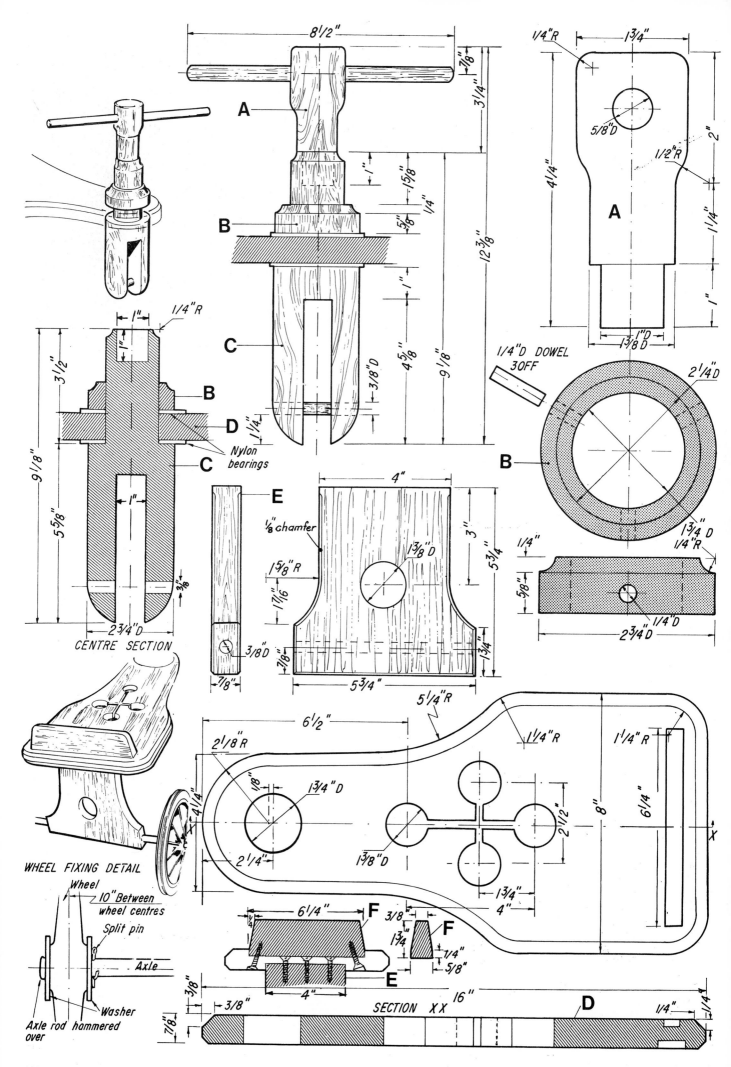

A

1/4"R

1 3/4"

5/8"D

4 1/4"

1/2"R

2"

1 1/4"

A

1"

1 3/8 D

8 1/2"

7/8"

3 1/4"

A

B

1"

1 5/8"

1/4"

5/8"

12 3/8"

C

1"

3/8"D

4 5/8"

9 1/8"

1 1/4"

1/4"D DOWEL
30FF

B

2 1/4"D

1 3/4"D

1/4"R

1/4"

5/8"

2 3/4"D

1/4"D

1"

1/4"R

3 1/2"

1"

B

D

C

*Nylon
bearings*

9 1/8"

5 5/8"

1"

3/8"

2 3/4"D

CENTRE SECTION

E

1/8 chamfer

1 5/8"R

1 7/16"

3/8"D

7/8"

4"

1 3/8"D

3

5 3/4"

1 3/4"

5 3/4"

7/8"

WHEEL FIXING DETAIL

Wheel

10" Between
wheel centres

Split pin

Axle

Washer

Axle rod hammered
over

2 1/8"R

6 1/2"

1/8"

1 3/4"D

4 1/4"

2 1/4"

1 3/8"D

5 1/4"R

1 1/4"R

2 1/2"

1 3/4"

4"

1 1/4"R

8"

6 1/4"

X

X

6 1/4"

F

3/8

F

1 3/4"

1/4"

5/8"

E

3/8"

4"

3/8"

7/8"

SECTION XX

16"

D

1/4"

1/4"

Kiddies' trike (from page 73)

not too large. The finished wood can be offered up to the underside of the seat and drilled to take the screws. This part must be glued and screwed to the seat before the bottom support part F.

BOTTOM SUPPORT

After making this part, it, too, can be positioned, glued and screwed to the seat. The housing joint in this part needs to be made well as it is always seen, and likewise the joint for the back wheel holder needs to fit well as this comes under heavy use.

AXLES

The front axle is, ideally, cut to the maximum diameter of the wood at the axle hole. It is not advisable to have any metal protrusions or even split pins or washers. Washers can be fitted either side of the wheel and between the forks if desired. The back axle needs to be measured and drilled to take ⅛in dia split pins as shown in the drawings. The ends can be rivetted over with the round end of a ball pein hammer just sufficiently to prevent the end washers slipping off.

ASSEMBLY AND FINISH

Assembling the front column and its constituent parts is assisted by a sash cramp to squeeze the top of the steering collar towards the wheel to keep the bearings tight. When the sash cramp is holding the collar, the latter can be drilled through three times at 120° intervals and locked in this position with ¼in dia dowel with glue. A little wear of the bearings is to be expected during running in so it is important to see that everything is fairly tight at the beginning. The handlebar can be locked in position with a ¾in panel pin.

The type of finish on the trike will vary with individual ideas but a good gloss finish polyurethane varnish needs some beating. It takes a lot of hard wear and offers some protection from the elements when the owner chooses to "garage" the model in the garden!

Parts List

Part Ref.	*No. reqd.*	*Description*	*Long ft*	*Long in*	*Wide in*	*Thick in*	*Remarks*
A	1	Crossbar head ..		6	2	2	Turned to shape
B	1	Steering collar ..		2	3	3	,,
C	1	Steering fork ..		10	3	3	,,
D	1	Seat	1	6	8½	1	Shaped
E	1	Back wheel holder		6	6	1	,,
F	1	Bottom support		7	2	¾	,,
Also							
	3	Plastic wheels ..		6 dia.			Rubber tyres, ⅜in hole
	1	Handlebar ..		9		⅝	dia. beech or ramin dowel
	1	Front axle ..		3		⅜	dia. mild steel rod
	1	Back axle ..	1	0		⅜	dia. ,,
	2	Plastic bearings		3	3	1/16	nylon, cut to shape

MINE OF INFORMATION ABOUT BRITISH STANDARDS

The tremendous expansion in the work of the British Standards Institution and the great effort made by this body to pave the way for the nation's change to the metric system are reflected in the 1972 BSI Yearbook, which is larger than ever before. This year, the volume contains almost 900 pages which list some 6000 British Standards, Codes of Practice and other publications used in industry, agriculture, commerce and other walks of life and states the contents and price of each.

Price, including postage £1·90 (plus 20p small orders charge for single copies). An interleaved version which can be kept up-to-date from BSI News is available for £5·25 from BSI Sales Branch, 101 Pentonville Road, London, NI 9ND.

GARDEN CHESS

by D. J. Laidlaw-Dickson

A sheltered little spot about twenty feet square in a pleasant corner of the flower gardens bordering an Austrian lakeside gave us our first sight of open-air chess. Squares follow metric sizes and at 50cm across – or 19½in. – are the same size as the popular carpet squares now in use as floor coverings. This gives a board just under 14ft. square and pieces are made to be large enough to handle and still permit players to walk on to the board to move pieces. Each piece has a large metal eye in the top, just big enough for a finger to be inserted.

On three sides the chess arbour was surrounded by shrubs and flowers, with park seats ranged round for spectators. Quite remarkably no one had removed any pieces and there appeared to be no kind of

supervision. Any likely looking passer-by could be approached to play (with a very high proportion of acceptances in a chess playing community, if not so high as reputedly in Russia!); failing this the lone player can start his own game, playing both sides, when sure enough a volunteer opponent will materialise in minutes . . .

Style of chessmen was as simple as can be based broadly on the ringed type in use in South Germany and Austria. Makers who fancy Staunton or other favourite pattern can make the necessary changes. Bases are all square with the pieces screwed up from the bottom. Wood chosen and thickness is not important. We have used oddments of salvaged wood and kept thickness within the softwood limits of our Black and Decker jigsaw.

Quite apart from the charm of a garden chess board using coloured Marley tile squares other options are open. Board could be laid out on a school playground, pieces made by a class – one piece per child, with the more expert doing knights and other difficult pieces; followed by a tournament with players seated on stepladders like tennis umpires with "movers" to shift the pieces. This, of course, is one of the problems of big chess, getting the feel of the board from ground level – we have unashamedly climbed on to encircling benches to get a birds-eye view!

Yet another thought, which we have not yet developed, is a half size set for the patio to play from garden lounges using a long pole with hook in the end to move pieces. This would be with small coloured tiles and only be 4ft. by 4ft. in board size.

Drawing is squared for ease of construction. If cardboard templates are made and pencilled round there should be no problems, and available wood used to best advantage. Completed pieces are then painted – black and yellow was the Austrian scheme – red and yellow is another pleasing combination. Any ordinary paint or enamel can be used, and pieces can be left out if desired or put away after play – they take very little actual wear.

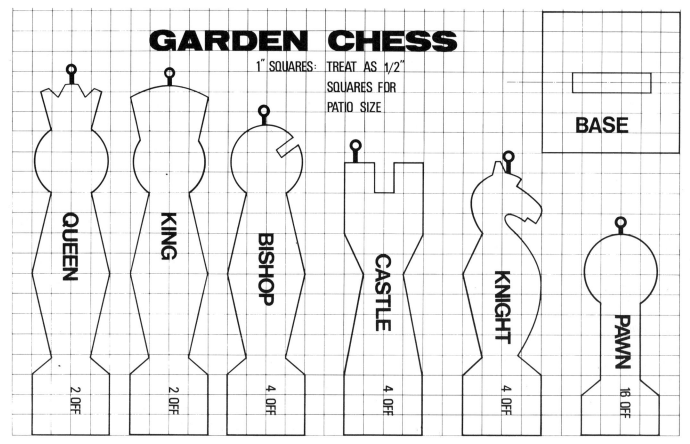

GARDEN CHESS

1" SQUARES: TREAT AS 1/2" SQUARES FOR PATIO SIZE

BASE

QUEEN 2 OFF

KING 2 OFF

BISHOP 4 OFF

CASTLE 4 OFF

KNIGHT 4 OFF

PAWN 16 OFF

An Antique Marbles Table

by Richard Irving

Some fifty years ago, I knelt on my knees in a school yard to use an aid to play the ancient game of marbles. The aid, Fig. 2, was made in the school woodwork room, and consisted of a piece of pine in which we cut small arches of various sizes, like a multiple bridge, through which we challenged our classmates to roll their marbles. The smaller the arch, the larger the number of marbles gained.

Recently I had an opportunity to examine an Antique Marbles Table, Fig. 1, the like of which I had never seen before. It bore evidence of having had much use over many years, indicated by the numerous light bruises caused by the marbles. These must have been larger than those used in my lifetime, judging by the height of the point of contact. The legs were detachable for storage purposes. The skill of the maker was particularly displayed in the table bridge. On both sides of this ran a band of boxwood carrying Roman numerals above its arches. So perfect were these numerals, that at first I thought them to be painted, until I noticed that one was slightly chipped, betraying that it was Rosewood. I imagine that the numeral bands had been built up as Tunbridge Ware was.

The authenticity of the table was supported by the old pointless screws which had been used to fix the frame to the table top, and the top to the rim. Numerous tack holes showed that the table top had been rebaized many times.

Because of the extreme novelty of this table, I'll describe it for the benefit of readers of the *Woodworker*.

THE RIM. The four corners of this were secret mitre dovetailed, as Fig. 3. Sides A and Ends B were rebated as Fig. 4. The baize-covered Table Top C was screwed up into

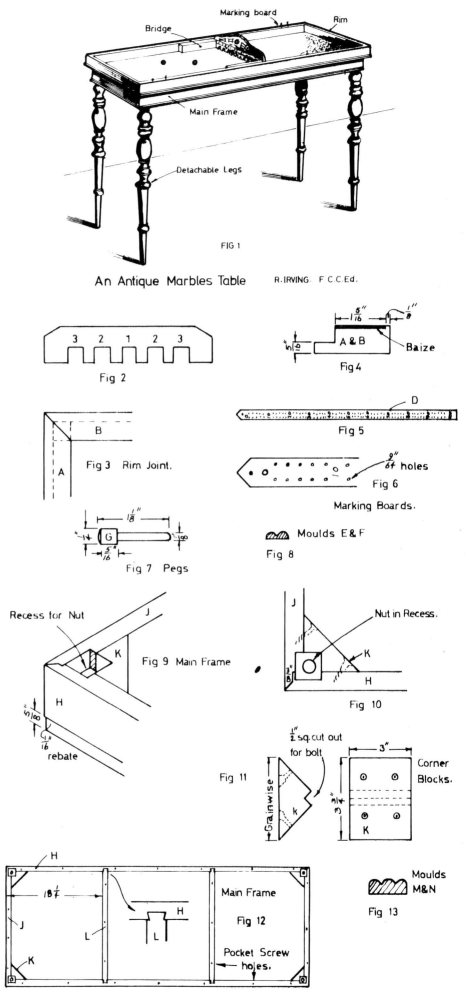

FIG 1

An Antique Marbles Table   R. IRVING. F C.C.Ed.

Fig 2

Fig 4

Fig 3   Rim Joint.

Fig 5

Fig 6

Marking Boards.

Fig 7   Pegs

Fig 8   Moulds E & F

Fig 9 Main Frame

Fig 10   Nut in Recess.

Fig 11   rebate   Recess for Nut

Fig 12   Main Frame   Pocket Screw holes.

Fig 13   Moulds M & N

Corner Blocks.

this rebate. At each end, the right hand corners carried a boxwood Marking Board D, as Figs. 5 and 6, into which pegs could be inserted to keep a tally of the score. The original pegs were missing, but G, Fig. 7, indicates what they could have been like. A double bead mould E, F, Fig. 8, embellished the bottom edge of the rim.

THE MAIN FRAME. For this, the four corners employed a form of mitre lap dovetail, Figs. 9 and 10. These corners were securely braced by Corner Blocks K, Fig. 11. The right angle corners of the Blocks were cut out to permit passage for ½in. dia. bolts used to attach the legs. Recesses were cut in the upper edge of the main frame to house the nuts into which the leg bolts were screwed. Two Cross Rails L were lap dovetailed into the Frame Sides H, Fig. 12. The Main Frame was pocketted inside for screws to fix it underneath the Table Top, with the nuts captive between the Rim and the Frame. A triple Bead Mould M, N, Fig. 13, put the decorative touch around the bottom edge of the frame.

THE LEGS. The originals were missing, so new ones were turned, as Fig. 14. Four 5in. by ½in. dia. bolts had their heads sawn off. They were secured in the tops of the legs with Araldite, supplemented by 1½in. round nails through holes drilled through one side of each leg and the bolts.

THE BRIDGE. This was a real masterpiece, fretted, shaped and arched as Fig. 15. Both faces of the Bridge carried the numeral bands previously mentioned. It was stop lap dovetailed into the Bridge Ends Q, as the small sketch, Fig. 16. The Back R was lap dovetailed into

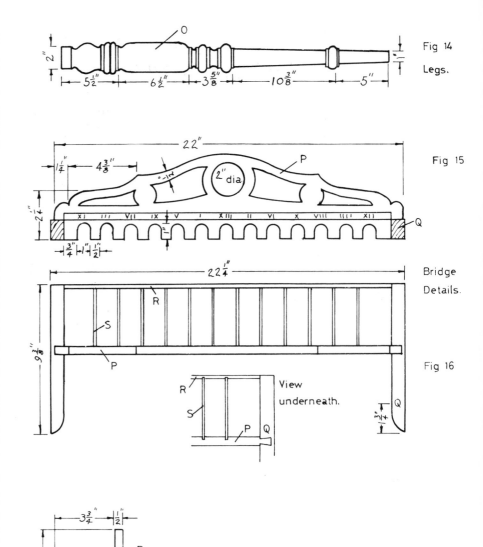

the Ends, Fig. 18. Twelve Divisions S were housed into the Bridge P and the Back R, to form a contain-

ing box for the marbles which had successfully passed through the arches.

BOOKS

the Editor reviews some new and re-issued books

RESTORING ANTIQUE FURNITURE by Leslie Wenn. Published by Barrie & Jenkins. Price: £3.75. Hardback

Some few years back the British Antique Dealers' Association, appalled by the ruination of antiques by incompetent attempts at restoration, decided, in conjunction with West Dean College, to promote the first professional course in conservation and restoration of antique

furniture. Leslie Wenn is the tutor of this course. His book is not for the beginner in woodwork – an adequate knowledge of cabinet making is taken for granted – but for those who have not attempted restoration work before and particularly for those who have done so blindly here is the necessary guidance. Mr. Wenn begins with the need for an understanding of antiques and the behaviour of

wood in furniture and goes on to describe the tools and equipment necessary for individual tasks. The reader is taken through the whole process of restoration, from the first examination to the final finishing and polishing.

The book, in itself, is a very readable item and I thoroughly recommend it to all those craftsmen who wish to take up antique restoration and to those whose interest runs no further than a thirst to know how things are done.

A delicate piece of reproduction and a very fine example of English craftsmanship —

P. J. F. CHILLINGWORTH'S

Georgian Style Toilet Mirror

• • •

This Georgian style toilet mirror would probably have been made in the reign of George III. Earlier mirrors were often walnut-veneered, the mirror being mounted between two posts which were fixed into a shaped box e.g. serpentine or bowfront, this would contain three or more drawers. Then came the oval and shield shapes often veneered with wood such as Satinwood, Tulipwood, King-wood or a fruitwood. Luckily I have restored quite a few different kinds of toilet mirrors over the years and I have tried to keep the construction and design as near original as possible. I have only seen a small number without a nest of drawers contained underneath possibly because being of a very delicate construction few survive today.

• • •

First mark out the mirror design full size on to 4mm. ply. Figs. 1, 2 and 3 show this set out on 1in. squares. Fig. 4 shows the setting out of the legs which is also drawn on 4mm. ply. Note the arrows drawn on the design indicating the direction that the grain should run on each piece of timber used on the finished job. When satisfied that the outer mirror shape is correct the oval mirror inner frame can be drawn, Fig. 9 shows how I set this out using the pin and string method. Briefly the method is as follows. Draw a line AB 16¾in. and a line CD 12¾in. to bisect it. Then measure

3in. from point A to find the position of the first panel pin. Measure 3in. from point B to find the position of the second panel pin. The third panel pin is placed at point C. A piece of fine string is then tied around these pins to form a triangle. The pin at C is then withdrawn and a pencil can then be moved along to draw the oval shape. I found that a notch made in the pencil about ¼in. from the lead held the string in place.

Cut out the outer ply frame shape. (Note: it will only be necessary to cut out half of this shape.) This will now become a template for

marking out on the timber but it should be kept in one piece as it can also be used to check your frame for trueness when glueing up later. Half the oval shape for the inner frame can also be cut, together with the leg pattern. Now the design can be transferred on to your timber not forgetting to allow extra timber for the top joints on the parts in Fig. 1, tenons on the bottom rail Fig. 3, and also the tenons on each leg. Each part of the frame can now be cut out together with the two legs. A bandsaw fitted with a narrow blade would be most helpful for cutting out these pieces but not having one myself, I found a coping saw was the next best thing. Make sure however to keep the blade square with your work. Finished off with a small round faced spokeshave and a sharp chisel. Final glasspapering is left until later. Note that the legs are rounded on the top edge only, Fig. 8.

When satisfied that the work is correctly marked out including all joints, and after these have been cut, the whole outer frame is finally glued up. Do not glue the legs in position at this stage, and note the top joint with the key insert, Fig. 5. This could, if you wished, be made to fit into the front so as to be hidden by the crossbanding. For some reason this was not done on the original. I used a resin glue to fix the outer frame together and it was assembled in two stages. First the joint at the top of the frame is glued to form a wish-bone shape and I cramped this to a flat board so as to eliminate any chance of twisting. The distance between the two points of the inside shoulder on the lap joints shown in Figs. 2 and 6 marked Y should be checked as it is vital that this be correct with your drawing. The bottom rail and the two lap joints can now be glued. The frame is again clamped to a flat board, paper placed under each joint so that the frame will not stick to the board. A final check with your ply template to make sure the frame is true and then work can start on the inner frame. Measure across the outer frame between the two points where the mirror screws will eventually pass through. This measurement will be the finished width of your inner oval frame. Subtract ⅜in. from this measurement which will give the size of the jig for making the inner frame. Blockboard is ideal for this job. Gauge ⅜in. around the half oval ply pattern; this will give the inside size of the oval frame. Check this before drawing on to the blockboard. After the blockboard has been cut finish off with a spokeshave to remove any imperfections. I then rubbed a candle around the edge at this stage to help as a release agent in the event of any glue coming between the frame and jig. Strips of pine ⅛in. thick by ¾in. wide are now bent around the jig to make up three layers to bring the frame to the thickness we require, ⅜in. In order to bend the pine easily around the jig saw, kerfs ¼in. apart are made along the whole length of each strip. Each layer need not be one continual strip but may be butt joined in places. Obviously these joins are staggered so as not to weaken the finished frame. Clear adhesive tape is used to hold the strips in place whilst the glue is drying. I used a resin base glue which gives plenty of working time. Note Fig. 10A, which shows how pine strips are kerfed.

The first strip fits around the jig and the second is then glued and taped on to the first and allowed to dry. They are made to stand proud approximately ¹/₁₆in. which will later be planed flush with the blockboard. Bend the strips carefully as the pine will break easily; tape along carefully without leaving any space between each piece of tape. When dry remove tape and clean off before gluing the final layer in place. After removing the tape from this last layer clean off ready for

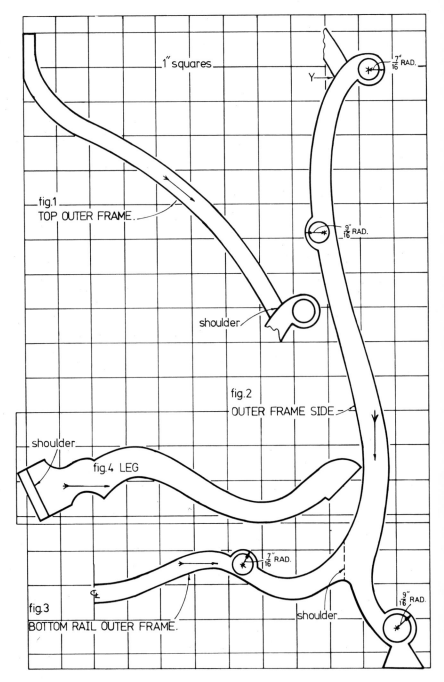

fig.1
TOP OUTER FRAME.

1" squares

fig.2
OUTER FRAME SIDE

⁷/₁₆" RAD.

⁹/₁₆" RAD.

Y

shoulder

shoulder

fig.4 LEG

fig.3
BOTTOM RAIL OUTER FRAME.

⁷/₁₆" RAD.

⁹/₁₆" RAD.

shoulder

veneering with Honduras mahogany veneer. I used scotch glue for this so a thin coat of size was required before veneering. The veneer can be joined on the centre line where the screws will pass through. As the join is not easily noticed when the centre mirror frame is in place, the veneer can be laid in one strip or two. This is left to dry for 24 hours and then the frame edge can be planed down to the blockboard jig. A cutting gauge is set to ⅜in. and from the blockboard face already planed, gauge around the frame. A veneer knife is taken around the gauge line to remove the waste. The frame can now be removed from the jig. Place this on to a piece of stout card or 4mm. ply and draw around the inside of the frame. This can be cut out to give a pattern for the mirror size. It is best to reduce

this by ¹/₁₆in. to allow for error when cut. The pattern can then be sent to the glazier so that the mirror glass will be ready for fitting later. The oak back can now be fitted. A well seasoned piece is vital; I used an old drawer bottom. The back is placed into a rebate which can be cut out with the aid of a cutting gauge fitted with a round faced stock to enable it to be taken around the inside of the oval shape. A veneer knife can then be used to remove the waste. The back is cut out, shaped and when a nice tight fit is obtained this is screwed in place with eight ⅜in. O gauge countersunk brass screws. Leave this in place while the cross-banding is glued to the front edge. Note that Fig. 1A shows the direction that the grain should run. The banding is made up with pieces

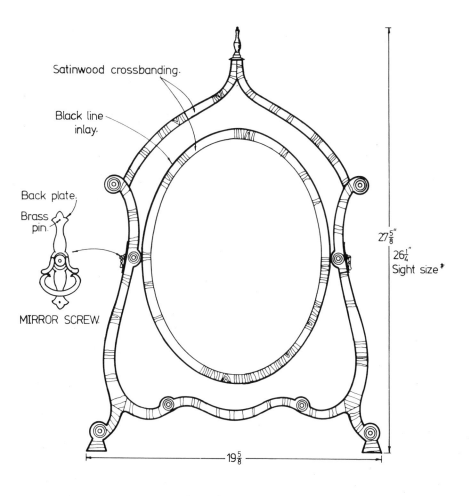

Satinwood crossbanding.

Black line inlay.

Back plate.

Brass pin.

MIRROR SCREW.

$27\frac{5}{8}"$

$26\frac{1}{4}"$
Sight size *

$19\frac{5}{8}$

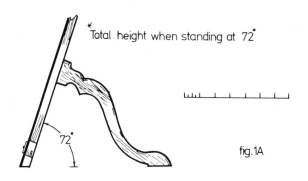

*Total height when standing at 72°

72°

fig. 1A

approximately 1½in. to 2in. wide. Allow the banding to overlap the outside of the frame for trimming off later and this also applies to the inside. To join the banding imagine that there are lines radiating from the centre of the oval frame; the joins are kept to the angles made by these lines. The crossbanding can be held in place with adhesive tape while the glue is setting. Again I used a resin base glue but scotch glue can be used and in this case the banding can be glued around the frame in three or four pieces at a time. It will be found that if this method is used no tape will be required as the glue chills quite quickly and this should be enough to hold it in position. When the glue has dried the banding can be trimmed down to the frame with a spokeshave. A mark-

ing gauge can be set to $^{11}/_{16}$in., the finished size of the banding. This is then taken around the outside of the frame. It will be necessary to use a gauge fitted with two trammel bars on the stock face for this job and then a round faced spokeshave is used to remove the waste. The banding can either be cleaned off to finish flat or rounded as in Fig. 10 B to form a nice round moulding. The more expensive Georgian mirrors were often treated in this way and it is well worth the extra work. A $^{3}/_{32}$in. square black line is then inlaid around the outside of the finished crossbanding. A rebate to take this line is made using a cutting gauge and a sharp chisel. Using a resin glue the line can be held in place with tape until the glue has set. Cross-banding can also be glued to

the outer mirror frame front, Fig. 1A shows the direction of the grain and also examples of the joins. Again I allowed for waste to be cleaned off later. The banding is also held in place using the same method. The two frames together with the two legs are then cleaned up to a good finish and polished. After polishing the two legs are glued into position making sure that they are both at 90° to the frame. Note Fig. 1A side view showing how the frame slopes backward at an angle of 72° when the legs are in place. Remove the oak back from the oval frame and fit the mirror in position. Small blocks are glued behind this to hold it in place and scotch glue is ideal for this job, see Fig. 10 and also the two mirror plates which can now be fitted. Before fitting the mirror however it is advisable to paint behind the crossbanding and also the edge of your mirror with spirit black or matt black paint to prevent any reflection from the inside. The oak back can now be refitted. The two brass back plates are pinned in place on the outer frame, which serve to prevent the mirror screws biting into the timber as well as being decorative. The finials and patrias can be turned and then glued in position. I used an epoxy adhesive for this job. If bone or ivory cannot be obtained for the finial or patrias there is a good ivory type resin on the market which is usually used to make chess pieces. Briefly the method used for making them this way is to turn the shapes required, using a good close grain wood. Wax polish while still on the lathe which will enable the rubber mould to be removed easily. Coat the wooden turning with either a cold liquid rubber or a hot meltable rubber which, when set, gives a perfect mould. These can be used several times so it is only necessary to turn one of each shape required. The resin is easily mixed and is poured into the moulds. Curing times will depend on the temperature of the room.

FINISHING

After sanding to a good finish all the mahogany was stained using bichromate of potash. The satinwood is left untreated and no form of stain was given as the natural colour of the wood is required. When the stain has dried this is rubbed down with OO grade or flour paper. Finally the work is given a coat of button polish and when dry this first coat is rubbed down again with OO grade paper. The second coat and following coats are rubbed down with wire

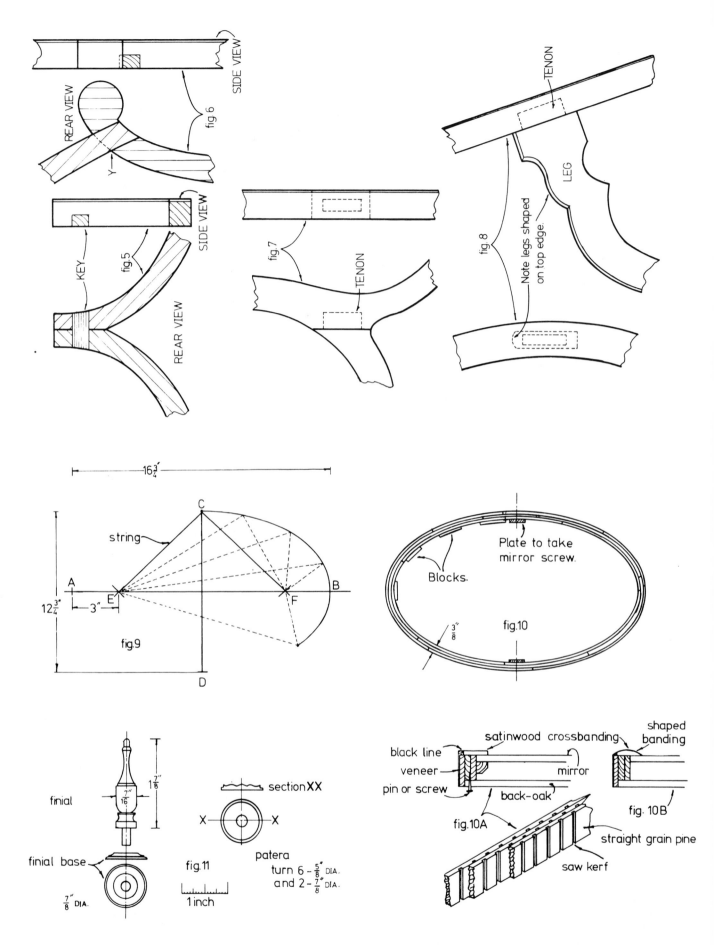

SIDE VIEW

REAR VIEW

fig 6

KEY

SIDE VIEW

fig.5

REAR VIEW

fig 7

TENON

TENON

fig 8

LEG

Note legs shaped
on top edge.

16¾"

C

string

A

E

3"

F

B

12¾"

fig.9

D

Plate to take
mirror screw.

Blocks.

⅜"

fig.10

finial

1⅞"

⁷⁄₁₆"

section XX

X — X

finial base

fig.11

patera
turn 6 – ⅝" DIA.
and 2 – ⅞" DIA.

⅞" DIA.

1 inch

black line
veneer
pin or screw

satinwood crossbanding

mirror

back-oak

fig.10A

shaped
banding

fig. 10B

straight grain pine

saw kerf

wool fine grade. I found four applications of button polish sufficient.
After the last coat has been rubbed
down with wire wool an application
of soft wax is given to the work
which plus a bit of elbow grease is

all that is required for a perfect
finish.

WOODEN TRACTION ENGINE

BY
E. D. FLETCHER

The design for this traction engine makes an excellent toy for any boy up to ten years old. Its robust construction will ensure hours of fun and amusement for the most boisterous boy— or these days—girl.

Friction drive for the flywheel is taken from the inner shoulder of the rear wheel.

As the toy is made up of reasonably small components, it is possible to use oddments of timber from the scrap box, or where available, old furniture. For example, on my model the wheels, flywheel and funnel came from an old school desk, whilst the school caretaker unknowingly provided me with the cylinder timber from the end of his sweeping brush handle!

Before starting work on the engine it is advisable to make a turning mandrel and a vee block.

Turning Mandrel

This consists of an 8mm (or imperial equivalent) by 150mm long pieces of M.S. bar, threaded for 50mm of its length and centre drilled at the threaded end. Also required are three nuts and two large diameter washers. Alternatively, a 5/16 coach bolt could be used with the head sawn off.

Vee Block

Whilst not essential, a vee block enables accurate drilling of the holes in the boiler. It should be approximately 150mm long and have an included angle of about 90°.

Body – Softwood

The body can be cut from the solid, or built up of smaller pieces. It is helpful if the body is divided into two pieces, a top piece which is 35mm and a lower portion which is 95mm. The two are glued together after shaping. This enables the end faces to be cleaned up by planing, giving a better finish than from a saw. After shaping and gluing, the hole which accepts the boiler spigot is cut, use an expanding bit. The centre for the 30mm radius boiler recess is outside the top 35mm piece and a 30mm thick piece of timber must be cramped against it and drilled through, stopping when the lower piece is reached. The tip of the bit will then have marked in the lower piece the centre for the 40mm spigot hole.

Alternatively, if an expanding bit is not available, the boiler can be connected to the body with dowels. If this method is used, the boiler recess will have to be pared with a scribing gauge.

The axle hole must be drilled vertically to ensure that the engine stands with all four wheels on the floor. At this stage, cut and drill the two 20mm square spacers and glue to each side of the body in line with the axle holes.

Do not drill the flywheel axle hole until assembly.

Boiler – Softwood

The turning of the boiler is straightforward, and being drilled after the hole in the body has been cut, allows the opportunity to amend the spigot diameter to suit any irregularities. The raised portion on the front of the boiler represents the smoke box door.

The vee block is used with a pedestal drill when drilling the various holes in the boiler to ensure that they are in line with the centre line.

Drill the 19mm Ø hole to accept the funnel, and at 27° to drill one forward canopy support hole. Turn the boiler through 54° and drill the other support hole.

Whilst not essential, the model is strengthened by dowelling as well as gluing the bogie and belly tank to the boiler. If this is to be done, holes should be drilled in the following manner.

At 180° to the funnel spigot hole, and in line with it, drill the front bogie dowel hole, and at the rear of the boiler, the belly tank dowel hole.

Rear Wheels – Hardwood

Here again, the timber can be built up, or turned from the solid.

The axle hole is first drilled in each piece of timber to ensure that it is at right angles to the timber face. The pieces are then mounted together on the mandrel with a locknut, nut and washer on the chuck end of the thread, and a washer and nut clamping at the other end. As the wheels are quite large, it is necessary to steady the mandrel with the tailstock centre to prevent whip.

The wheels are turned to the correct external diameter, and once this has been done, they may be treated as two separate items. The depression on the outside of the wheel represents the lacing of the spokes; the grooves and fillets on the edge, the rubber tyres; and the shoulder on the inside provides the drive for the Flywheel.

Front Wheels – Hardwood

The procedure is the same for the front wheels as for the rear, but without the inner shoulder.

Flywheel – Hardwood

Clearance between the hub of the flywheel and the edge of the rear wheel is close, so care must be taken with the turning of the flywheel hub. The turned groove is for decoration only, and is entirely at the discretion of the maker.

Funnel – Hardwood

The only critical dimension is the diameter of the plain spigot at the base of the funnel, which has to fit into the drilled hole in the boiler. The hole in the top of the funnel is drilled in the vice after the turning operations.

Canopy – Softwood

Cut and shape the canopy and drill *only* the holes for the rear canopy support dowels.

Belly Tank – Softwood

The recess for the boiler is cut with a coping saw and finished with a half round file. The dowel hole is drilled to mate with that in the boiler.

Front Bogie – Hardwood

Cut and plane a piece of hardwood 105mm by 55mm by 35mm. Mark out the frontal shape on the timber, and drill the axle hole taking care that it is perfectly in line. Cut out the frontal shape and drill the dowel hole, ensuring that it is at right angles to the axle hole. Finally, plane the front and rear faces to give the desired taper.

Canopy Supports – Dowel

Each rear support is cut from 12mm dowel, 95mm long. The front supports are 12mm dowel, approximately 120mm long.

Axles

These are made from 8mm Ø Bright Drawn Mild Steel, each end slightly chamfered, drilled and tapped 2BA. The axle for the flywheel is tapped at one end only.

Hexagon headed bolts for the axles are visually more pleasing than domed bolts, but are not essential.

Front Axle .. .. .. 8mm Ø by 148mm
Rear Axle .. .. .. 8mm Ø by 168mm
Flywheel Axle .. .. 8mm Ø by 48mm

Assembly

Heavily chamfer or round all sharp edges.

Fit the rear axle and on the flywheel side, fit a rear wheel. Position the flywheel so that its centre is 16mm from the top of the body, mark the centre position, and drill for and fit the flywheel axle.

If dowels are to be used to assist in the fastening of the bogie and belly tank to the boiler, position these before gluing the boiler to the body.

Alternatively, drill and fit the dowels after gluing the bogie and tank in place, remembering to drill through the dowel in the bogie axle hole.

Whichever method of gluing is adopted, however, it is necessary to position the axles and wheels before final cramping, to ensure that all four wheels touch the ground, and that the funnel hole is vertical.

Glue the cylinders to the body. Temporarily fit the front and rear canopy support dowels in place, position the canopy on the rear dowels, and mark the centres for the front dowels. Drill the holes at an angle of 27° to the vertical.

Fit and glue the funnel, canopy supports and canopy.

Glue to the inner shoulder of one rear wheel an 8mm wide elastic band. This provides the friction drive for the flywheel.

At this stage it is as well to apply a finish to the model, either of clear varnish or paint. Painting the individual spokes in the wheels and lining the body and boiler should provide endless amusement!

Finally fit the axles and wheels with washers in the following order:

Axle in body, 9mm washer, wheel, 9mm washer, 2BA washer and 2BA nut.

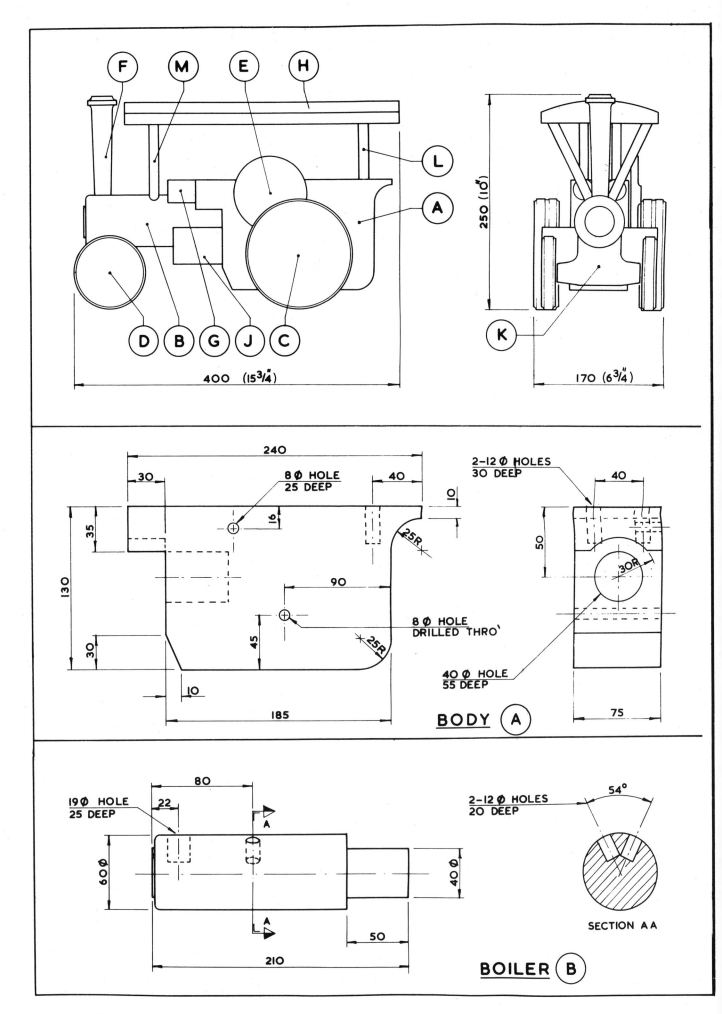

BODY (A)

8 Ø HOLE
25 DEEP

2-12 Ø HOLES
30 DEEP

8 Ø HOLE
DRILLED THRO'

40 Ø HOLE
55 DEEP

BOILER (B)

19 Ø HOLE
25 DEEP

2-12 Ø HOLES
20 DEEP

SECTION A A

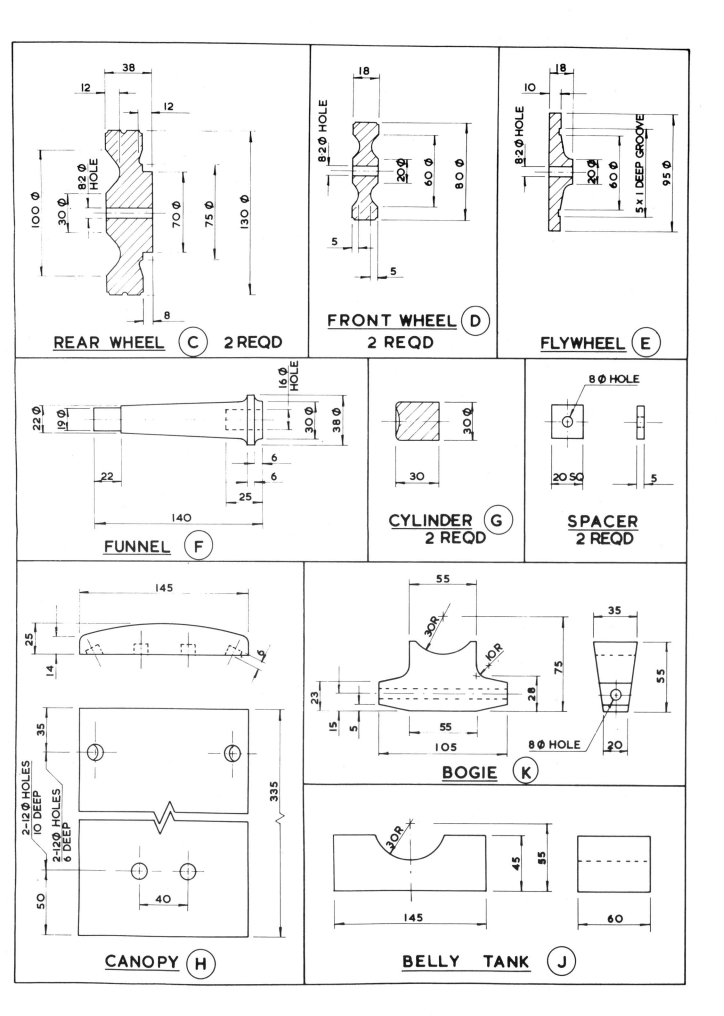

REAR WHEEL (C) 2 REQD

FRONT WHEEL (D)
2 REQD

FLYWHEEL (E)

FUNNEL (F)

CYLINDER (G)
2 REQD

SPACER
2 REQD

BOGIE (K)

CANOPY (H)

BELLY TANK (J)

Pine Cottage Style

COFFEE TABLE

by D. J. Sneade

Because of the particular design of this coffee table my choice of wood was pine. Apart from being reasonably cheap compared to hardwoods, a light timber does enhance the appearance.

When buying the timber, try and get kiln dried stuff with a moisture content around 10% and store it in a dry place for as long as possible beforehand, because most timber yards, in my area anyway, stack their timber in open-sided sheds and it will absorb too much moisture especially in damp weather.

The timber I used was a full 5″ × 1″ only because it was readily available, but an inch or so on the width will not upset the design. Three-quarter inch thick stuff could be used for the legs and feet, but 1″ or 1¼″ should be used for the top.

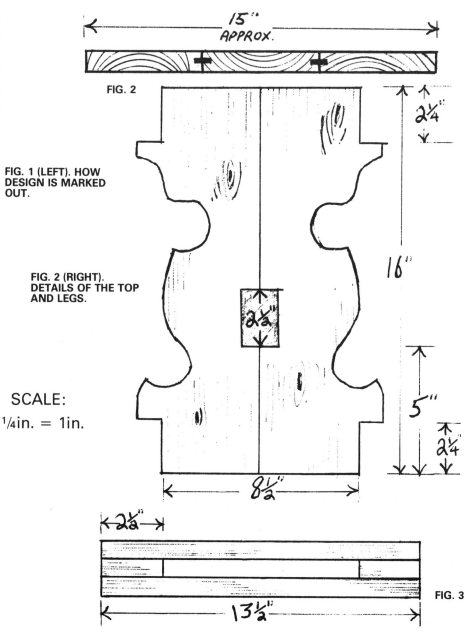

FIG. 1 (LEFT). HOW DESIGN IS MARKED OUT.

FIG. 2 (RIGHT). DETAILS OF THE TOP AND LEGS.

SCALE:
¼in. = 1in.

FIG. 2

15″ APPROX.

2¼″

16″

2½″

5″

2¼″

8½″

FIG. 1. LEG AND FEET DESIGN MARKED OUT IN SQUARES.

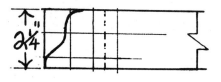

2¼″

2½″

13½″

FIG. 3

FIG. 3. DETAILS OF THE FEET. ALL MEASUREMENTS CAN BE ADAPTED TO THE TIMBER USED.

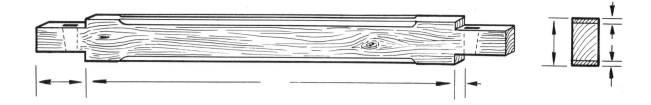

FIG. 4

CONSTRUCTION

The table can be made with the minimum use of power tools, but of course they do help to cut the time down, especially if you are fortunate to own a belt sander, planer or thicknesser. A surface planer is a must for truing up the edges to be joined together.

Start by making the templates out of ply or hardboard (see Fig. 1). Half a side for the legs and a complete one for the feet. Divide them into squares, draw the design and cut the shape.

Next make the two feet and two top supports, which are all identical. See photo and drawing. Cut out the pieces making sure that the inserts are square and glue together. The inserts could be put through a thicknesser (before cutting to length), at the same time as the legs thus ensuring a good fitting mortise. No dowel joints were used, but a strong glue such as Aerolite 306 is recommended.

The difficulty when butt jointing wood is that it often slides when cramped up. To overcome this, nail two veneer pins on one of the mating edges and cut the heads off 1/8" proud of the surface.

When the glue has set, use the template to mark the shape, cut out with a coping saw and finish off with a belt sander.

An alternative method of making the feet is to cut them from a solid piece of wood and mortise them afterwards.

Now for the legs. The width is made up by gluing two pieces together, but before cramping, it is best to cut the mortise for the stretcher at this stage. Clamp the two pieces side by side in a vice, mark them carefully, cut out, and cramp up. When the glue has set, mark one side with the aid of the template, reverse and mark the other. Cut out the shape with a coping saw, or bandsaw (if you are lucky enough to own one), then cut back the tenons ensuring a good fit in the feet.

I used a small drum sander to finish the concave shapes and a spokeshave the convex.

The stretcher is made out of 1½" × 3" stuff. After planing to the correct size make sure there is no twist in the length. It is also important that when the tenons are sawn the shoulders are parallel because the legs rely on this vertical hold when the peg is driven home.

Cut the stretcher mortises next. To avoid any binding and to ensure a tight fit when the peg is inserted they should be cut back 1/8" under the leg thickness (7/8" from shoulders if you use 1" stuff). A finishing touch is to stop chamfer the four edges.

An alternative stretcher can be made out of 3" × 1". The peg driven in sideways instead of vertically, but you must cut a different size mortise in the legs.

The pegs are marked free hand and cut to shape. A slope from top to bottom of 1/4" to 3/8" is sufficient.

THE TOP

Because of their short lengths up to now all the various parts have been butt jointed, but the top should have either dowels or loose tongues in the edges for extra strength. I used plywood tongues slightly narrower than the combined depth of the grooves to allow for any excess glue that could not escape. Three pieces 3'1" long are used to make up the 15" wide top. The heart side of the planks alternated to help prevent warping. Glue and cramp up. (See Fig. 2).

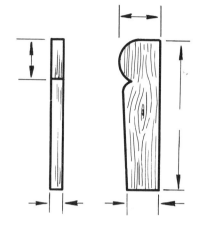

THE TEMPLATES NEEDED.

THE FOUR PARTS OF ONE OF THE FEET.

CRAMPING UP ALL THE FEET AT ONCE.

CUTTING THE LEGS TO SHAPE ON A BANDSAW.

ASSEMBLING

Before assembling, any blemishes especially bad knots should be carefully inspected and filled with stopping if necessary. Sometimes a darker stopping looks better and often saves the tedious task of colour matching.

When dry, sand down all pieces. Glue the legs to the feet, wedges can be inserted at the ends of the mortise through the bottom, but is not really necessary if they are a good fit.

Now insert the stretcher in the legs and gently knock in the locking pegs. No glue is necessary, but make sure they are a good snug fit.

The top was fixed with four steel shrinkage plates to allow for any movement in the timber.

CUTTING OUT THE MORTISES IN THE STRETCHER. TO AVOID ANY TEARING OF THE GRAIN CUT THE SHOULDERS OFF FIRST.

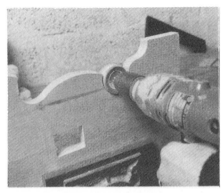

FINISHING OFF THE EDGES OF THE LEGS WITH A DRUM SANDER. THIS IS A VERY USEFUL TOOL AND LEAVES A BEAUTIFUL FINISH.

LEFT: CHAMFERING THE FOUR CORNERS OF THE STRETCHER WITH A SPOKESHAVE.

BELOW: CUTTING THE GROOVES FOR THE LOOSE TONGUES ON A CIRCULAR SAW. THE WOOD HAS TO BE PASSED OVER A SECOND TIME, AFTER MOVING THE FENCE TO INCREASE THE WIDTH. THE GUARD HAS TO BE REMOVED FOR THIS OPERATION.

FINISHING

The finish is a matter of personal choice, but remember at some time or other, the top especially will suffer a lot of tough treatment.

Pine darkens with age, so a clear finish, whatever, is best. My choice was clear mat polyurethane. Three coats were applied, carefully sanded between coats and finally finished with ordinary furniture wax to give it that silky sheen.

Carved Oak Reading Stand

The woodwork of this stand is fairly obvious; little explanation is required. The two middle rails are pivoted on screws enabling the stand and its strut to fold as shown by the dotted lines in Fig. 2. The joint of the uprights to the top rail (Fig. 2) needs careful planning owing to the cutting away of the top rail. It should be set out in full size and the carving plotted first.

FIG. 1. STAND FOR MAGAZINES, BOOKS, MUSIC, OR FOR COPYING
This design is founded upon a book rest in the Victoria and Albert Museum, South Kensington. The original is in oak and dates from about 1700. Apart from its usefulness the stand is a good subject for carving.

Since the carving of the uprights and bottom rail is little more than incision work with the background merely sloped into the leafwork, we may deal here with the top rail only. This is pierced right through and the scroll work is deeply and vigorously cut. Draw in half of the design on paper and transfer it to the wood using carbon paper. The other half is put in by reversing the drawing. Certain parts are pierced right through (see right hand side of elevation in Fig. 2), and cutting these is the first step. Bore holes and cut out with the bow saw. Any unevenness is cleaned up later as the carving progresses.

Fig. 4 (see opposite page) shows two stages in the carving, from which it will be seen that a cut with a small, fairly quick gouge such as ¼in. No. 7 is first made around the end scroll. It can be deepened and made wider as it curves out of the spiral. This frees the rib of the spiral and enables a downward cut to be made with the gouge without danger of the substance of the rib crumbling. The lower illustration in Fig. 4 shows how the downward cut is made, and how the waste is eased away by a sloping cut. The gouge will have to be changed as a different part of the spiral is cut.

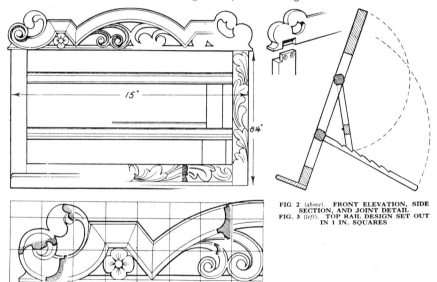

FIG 2 (*above*). FRONT ELEVATION, SIDE SECTION, AND JOINT DETAIL
FIG. 3 (*left*). TOP RAIL DESIGN SET OUT IN 1 IN. SQUARES

QUICK-TIP
ASSEMBLING WOODWORK

Before you begin to glue up a piece of woodwork always consider first whether you can with advantage assemble parts individually. Remember that to glue a whole number of joints in one operation is a difficult job, especially if you have to work single-handed. It may result in the glue becoming chilled before you can apply the cramps. Take the simple case of a table. It simplifies the work tremendously if two opposite sides can be put together independently and the glue allowed to set. These can then be handled as complete units in themselves. The same idea can be carried out in a larger piece such as a sideboard. The ends can be glued up by themselves as a preliminary operation. Possibly too the back and part of the front could also be assembled before the whole is dealt with. Make sure however that this procedure does not prevent the final assembling.

The main broad band is next dealt with, and it will be found convenient if this is chamfered before any hollowing is attempted. Mark in the extent of the chamfer around the edge by using a pencil and holding the finger to act as a gauge. Cut away the wood with the chisel, following the grain as closely as possible. At the internal mitre it will be convenient to make a cut with the V tool. For hollowing use as wide a gouge as possible and make long cuts.

The mitres call for special care, especially the internal ones. The outer ones are formed automatically by the hollowing of the scrolls and are an indication of the truth of the working. This applies in a measure to the internal mitres, but the chief difficulty is that the tool must stop exactly at the mitre, otherwise it cuts into the adjoining scroll. A good plan is to cut down along the mitres with the V tool, stopping short of the finished depth. This forms an opening into which the tool can run. When the finished depth has been nearly reached a downward cut is made along the mitre with knife or gouge and the wood cut into this from each side. This ensures the mitre being accurate.

Fig. 4 shows how the leafwork at the ends is sloped away. After working to the approximate shape the gouge can be used hollow side downwards. Very little modelling is necessary on the small flowers. The separation of the petals is cut in and sloped away at each side. Rounding over the ends of the petals and one or two cuts with a quick gouge towards the round centre completes them. At the back all edges are lightly chamfered.

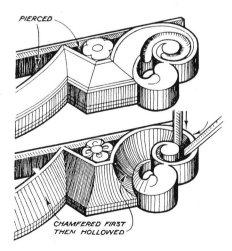

PIERCED

CHAMFERED FIRST THEN HOLLOWED

FIG. 4. STAGES IN THE CARVING

An Interesting Little Exercise . . .

SIMPLE BAR SKITTLES GAME

. . . That Can Provide Hours of Fun

by R. G. Large

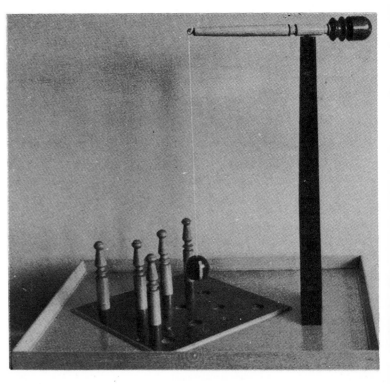

These bar skittles are easy to make and provide a good opportunity for a newcomer to wood turning to use a lathe. Mine were made with a very small Godson in mind, but a more sophisticated version would amuse adults. The game would be more difficult if the skittles were smaller and futher apart, set out as I have shown them the adult is highly amused for a short time and then becomes bored.

The arm rotates and to play, it is swung away from the board and the ball is thrown out so that it swings round through 180 degrees and back on to the skittles.

The choice of wood is a matter of individual taste – I used ramin and mahogany to give a two-tone effect. Similarly the dimensions can be varied, mine are shown to give some idea of the size and proportions. As always shapes are a compromise between ambition and available skill – those shown in the diagrams are simplified for convenience.

The base board is ½in. plywood, white faced, 2ft. by 1ft. 6ins. It is edged with heavy picture framing, mitred in the normal way. When using a mitre box I find it is essential to watch the saw and keep it going down the wood dead on 90 degrees, so that the mitres fit flush and true.

Because the board rocks slightly during play it is necessary to locate the skittles in shallow holes to prevent them falling accidentally. The base could be drilled but I used a separate piece of mahogany-faced ¼in. ply, set diagonally to look more attractive. This was edged with ¼in. quarter round beading to finish it off. The diagram shows the skittles as I placed them. The easiest way to mark the positions is to draw in the diagonal lines and then work from there marking the hole centres 3ins. apart. Ideally this job should be left to the end so that one can experiment as to exact positions, making them hard or easy depending on the likely age and sobriety of the eventual players. One in. diameter holes were drilled with a flat bit and electric drill.

The pillar and its foot are in mahogany, the pillar slotting into the foot as shown to give a simple but strong joint. The foot is glued to the pillar and screwed to the base board, though bolts and wing nuts could be used to remove it for storage. The more ambitious could turn the pillar too.

The swinging arm is a piece of ⅞in. dowel turned to a fancy shape and glued into a larger diameter piece of mahogany which acts as a counter weight. My dimensions will produce a tip heavy effect and this pre-

vents the ball swinging too freely and, more to the point, too dangerously. It is screwed to the top of the pillar with a couple of washers to make a bearing.

The ball is mahogany turned from 1½in. square wood. Before turning it I cut ¼in. grooves along the centre of each face with a plough plane and glued pieces of ramin into the grooves. The grooves should be about ⅜in. deep. When turned the effect is very pleasing and it echoes the two-tone theme. A sharp gouge seems to be the thing for turning balls.

Skittles are made easily from ⅞in. dowel, 5½ins. long. They should be shaped so that they are not top heavy, and I chose nine as a usual number – (11 housings in board).

Assembly is a matter of fine adjustment and positioning before drilling and screwing. Make sure that the pillar and arm are so placed that the ball is in line with the centre skittle – it helps if the arm is slightly too long so it can be cut down finally. If the cord is long enough to let the ball hang about 1in. below the centre skittle it should be about right – it must be able to reach all the skittles.

I dare say my bar skittles are not authentic, they were made from one brief memory and are, as I have said, simplified.

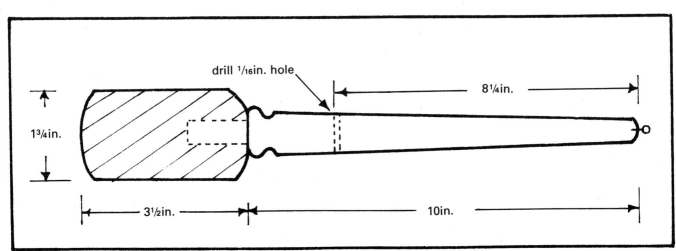

drill ¹⁄₁₆in. hole

8¼in.

1¾in.

3½in.

10in.

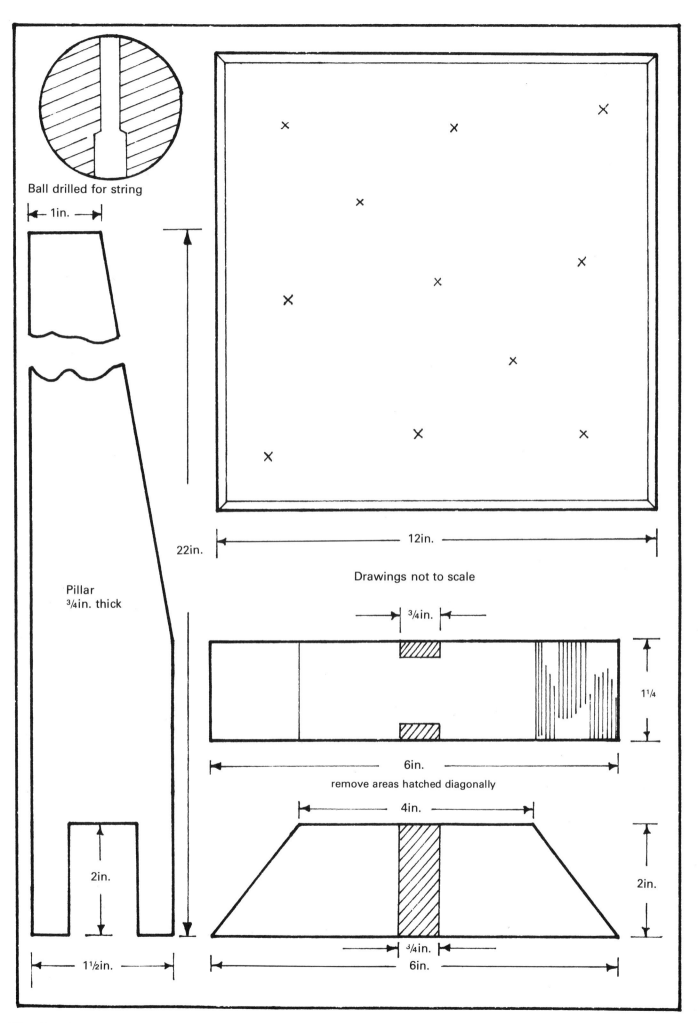

Ball drilled for string

1in.

Pillar
3/4in. thick

22in.

2in.

1½in.

Drawings not to scale

12in.

3/4in.

1¼

6in.

remove areas hatched diagonally

4in.

2in.

3/4in.

6in.

Traditional Style Dancing Dolls

MALCOLM P. BESTWICK

tells of his experiences in carving and dancing these 'jig dolls'

Dancing dolls, also known as 'jig dolls' or 'dolly men' have been made and danced for many years although the origins of the doll are not clear. One, made during the Napoleonic wars is only 2½" high but has ball joints skillfully carved for the arms and had obviously been made with a great deal of skill and patience.

Two rather unusual dolls which were exhibited at a folk festival in Wadebridge 1976, were made from tin plate and beautifully painted to portray railway characters — there being a strong railway tradition in the family of the dolls' owners. Another doll which is still danced regularly in the Dartmoor area belings to a well known folk musician; Bob Cann.* This doll was made at about the turn of the century and is apparently made from alder, which, after carving the green wood, was baked in the oven for about 20 minutes to harden it.

When danced, a doll has a stick inserted into a hole in the back and this is held in the hand with the doll standing on the end of the dancing board. The board, which is made of 6mm ply, is placed on a table or hard chair with the board overhanging the chair or table by about 18". The operator sits on one end and repeatedly taps the board sharply with the closed fist of one hand whilst holding the doll by the stick with the other hand. As the end of the board bounces up and down the legs and arms move in a most lifelike manner, Fig. 1 (below).

The doll illustrated here was made out of mahogany and has stood up to a lot of 'dancing' without serious mishap, (I heard of one doll, owned by a friend, whose head fell off whilst dancing, which the audience found highly amusing!).

A few dolls of this kind of various dates are among the collections at the Bethnal Green Museum, Cambridge Heath Road, London E29 PA.

Fig. 1

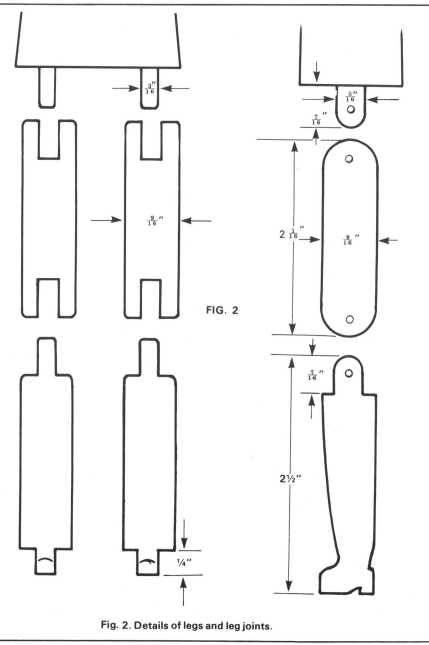

FIG. 2

Fig. 2. Details of legs and leg joints.

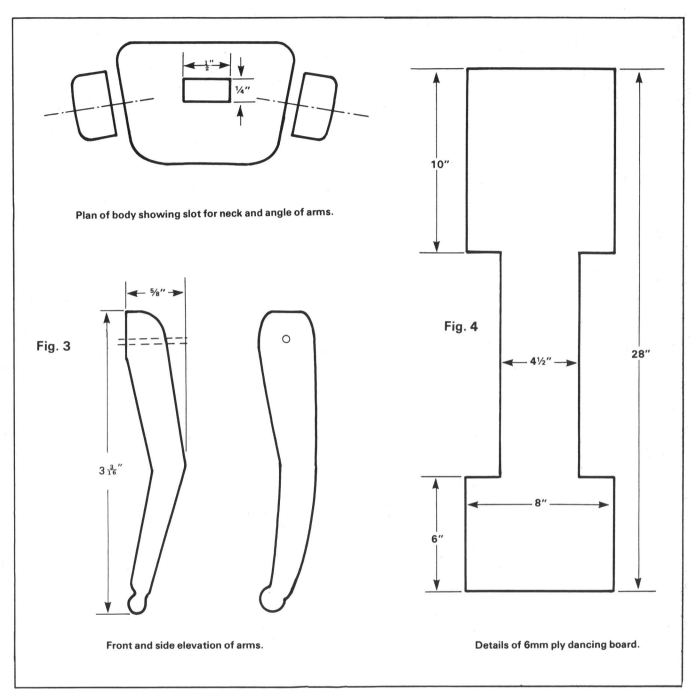

Plan of body showing slot for neck and angle of arms.

Fig. 3

Fig. 4

Front and side elevation of arms.

Details of 6mm ply dancing board.

The leg joints should be slack enough to let the legs swing freely both forwards and backwards without jamming at the end of each movement (Fig. 2) some final shaping usually being necessary when fitting the legs together. I have heard of dolls with lead feet attached to make them dance better, but I have not found this to be really necessary. The legs are secured at the joints with a ⅝" No. 4 screw, having first drilled the inside joint with a ⅛" hole to let the legs swing freely. The arms are set at a slight angle on the body (Fig. 3), so that the hands when moving forward, come across the body rather than parallel to it, giving the doll more character when dancing, the hands almost touching when in front of the body.

The body was roughly cut out with a coping saw from a block 3⅝" x 2" x 1¼" before finishing with carving chisels. It is important to allow ample depth on the joints at the base of the body and the joint on the lower leg, as this is where any weakness will show up when in use. A ¼" hole is drilled into the back 1⅛" down, to receive the operating stick. The 18" long $\frac{5}{16}$" dowel

stick is slightly tapered to make a tight fit into the¼" hole. The slot for the neck and the hole in the back should be made prior to carving.

The head was made from a block 3½" x 1½" x 1½", the waste at the base of the neck being used to hold the head while carving. The character of the doll is largely governed by the face and it is well worth taking a little trouble to create your own character, the one illustrated here is a caricature of my father-in-law. The neck is oblong shaped being ⅜" wide and $\frac{3}{16}$" thick, and is fitted into the corresponding hole in the body by a ⅝" No. 4 screw to allow the head about ½" lateral movement.

The board is an important factor in the successful operation of the doll. Various shaped boards can be used but the one that I use is 28" long by 8" wide at each end with a narrow centre section of 4½" wide 6" and 10" from each end, (Fig. 4). I have one board made of 5 ply which operates better than another one made of 3 ply, the 5 ply being a lot more springy as opposed to the spongy action of the 3 ply board. Readers may like to

experiment with different boards made of various other materials, such as plastic faced ply.

A ¼" gouge was used throughout for final shaping with the chisel marks being clearly left. Finally the doll was painted with acrylic paint, putting the paint straight onto the bare wood. I have found that legs painted white illustrate the dancing feet far better than a darker colour, but this is a matter of choice. Traditionally these dolls were danced to various country dance tunes, either played on fiddle, melodeon or concertina. When operating the doll without any musicians on hand, a tune can be whistled or sung, jigs, reels and polkas being ideal tempos for dancing.

*Bob Cann lives on the edge of Dartmoor and plays regularly in the Dartmoor area for dances. He has a record called *West Country Melodeon* on Topic 12TS 275. The tunes are very suitable for dancing dolls.

If any readers have further information regarding the history of dancing dolls Malcolm Bestwick would be pleased to hear from them. Letters c/o *Woodworker* at the usual address will be forwarded to Mr. Bestwick in Cornwall.

KITCHEN RACKS
in pine for spices and crockery

The spice rack

A. Yarwood gives drawings and details for making traditional-style kitchen wall racks in pine *(Pinus sylvestris)*; and a method for boring angled holes.

Traditional-style kitchen racks made from pine finished natural colour and grain, make attractive wall features in the modern kitchen. They form pleasing contrasts to the straight lines, square edges and plain colours of so many kitchen fitments. Here are two such racks, one designed to hold spices, the other to contain plates, cups and saucepans.

The term pine is used here to describe the wood from Scots pine *(Pinus sylvestris)*. This common building timber comes under the guise of a variety of names — yellow deal, red deal, Scots pine and redwood — to name a few. British Standard specifications recommend the use of redwood to describe the timber from Scots pine.

Indeed the term redwood or red deal is commonly used in the Scandinavian countries from which this timber is often exported. The term deal refers to the size of the planks into which the logs from the trees are sawn. A deal is usually 9 × 3in. or 11 × 3in. The deals are re-converted by sawing into the market sizes we use in the workshop.

Good quality redwood is a joy to work with. Providing all tools are very sharp it planes sweetly, saws easily and cleanly and chisels quite freely. As you work with this timber, the workshop becomes redolent of the forests from which the wood was obtained. As the tiny resin canals of the wood are cut, so the air becomes scented with the sweet smell of resin. The second wood used, in the wall rack, was ramin, from which the dowels were made. Ramin comes from the Pacific area of the world, chiefly from Malaya. It is a tough and strong wood, hard and with an even texture. It is straight grained and of a uniform golden brown colour. This wood is commonly used for the manufacture of dowels.

The spice rack was made first. To find suitable dimensions for this rack, all the spices (in their containers) from our kitchen cupboard were placed in lines on the kitchen worktop. This allowed measurement of the lengths which each row would take up in the rack. After measuring this length and the required depths, a drawing of the design for the rack was made. This is given in Fig. 1. Then all parts for the rack were planed to their finished width and thickness and the ends of the side pieces shot to their final length in a shooting board. The construction of this rack can be seen in Fig. 3. After making the dovetails by which the box corners are jointed, its front rails and shelf were jointed to the sides with mortise and tenons and stopped housings respectively. The tenons are only ¼in. (6mm) long and the housing grooves only ⅛in. (3mm) deep.

When satisfied that all the jointing fitted well, the curves on the front edges of the ends were sawn, filed to shape and sanded. Now the various parts of the assembly could be sanded clean and the rack glued together, taking the precaution of ensuring all was square before putting the glued-up work to one side for the glue to set hard. A final planing and sanding of the outer surfaces of the construction completed the work. More about finishing and fitting to the wall later.

Dimensions for the second rack were obtained by measuring such items as plates, saucers, cups and saucepans. When satisfied that suitable sizes had been found a working drawing was made (Fig. 2). Again apart from the dowels which were purchased, all parts for the rack were planed to finished widths and thicknesses before work on the jointing commenced.

The wall rack

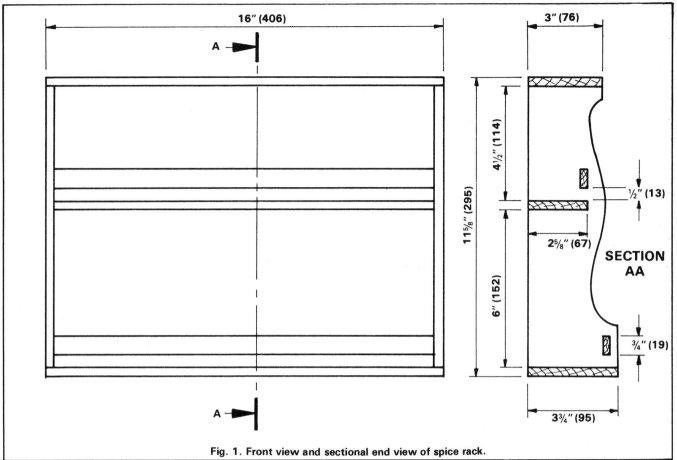

Fig. 1. Front view and sectional end view of spice rack.

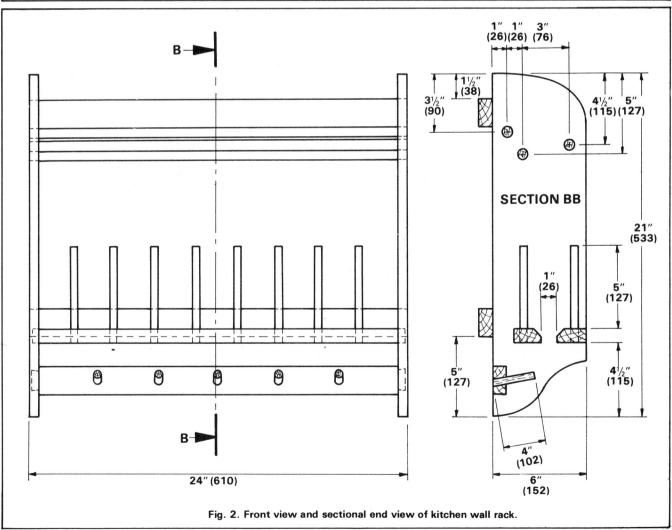

Fig. 2. Front view and sectional end view of kitchen wall rack.

RACK FOR COOKERY BOOKS

'I made this book rack to hold my wife's cookery books and also to show her what she had missed in the days before I acquired a lathe, writes Richard Large. 'It was also an exercise in turning; leaving part of the wood square in section and part round. This is something which furniture often demands yet writers on turning do not always deal with it.

'The process is quite simple. Maybe this is why no one bothers to explain it. To produce a sharp shoulder between the square and the round (as with the tenon joints on the bottom of the front uprights), I gently offered the parting tool up to the wood until it cut it round. To make a more elegant and rounded shoulder, as on the top of the front uprights, I used a skew chisel, though it may help to make the first cuts with the parting tool.

'Dimensions and construction of the rack will be evident from Fig. 1. I found it was important to ensure that the back rail was low enough to prevent small books slipping through: a cascade of literature into the pudding mix should the rack have to be moved would hardly please the cook!

'Ideally the tenons of the side rails should fit through those of the back rail. One thing I

Rack for cookery books.
The material is pine.

Fig. 1

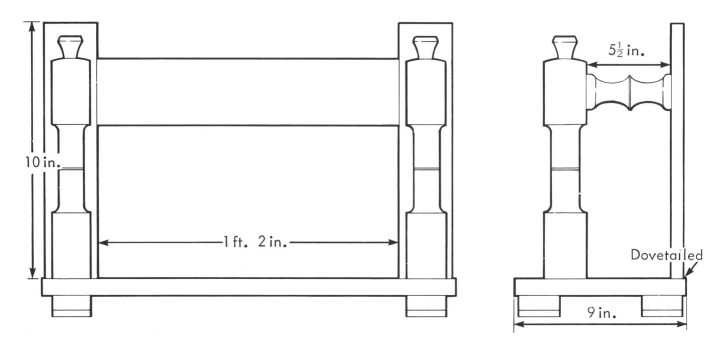

10 in.

1 ft. 2 in.

$5\frac{1}{2}$ in.

Dovetailed

9 in.

overlooked in making the rack is that when glued joints dry-out (as they did) the shrinkage of the glue may pull the joints out of true so that carefully set right-angles disappear. This should not happen of course with accurate, tight joints but it pays to cramp them nevertheless. The front uprights, being unsupported by other joints, are prone to movement and can be held as in Fig. 2.

'The back uprights are dovetailed into the base but all other joints are mortise and tenon. The feet are turned, drilled through and screwed on. I used pine for the rack though it might have looked better in beech.'

Front uprights $1\frac{1}{4}$ in. square
Back uprights 2 x 1 in.

Fig. 2

String

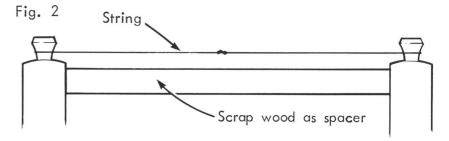

Scrap wood as spacer

RECORDER

'The design given here,' says the author, Peter Tomlin, 'is simply a reproduction of the Stanesby recorder of 1700 and should prove perfectly adequate . . . exceedingly cheap and, properly played, a very beautiful instrument . . .'

The recorder is an instrument of the flute family, having the acoustic qualities of a tube open at both ends. Thus it overblows at the octave, unlike the clarinet which overblows at the twelfth. It differs from the transverse flute mainly in that the player's breath is channelled down a wind-way so that it cannot fail to strike the edge of the aperture at the correct angle. It is this which makes the instrument so easy to play — or rather sound. Playing as distinct from just blowing the recorder is quite exacting. This characteristic of easy blowing, unfortunately, also reduces the flexibility of the instrument in the matter of intonation.

In the baroque flute the intonation is under the control of the player to a very large degree. By altering the angle at which the stream of air strikes the far side of the embouchure hole; by slackening the throat muscles; or by altering the size of the mouth cavity the intonation and quality of the note can be infinitely varied. The way the player secures exact intonation, however, depends entirely upon the speed at which the breath strikes the edge of the slot.

Consequently, much recorder playing is out of tune. Moreover, instruments by different makers are often not in tune with each other, while imported instruments have different fingerings from British-made recorders. Of course this is largely due to the fact that the revival of the recorder was school-oriented, where cheapness is all, and there is no great worry beyond actually getting the children to perform something recognisable as music.

Essentially then we see the recorder in a state of arrested development. The modern instrument is exactly what it was in the early 18th century: doubtful intonation, low volume of sound and all; but nevertheless, exceedingly cheap and when properly played a very beautiful instrument. Perhaps some modern Boehm will do for the baroque recorder what was done for the baroque flute. The design given here is simply a reproduction of the Stanesby recorder of 1700 and should prove perfectly adequate.

Making this instrument begins by taking a block of hardwood, preferably box or maple and turned to a length of 180mm with a diameter of 50mm. One end is deeply drilled with a pilot drill, followed by a 25mm flat bit, to a depth of 25mm. This is for the socket of the middle joint. The flat bit is then replaced by a 19mm or ¾in. twist bit and the head joint is bored right through concentric with the socket.

To strengthen the rim of the socket an ivory or bone ring can be made and fitted. Ivory is more easily worked than bone and is superior in appearance. Personally I prefer not to have ivory as its use means another elephant has come to an untimely end. So of course does bone; but the cow is not facing extinction as is the elephant.

The exterior contour can be turned largely as a matter of taste. A restrained baroque outline, using the characteristic reversed curve, and perhaps a pair of balanced ornamental rings seems about right. I do not recommend incised rings which are a source of weakness in the swelling round the socket; raised rings are much superior.

Next comes the really difficult part: cutting the slot and chiselling the wind channel. The slot is situated 65mm from the top end of the mouthpiece and is 14mm in width and 4mm across; its edges must be sharp and clean cut. Size seems to be important; in practice it makes the recorder harder to blow if the slot is made wider, possibly because a wider slot dissipates the wind pressure. When chiselling the slot it is well to put a spare piece of ¾in. dowel under the slot to prevent any ragged edges occurring, and to act as a temporary support to the bore of the mouthpiece.

With the slot cut the next thing to be worked is the wind channel. Recorders are classed as fipple flutes, the fipple being the piece of dowel which blocks up the top end of the mouthpiece. This is 65mm in length and should be a tight fit in the bore. On the top of the block (before it is inserted in the mouthpiece) is planed a flat surface 14mm in width to form one side of the wind channel. In section this is rectangular being 3mm by 14mm wide. The other three sides are chiselled out of the solid, from the rounded surface of the bore, in line with the slot already cut. It is useful to insert a slip of wood into the slot in case the chisel should slip and damage the lip of the slot.

Some instruments have a wind channel larger at the outer end and having a slight taper down towards the slot. The purpose of this is to concentrate the stream of air as it passes down the windway, thus increasing its pressure as it strikes the edge of the slot. However, the recorder seems to blow quite easily without it so perhaps it is not so necessary.

Next to be made is the lip which causes the air stream to divide (and vibrate in dividing) causing the air column in the tube of the instrument to vibrate also. The top surface must be chiselled down towards the slot to form a sloping surface. This sloping surface fans out from the edge of the slot and makes an angle of 15° with the centre line of the mouthpiece. The wood is pared carefully away leaving a pair of vertical edges to the left and right of the fan-shaped slope. These two little vertical edges also help concentrate the flow of air where it is needed.

When this has been done the lip of the edge is still curved on its underside where it faces the windway. It should now be under-cut at about 60°, the actual edge being blunt (about 1mm in thickness). This is best carried out with a small flat file so that the central blunt portion comes immediately opposite the centre of the wind channel. The under-cutting is necessary to convert the interior rounded surface of the bore into a flat surface to match that of the windway.

The fipple is then glued into the mouthpiece so that the inner end comes level with the beginning of the lateral slot. You should now have a windway leading down to a blunt edge and be able to blow a note, rather like a whistle. Shape the mouthpiece and cut away the waste with a coping saw to make a comfortable shape for the mouth.

When the mouthpiece is completed, the next part to be made is the foot joint. Like the mouthpiece, it has a socket for the middle joint, and as it is easier to fit tenons to sockets than the other way round, it is better to make these first. A piece of timber is turned to 100 × 35mm and the ends squared. This is then held in a three-jaw chuck centre-drilled and pilot-drilled from end to end. This is important because it is so easy for a drill to wander off-centre. At least three diameters have to be concentric with every joint made: the bore itself; the sockets for the tenons; and the external contours.

As the flat bit to be used for boring the socket hole has a triangular point about 5mm across the base, a pilot drill smaller than this should be used. When drilling deep holes I find that overheating can be prevented by using the slowest speed of the lathe and rubbing candlegrease on the drill from time to time.

After the pilot drill has been used, a 20mm flat bit is put in the three-jaw tailstock chuck and the socket hole bored to a depth of 20mm. The flat bit is removed and replaced by a 15mm drill and again the foot joint is bored right through. This completes the interior of the foot joint.

The exterior contour consists of the bone ring for the socket, a swelling around the socket to prevent cracks and the traditional flared end, plus any decoration in the form of raised (not incised) rings. The Sunday joint will probably provide a bone ring about 25mm internal diameter. I usually cut a slice of bone off, put it in the three-jaw chuck, turn the interior to the largest size the piece of bone will take and turn its seating round the socket to match its diameter. It is fixed in place with Araldite or similar glue. When set the irregular surface of the bone ring can be turned to a smooth finish. ·

The foot joint has one hole in it, for right little finger. Its centre is 20mm from the rim of the socket. If it is drilled at right-angles to the bore of the recorder it will break into the socket hole. Therefore it has to be angled towards the bottom end of the foot joint so that it enters the bore farther down than its exterior position. A similar idea is found in the bassoon and also in the clarinet. The purpose is to make the holes suit the spread of the fingers, and prevent the necessity of fitting a key at this place.

If the swelling around the socket is left at 35mm diameter and the 6mm finger hole drilled at an angle of 60°, the hole will just miss the socket for the middle joint and enter the bore at the correct acoustical point. The exterior can be turned by mounting the foot joint on a mandrel.

When the mouthpiece and foot joint are complete, the middle joint with its two tenons can be started. It has seven tone holes; six on the front and one on the back for the left thumb. The finished length is 265mm. A piece of hardwood is turned to a diameter of about 35mm and bored through from end to end with a 15mm drill. This parallel bore has to be converted to a diminished taper, as in the baroque flute. If a flute has already been attempted, the reamer for that can be used for both the recorder and the bassoon.

Two pieces of 20 × 10mm flat steel and 400mm in length are soft-soldered together (making in effect a piece of 20mm square bar 400mm long). This is then turned to a cylindrical section. The drawback is that to do the job a large lathe is required, one with a headstock spindle bore of 30mm and a large four-jaw chuck. If you can get half-round steel it is

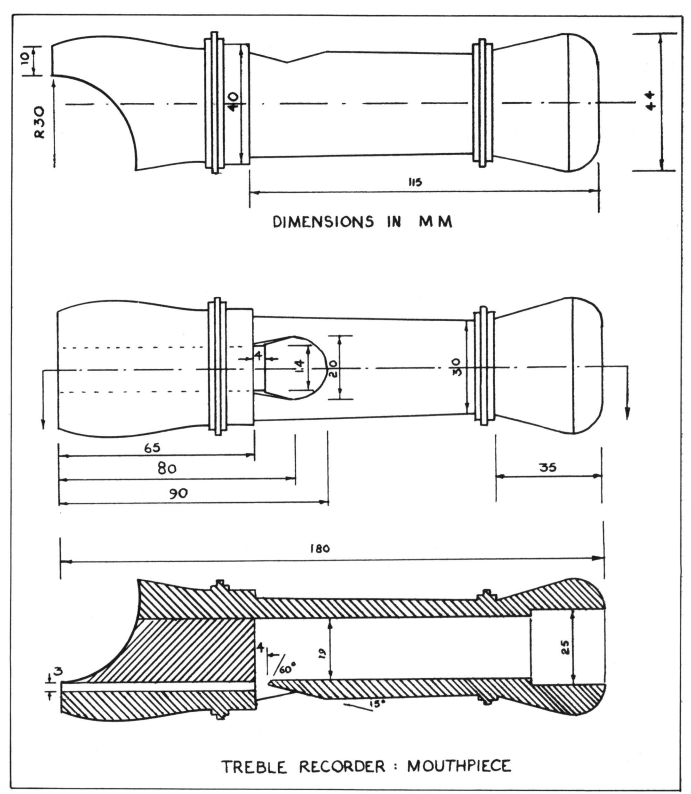

DIMENSIONS IN MM

TREBLE RECORDER : MOUTHPIECE

obviously better but nobody seems to stock it in my county, so I laboriously turn a square section to round section. Fortunately it is a one-off job.

The end of the bar is faced-up to 90° and centre drilled. One end is held in a three-jaw chuck and the other end supported by the tailstock centre which must be set over 2mm, thus turning the steel bar to a taper 19mm at the top and 15mm at the bottom. If the tapered bar is now heated, it will separate into two D-section reamers. The solder can be cleaned-off and the bar hardened if it is cast steel. I have found that mild steel will do the job quite well, though it does not hold its edge very long.

In use the reamer can be held either in the

tailstock chuck or in a tap wrench held in the hands. The lathe is set to run at its slowest speed and the bored piece of timber is held in the three-jaw chuck. Then the reamer is fed slowly into the hole. It should be withdrawn at frequent intervals as it gets hot. It will produce a clean, tapered bore if the cutting edge is kept sharp. Rubbing candlegrease on the reamer prevents overheating and the grease gives the bore something of a polish, which is all to the good.

Once the bore has been reamed the wider end is turned down to a good tight fit in the mouthpiece socket and the lower end turned down to fit the socket of the foot joint. The three parts can then be assembled and the first note blown. With the little finger

covering the hole already drilled the note should be middle F, slightly flat. Blowing a little harder will produce F an octave higher and blowing harder still the F above that slightly sharp.

The foot joint can be reamed to match the taper of the middle joint, though in practice I have found that it does not seem to make much difference. Perhaps this is because the foot is too short to exercise much influence on the rest of the recorder. The reamer will be found to be longer than is strictly required to ream a tapered bore for a recorder, but this is because it has to be used for other instruments. It should be put into the bore of the recorder as far as it will go; there must be no 'steps' to break the continuity of the bore.

Once the bore is completed, the exterior contours can be turned. In this case the exterior is perfectly plain. The thickness of the wood should be about 5mm with the outside taper reflecting the interior taper. A groove can be turned on the tenons so that a cork lapping can be glued in it to ensure the joints are airtight.

The tone holes, seven in number, are then drilled at the positions indicated. They are slightly undersize and have to be enlarged to bring the instrument up to pitch (starting with the lowest holes) using a round file. It will be necessary to have a fingering chart (obtainable from most music shops) so that the correct holes can be worked on. Then all you have to do is play it!

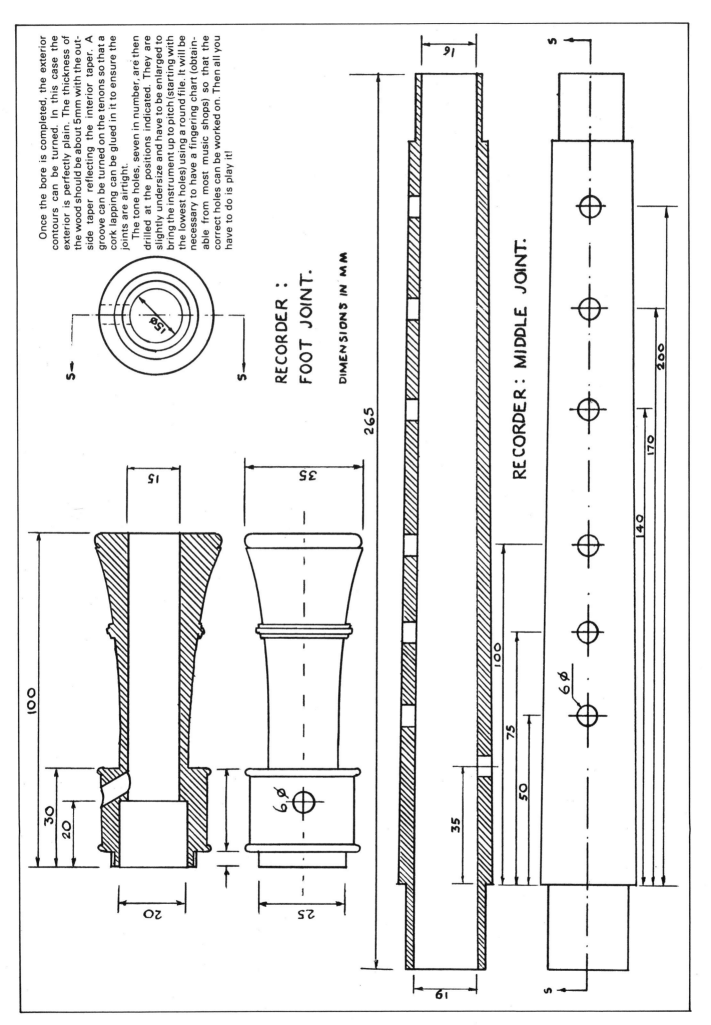

RECORDER :
FOOT JOINT.

DIMENSIONS IN MM

RECORDER : MIDDLE JOINT.

1▶

ABOUT TIME

But Alan Holtham points out that time is of no importance when turning a clock

One of my regular customers came into the shop and said that it was about time I wrote some more woodturning articles, so here is one just for him!. . .

In recent years there has been a tremendous increase in the number of gadgets and devices in the field of cheap electronics. One of these pieces of wizardry of interest to the turner is the accurate quartz clock movement currently retailing at around £7. With the addition of a suitable face and frame it is a useful thing to have about the house (Fig. 1). The finished result is quite impressive; yet the clock is quickly made up, the procedure being as follows:

Select a suitable piece of sound timber about 8-9in. diameter and 2-2¼in. thick and mount this on the faceplate using three or four small screws. My faceplates are about ¼in. thick so ¾in. screws should be more than long enough.

With the lathe revolving at about 1000rpm trim up the edge and face of the disc (Fig. 2) using the ⅜in. bowl gouge. The aim is to make a frame with a suitable rebate to allow the clock face to be set in from the rear, so start work on what will become the back of the clock. If you are going to use one of the commercially produced ceramic 6in. faces, mark out a circle a shade over 6in. diameter and cut this in to a depth of about 1½in. using the parting tool (Fig. 3).

When making deep cuts like this on the edge of a radius, take care to cut the groove slightly wider than the parting tool to allow clearance. If you fail to do this there is a danger of the tool sides becoming jammed in the groove. This happened to me once and resulted in the parting tool bending like a banana at the tang and splitting the handle cleanly into two, including the ferrule! So take care.

Form the rebate to the shape shown in Fig. 4(i), then with the lathe stopped check that the face actually does fit (Fig. 5). This may seem obvious, but more than once I have gone ahead and parted the frame off only to find that the face does not fit. Then I had to spend hours making fancy chucks so that I could enlarge the rebate to what it should have been in the first place. If you check it and all is well you can go ahead and part the thing off as in Fig. 4(ii). However the safer way is to unscrew the block and reverse it on the faceplate, mark out the inner edge of the rebate (Fig. 6) and part off from the front (Figs. 7 and 4(iii)). This leaves the centre piece intact, rather than turning it away to waste.

2▲   **3▼**

With the frame now free the face should be a snug fit, deliberately being left slightly loose to allow for wood shrinkage (Fig. 8). We are now half way home, the only remaining job being to turn the front. This creates a minor problem in that there is

1. Quartz clock movement used to good effect. 2. Trimming up the edge and face of the disc with a ⅜in. bowl gouge. 3. Circle cut to 1½in. using the parting tool.

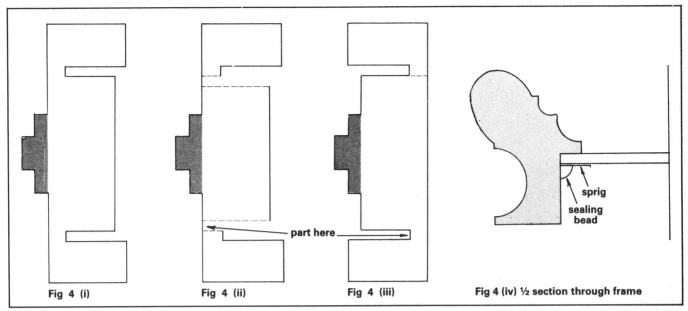

Fig 4 (i) Fig 4 (ii) Fig 4 (iii) Fig 4 (iv) ½ section through frame

part here

sprig
sealing
bead

nothing left in the centre to screw the faceplate to, and yet the recess is too large to take one of the expanding chucks. I rechuck by turning up a scrapwood disc (Fig. 9) to be a tight fit in the rebate (Fig. 10). With the frame pushed on tight, the front can be shaped to your design (Fig. 11).

Beware of making the frame fit too tightly or you will split it across the short grain. Maybe not when you put it on but possibly when you pull it off after the shaping has weakened the section that much more. If by any chance you go to the other extreme and the frame is too loose on the scrapwood disc, try wetting the disc with water to swell the fibres. This will probably solve the problem.

When the turning and finishing is completed the face and mechanism can be assembled and fixed to the frame. My preference for this is to hold the face in place with a few small glazing sprigs or panel pins, then seal round with a bead of flexible adhesive (Fig. 4(iv)). This system holds the face securely in place but allows for any timber movement that would crack or distort the face. The mechanism itself incorporates a hanger so the job is now complete.

I am often asked how long I take to do a particular job? I always reply that time is not a yardstick by which to judge turning ability. A job like this clock would probably take me something like 45min from start to finish but I am rather a slow turner. On the other hand it might take you three hours to complete so you are going to feel rather disheartened if I say you should do it in half an hour. As long as the job is done to your satisfaction and the best of your ability, time is of no importance. The finished result is what counts. If you are making these items for a living then things are a bit different, as you nearly always have to work to a time in order to remain competitive. It is then that quality might begin to suffer a little in return for quantity. Be aware of this bearing in mind the type of market you are aiming at.

(Continued on page 102)

4 (i). Shows the rebate shape.
4 (ii). Shows parting off.
4 (iii). A safer way of parting off by reversing on the faceplate, leaving the centre piece intact.
4 (iv). Method of holding face in place.

5 ▲

5. Mark out the inner edge of the rebate.
6. With the lathe stopped check the face actually does fit.

6 ▼

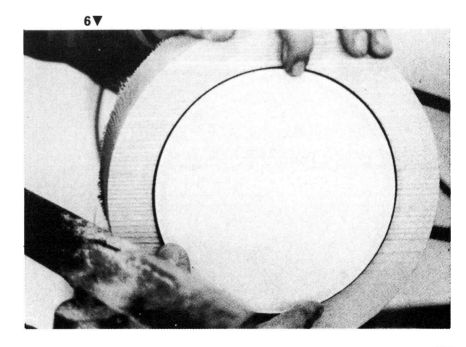

About time

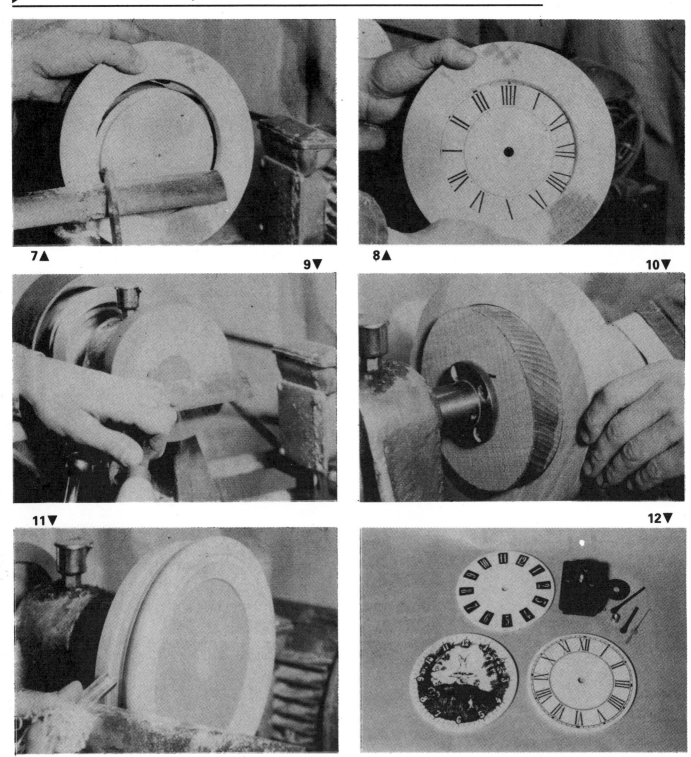

7▲   8▲   9▼   10▼   11▼   12▼

7. Part off from the front. 8. The face should be a snug fit, but has been deliberately left loose to allow for wood shrinkage. 9. Rechuck by turning up a scrapwood disc. 10. To be a tight fit in the rebate. 11. Front shaped to personal choice of design. 12. Variations on the theme.

ADJUSTABLE STOOL

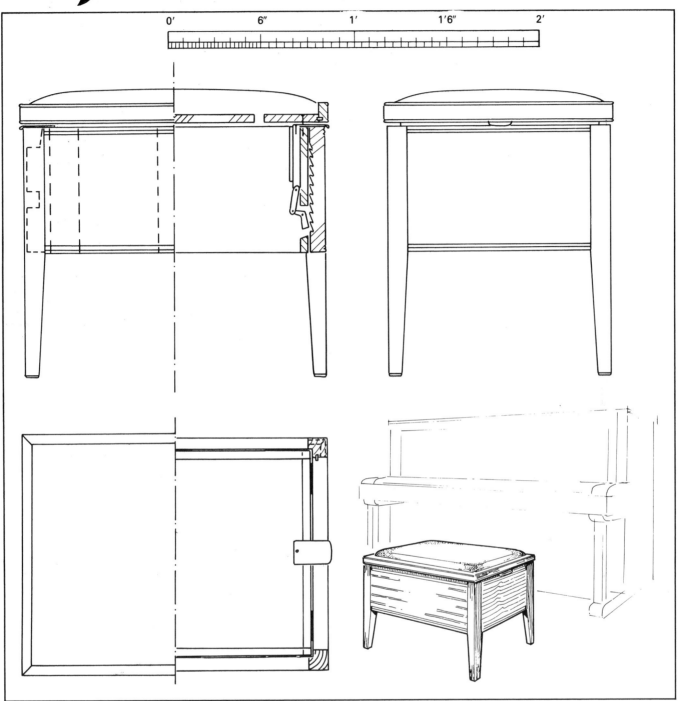

Readers have asked for details of an adjustable (music) stool. Of such stools available commercially some employ a patent all-metal scissors-type adjusting mechanism, others an all-metal underframe similar to a typist's adjustable chair and are therefore not applicable to a woodworking job.

At the request of WOODWORKER, R. W. Grant DLC FRSA MSIAD has designed and illustrated a stool which employs a simple yet effective ratchet mechanism within a telescopic box. The mechanism could be adapted for other projects such as adjustable lecterns, artists' easels etc.

Construction of the inner and outer boxes and seat is straightforward work but it should be noted that the ends of the outer box are made from thicker material. This is

Cutting List

Net sizes shown. Dimensions in in.

Number	Description	L	W	Thickness	Material
4	Legs	16	1¼	1¼	Oak
2	Outer box sides	19¼	8	¾	Oak
2	Outer box ends	12½	8	1	Oak
2	Inner box sides	17½	8	½	Oak
2	Inner box ends	12¾	8	½	Oak
1	Seat baseboard	18½	14	½	Birch ply
2	Side seat strips	20	1¼	⅝	Oak
2	End seat strips	15	1¼	⅝	Oak
1	Foam pad and upholstery materials to suit	18½	14	2	Medium density foam
10	Beize strips	8	2	1/16	
4	Guide bars	3½	¼	¼	Oak
2	Cover plates	3½	⅞	3/32	Brass
2	Handles	2½	1½	3/32	Brass
2	Pawls and respective linkage pieces to suit;	¼in. square section minimum			

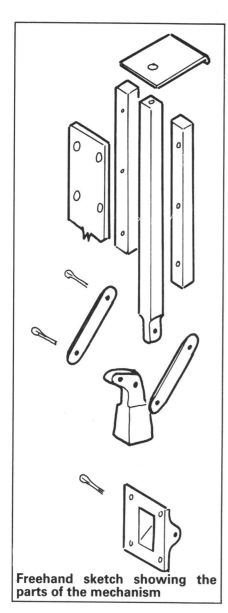

Freehand sketch showing the parts of the mechanism

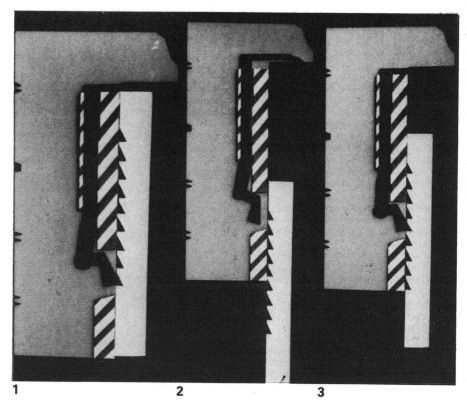

1 **2** **3**

Above: Action of the ratchet-and-pawl mechanism

ADJUSTABLE STOOL

because they carry the weight of the sitter and tough wood such as oak must be used to give the toothed rack the necessary strength.

The scaled drawings comprise a front elevation and plan with half sections about the centre line, plus an end elevation which shows the scratchstock reeding employed as decoration. The principal point to remember about the construction of the outer box is that the inside must be flush to allow the inner box to telescope. Thus the tenons are offset to give better penetration into the legs and the joints may be further strengthened by inserting a hardboard tongue into the length of the tenon shoulder as indicated on the plan.

The insides of the legs will need to be rebated to accommodate the inner box and may be stopped at the bottom at the point at which the seat comes to rest. The inner boxing is through dovetailed and made ⅛in. smaller all round than the outer box.

It should be appreciated that the depth of the boxing is to ensure stability and smooth working, which is further assisted by gluing 2in. wide strips of felt or beize (as indicated on the elevation and plan) to the outer box as packing. These strips may be liberally dusted with talcum powder to assist smooth running and they will, of course, prevent unsightly scoring on the inner box when it is raised.

The seat is formed on a baseboard of ½in. plywood which is screwed to the top of the inner box. Ventilation holes must be bored in this baseboard to prevent 'ballooning' of the foam seat which may be covered in any suitable fabric. The seat edge strips are tongued and glued on with mitres at the corners. These also have the characteristic scratchstock mould worked on the top and bottom edges.

The lifting mechanism is shown in the sectional elevation and its metal parts (preferably brass) in the freehand sketch. Remember that a pair will be necessary. The metalworking involved is not difficult and most workshops are likely to have the few simple tools needed.

The photographs demonstrate the action of the ratchet-and-pawl mechanism in the form of a model: No. 1 — the seat in its lowest position; no. 2 — a pull upwards on the seat (or handle) will disengage the pawl from the rack and allow the inner box to be lifted to any desired height; no. 3 — once upward movement ceases the pawl, by its own weight and inclination, will re-engage in the nearest point in the rack and securely hold it there.

To lower the seat it will be necessary to raise the handle slightly to free the pawl. The exact sections of the metal parts are not critical but they should not be less than ¼in. square and strong enough to take the weight of the user. The outer guide bars can be made of hardwood and the whole mechanism must have free play. The handle can be secured to the central bar by a self-tapping screw and solder while the lower end should be rounded over and drilled for a steel splitpin. This secures the pair of link pieces which are drilled at each end, the holes being pitched 1¾in. apart.

The cranked pawl is best cast and thickened at its lower end to give it sufficient weight. This is pivoted to a brass bracket which is slotted to receive the pawl and to allow it to work freely through a hole cut in the inner box to engage the rack. The rack itself should be carefully chiselled out of the end, although a suitable modification might be to employ a metal 'ladder' which could be made from a length of 'Tonk' strip as used for adjustable shelving.

The teeth are pitched ⅜in. apart commencing some 1½in. from the top and stopping at a point reached by the pawl when the seat is at its lowermost position (photo no. 1). It would be as well to make a full size drawing, or rod, of this to establish critical lengths and points. The points of the rack should be rather blunt. The whole length should be dressed with a mixture of vaseline and ground pencil lead to act as a lubricant.

The stool may be finished as desired, though waxing is suggested. Carrying handles may be added as any attempt to directly lift the stool by its seat will result in the boxes becoming separated. This, incidentally, is the way in which they are initially assembled.

Happy hours

Colin Murdoch's cocktail table promises (nearly!) as much pleasure in the making as the using

There is definitely something elegant about the basic design of a cocktail table. Unfortunately, the market is littered with cheap, shoddy models which don't do it full credit.

There are no intricate processes involved in making the piece, although patience and care are required to make a good job of the top ring. The project is fairly simple and very enjoyable to make, and does not require a lot of material. I chose four legs partly for ease of manufacture and partly for stability. I used sapele mahogany, mainly for its working qualities.

The first step is to select a piece of timber for the centre post measuring 460×60×60mm, and to mark out the four mortises using a mortise-gauge. Next, make a template for the legs as shown in fig. 1 and

cut the legs out, taking note of the direction of the grain. Obviously you don't want the grain to run vertically.

The tenons can now be marked out and the joints cut and fitted. The centre post is mounted on the lathe and shaped. The legs can be finished with a spokeshave and scratch-stock. For the uninitiated, the latter is simply a cutting-gauge with the blade turned at right-angles and the stock set close to it. It can also be used to form the grooves on the legs as shown in fig. 2.

The top is made by dowelling together three pieces of timber 500×70×15mm, as shown in fig. 3. A face-plate is then mounted on it and a 500mm circle drawn on. The corners are removed before it is mounted on the lathe, flushed off at the face and turned down to round. Two grooves are then put in the edge for decoration and the recess made for the leather insert. Obviously, you will need the leather on hand to ensure that it is an exact fit.

The twelve pedestals were made two at a time, using six pieces measuring 200×25×25mm. The easiest way is first to turn the pieces of timber until round, and

then mark the various lengths with a pencil and turn to shape. I used calipers to check the end sizes and visually checked the shape. Fig. 4 shows a finished version.

Finally the ring must be made. The first step is to take a piece of chipboard or blockboard and draw two circles on it, one the same size as your top and the other 25mm less (fig. 5). This will be the actual size of the wooden ring you are making. The circles are then split up into six equal parts as shown. Holes are drilled in the 12 places marked, and countersunk at the back to accept a suitable screw. Six pieces of timber measuring 270×70×20mm are then cut, mitred, and placed on the blockboard as in fig. 6. Make sure they fit tightly.

The next step is to dowel these pieces together. The easiest way is to tap a small panel pin into the end of one of the pieces and snip the end off, leaving 2mm protruding. It can then be pushed in place, where it will leave a mark on the next piece. The two pieces can then be drilled and a dowel put in place ready to mark the next piece.

● A delicate design for the circular-work specialists. The top ring demands very accurate jointing; note the scratch-stock moulding on the legs and leather insert in the top

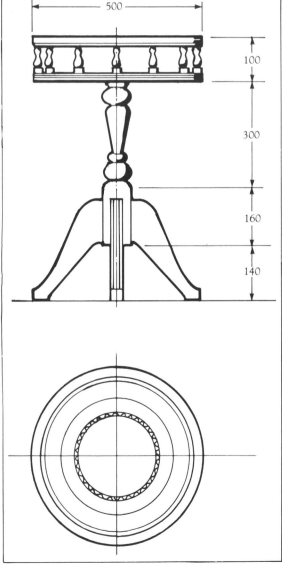

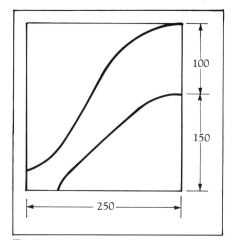

Fig. 1

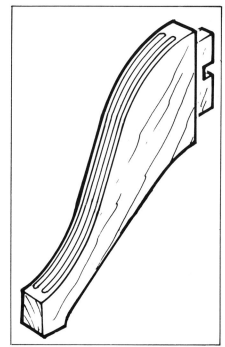

Fig. 2

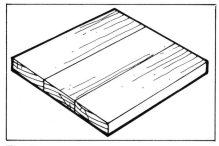

Fig. 3

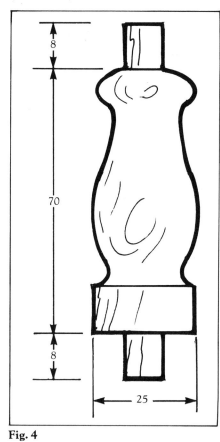

Fig. 4

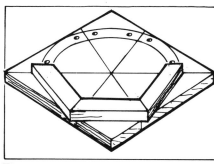

Fig. 6

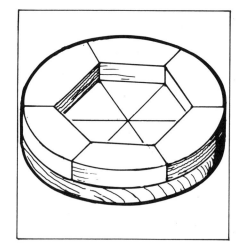

Fig. 7

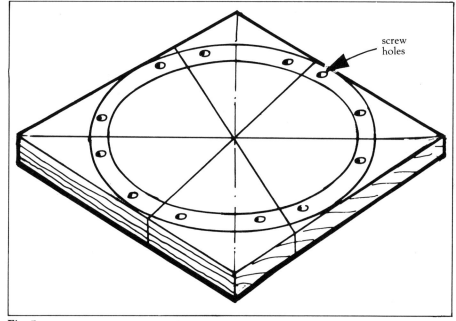

screw holes

Fig. 5

Once all the pieces have been dowelled together the hexagonal frame is screwed to the blockboard — dry at first — to ensure there are no gaps. Once fitting properly it is removed, glue is applied to the dowels, and it is screwed back to the board. It is then trimmed with a saw as in fig. 7. Using a faceplate, you can now mount it in the lathe and turn it to a ring shape. I put two grooves in the top and sides on this model, but obviously you can shape it to any design you like. After this has been glasspapered, it is removed ready for fitting.

The easiest way of doing this is to mark out the tabletop in 12 segments like a clock face. Again panel pins are tapped in and

snapped off 2mm from the surface. The ring is pressed on and then carefully removed. There should now be 12 marks in the ring and tabletop, all of which may be used for drilling to accept the pedestals. The tabletop is fixed to the centre post with three dowels which can be marked out the same way.

Before gluing, all pieces were glasspapered to a smooth finish. I used PVA glue to assemble the entire table, since it is water-soluble and sets slowly. Gluing up is obviously easiest done in stages.

The table was finished with polyurethane varnish, glasspapering between coats. After four coats, the gloss was toned down using

steel wool and wax, leaving a satin finish. Finally the leather was glued in place with Evo-Stik contact adhesive.

The result: a handsome cocktail table radiating quality! ■

Cutting list

Dimensions in mm				
centre post	1	460×	60×	60
legs	4	250	250	20
top	3	500	70	15
pedestals (2 from each)	6	200	25	25
top ring	6	270	70	20
blockboard or chipboard	1	500	500	20

Bathroom enhancers

Tony Lord's neat array of bathroom fittings are all in pine, to go with a boxed-in bath, but they can just as easily be of a hardwood.

Except for the toilet-roll holder, which needs a lathe for the bar and cap, they can all be made with hand tools alone. Some dimensions are changeable; some are defined by reference to the articles held, hung or hoarded! ■

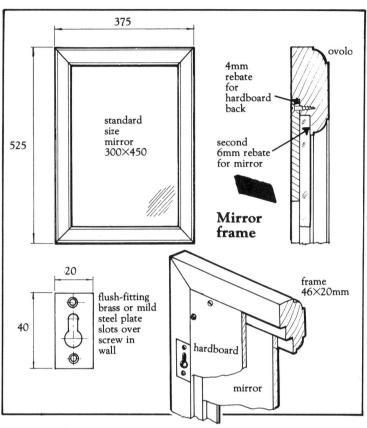

Mirror frame

- flush-fitting brass or mild steel plate slots over screw in wall

ovolo

4mm rebate for hardboard back

second 6mm rebate for mirror

frame 46×20mm

hardboard

mirror

standard size mirror 300×450

● **Above:** *The mirror is a standard size – 12×18in – held in a rebate by 4mm hardboard, fixed with no4×½in screws. Be careful to make the rebate for the back wide enough to take the screws without splitting; the frame section, ovolo-moulded by hand or router, is a hefty 46×20mm. Note the laminated construction of the mug-holder, **below left**, which avoids shrinkage and cupping; the toilet-roll holder, **below**, sports a 26mm-diameter bar with a 16mm spigot, taper-turned for a push fit into the end-cap. All dimensions are in mm*

Toothbrush- and mug-holder

rounded edges

grain direction

5mm thick

mortise for pinned tenon

mug-holder shaped after drilling

screw-holes countersunk or counterbored and plugged

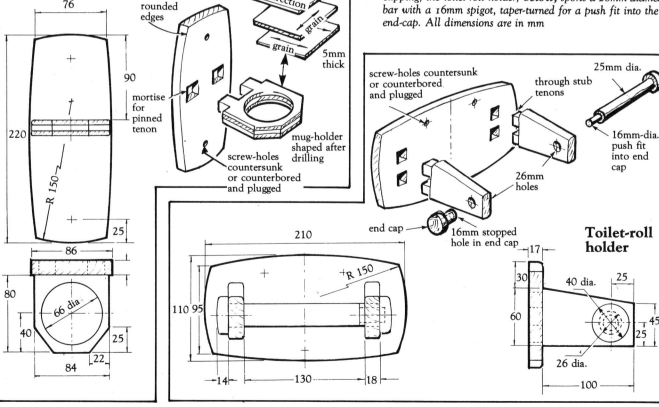

screw-holes countersunk or counterbored and plugged

through stub tenons

25mm dia.

16mm-dia. push fit into end cap

26mm holes

end cap

16mm stopped hole in end cap

Toilet-roll holder

40 dia.

26 dia.

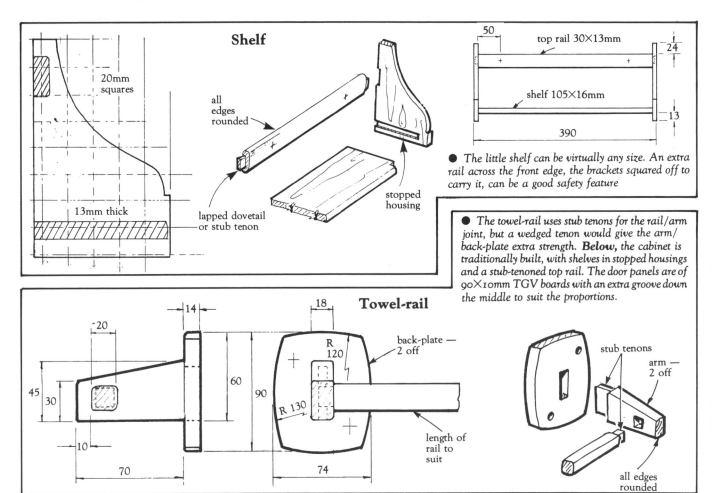

Shelf

20mm squares

all edges rounded

13mm thick

lapped dovetail or stub tenon

stopped housing

top rail 30×13mm

50

24

shelf 105×16mm

13

390

● *The little shelf can be virtually any size. An extra rail across the front edge, the brackets squared off to carry it, can be a good safety feature*

● *The towel-rail uses stub tenons for the rail/arm joint, but a wedged tenon would give the arm/back-plate extra strength.* **Below,** *the cabinet is traditionally built, with shelves in stopped housings and a stub-tenoned top rail. The door panels are of 90×10mm TGV boards with an extra groove down the middle to suit the proportions.*

Towel-rail

14

20

18

R 120

back-plate — 2 off

45

30

60

90

R 130

10

length of rail to suit

70

74

stub tenons

arm — 2 off

all edges rounded

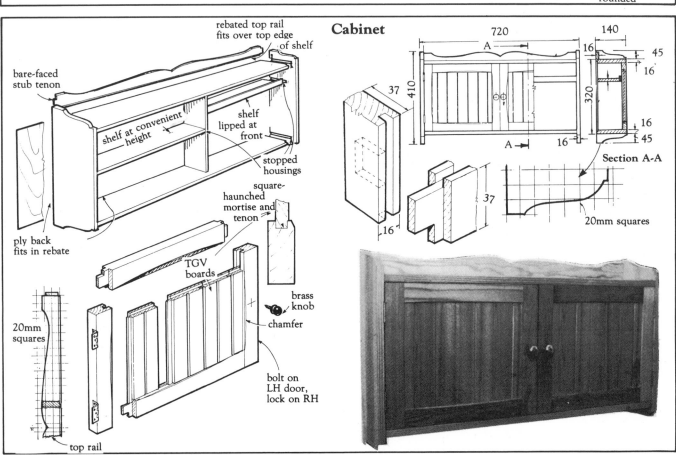

Cabinet

rebated top rail fits over top edge of shelf

bare-faced stub tenon

shelf at convenient height

shelf lipped at front

stopped housings

ply back fits in rebate

square-haunched mortise and tenon

20mm squares

top rail

TGV boards

brass knob

chamfer

bolt on LH door, lock on RH

720

140

A

16

45

16

37

410

320

16

16

45

A

16

Section A-A

37

20mm squares

Making equipment boxes

Bill Gates writes: It's often difficult to replace power tools in their original packing — particularly when a plug has been added to the cable! Yet some require protection when not in regular use. So you need to make a box.

Shown in the drawings are three possible constructions — A, B and C: rebated corners, tongued joints and dovetail joints. The top and the bottom of the two larger boxes were glued to the sides and the ends and then place under pressure until the adhesive had set, thus avoiding the use of pins. Shaped blocks and cut-outs in plywood are required to hold the articles in position; these can be made up in a number of pieces, which will make the cutting-out easier to perform. You need not fit the blocks exactly, because the thickness of the covering material must be allowed for. Softwood is quite suitable for those blocks which are to be covered; assemble them dry first and check the fit of the article — any adjustment should be made before gluing the blocks in their places.

Cabinet cloth was used for the lining, fastened with an impact adhesive.

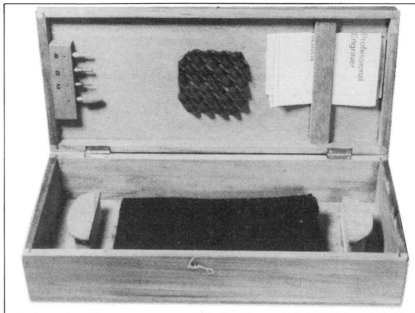

● A neat home for your engraving tools; the shaped covered blocks hold the tool, the blocks at either end retain the cable. This is Box B

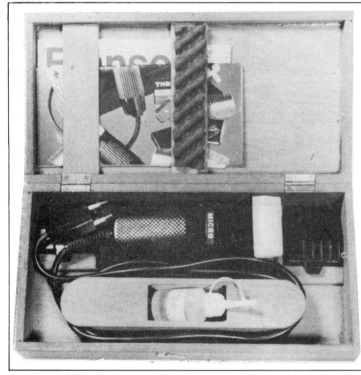

Box A; this one, like the scalpel and the engraver box, sports a sponge cushion to keep the equipment in tightly. Provision for the leaflets to be kept in the lid is also made

together, with the bottom only glued to the frame. 5mm plywood was prepared with cut-outs for the knives and glued to the inside of the bottom, a division being included to accommodate spare blades. The whole of the bottom is lined with cloth. To prevent the knives from moving, a piece of sponge rubber is glued to the lid to provide pressure when the box is closed. The lid is secured with a brass side hook and a screw eye.

I have made several jigs for making such boxes, which are adaptable for various operations in conjunction with a router or a plough. One consists of two parallel pieces of timber held together with screws — this makes it easier to hold and adjust before applying the cramps. The pieces of timber need to be large enough to provide a good surface bearing for the router base, and long enough to control the fence. The other is a jig for face work; waste pieces are required to support the base of the router and to prevent damage when grooving across the grain. ■

It is best to begin with sketches, drawing the outline of the article to determine the shape of the blocks, etc., and the space required. Then make the box, complete with top and bottom. Next, clean up the box, mark the depth of the rim with a gauge line, and use a tenon-saw to cut through the box to form the lid. When dovetailed joints are employed for the corners, care must be taken to arrange their positions to suit the depth of the lid.

Rebated joints are suitable for small boxes holding lightweight articles. For box C the joints were pinned and glued

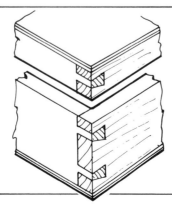

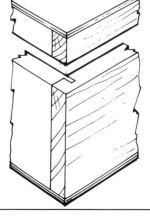

● Alternative corner joints. Box A is on the left, Box B on the right, but you can ring the changes on these and other methods

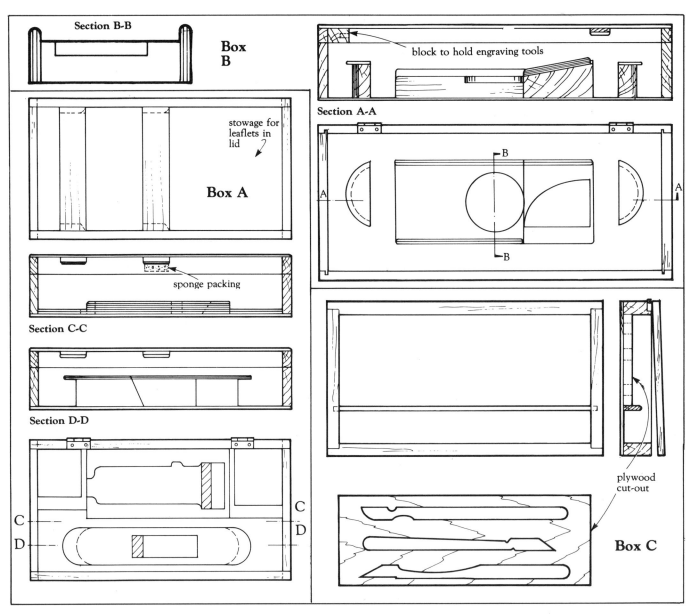

Section B-B

Box B

Box A

stowage for leaflets in lid

Section C-C

sponge packing

Section D-D

block to hold engraving tools

Section A-A

plywood cut-out

Box C

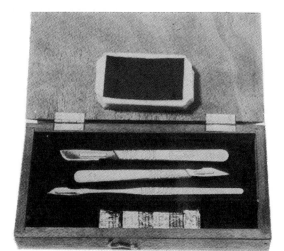

● *Another variation, this time for scalpels, modelling and artwork tools. Decide your own shapes and sizes for the precious pieces you want to keep neat and tidy*

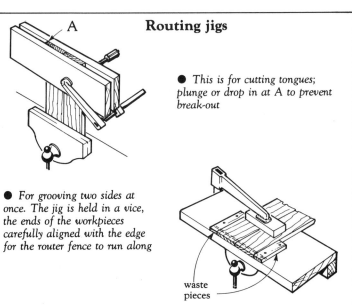

Routing jigs

A

● *This is for cutting tongues; plunge or drop in at A to prevent break-out*

● *For grooving two sides at once. The jig is held in a vice, the ends of the workpieces carefully aligned with the edge for the router fence to run along*

waste pieces

Making games people play

We present three surprisingly tricky board-game projects for profit in the making and pleasure in the playing

---

Martin Bulger recounts how and why he made his solitaire board triangular ...

I had two aims in designing this game. To ease the boredom of long car journeys, and to destroy the belief (widely held among my school pupils) that all boxes should have four sides.

As a table game, triangular solitaire is quite common, and it is reasonably simple in design, but as a travel game it must obviously be compact and self-contained; perhaps even small enough to go into a coat pocket!

The grid is best marked out with a 60° set-square, or perhaps a protractor. Divide a base line into eight units, the size decided by the size of the pegs you will be using (fig. 1a); I used ⅝in (15mm) spaces for pegs made from ⅛in-diameter dowels. Reverse the set-square and draw more lines from the same points (fig. 1b); then the pattern of the holes and the shape of the base can be picked out (fig. 1c).

Drill the holes, then cut away the waste. Sand the playing surface and carefully plane the edges to size — the sides are best glued on one at a time so you can cut them long and trim them to size when the glue has set.

They can be held for gluing with a G-cramp and cramping block (fig. 2), or just held with masking-tape. Cut the sides about ⅛in deeper than finished height, because the top is glued on and the whole lid then sawn off; which makes certain that lid and base are the same size. When gluing the top, make sure the grain is in line with the grain of the base.

The biggest difficulty with this design was securing the hinged lid. Fixing a block or catch to one side looked distinctly lopsided, so I decided it had to be something fitted at the leading corner.

My solution was the sliding hinge, which I produced by filing slots in one of the leaves of each of the pair (fig. 3) so I got a closing and locking action in one movement. It may break a few hinging rules, but it works!

● *Traveller's triangle... open the box for a neat, portable game. Exact size, construction and ornamentation are up to you*

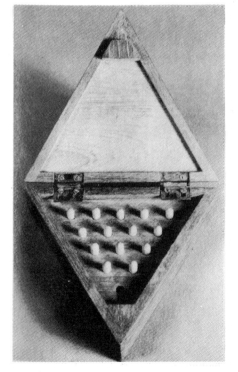

● *This version, about 5in along each side, is a solid triangular base with facings, plus a solid top*

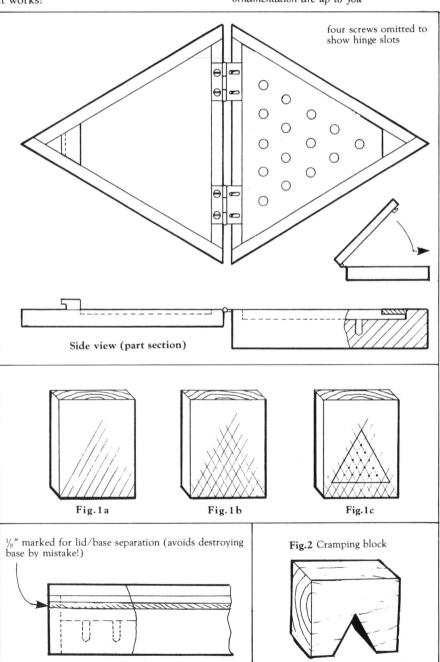

four screws omitted to show hinge slots

Side view (part section)

Fig. 1a   Fig. 1b   Fig. 1c

⅛" marked for lid/base separation (avoids destroying base by mistake!)

Fig. 2 Cramping block

Making games people play

. . . and Michael Sylvester tells the secrets of nine men's morris

Nine men's morris is absorbing to play; the rules are easy enough for a young child to learn, but my own set has witnessed many a titanic and protracted struggle between adults. If you choose your timber well, and make the board carefully, you will also have a simple yet elegant ornament.

Many people will recognise the name without knowing much about the game. It was played in medieval England by country folk, the commonest board or 'pound' being that cut in any convenient piece of turf. This rustic outdoor image is, however, only part of the truth. The game translates very pleasingly into wood, and has the double merit of being a simple construction for the inexperienced woodworker and a source of endless possibilities for the more skilled and ambitious. The construction details that follow can be seen as complete or as a basis for something more elaborate.

Nine men's morris is one of those games that has stood the test of time. Although it was widely played up till the 19th century, it has in fact a much longer and more distinguished history. It was played 4000 years ago in ancient Egypt, 2000 years ago in Ceylon, and 1000 years ago in Ireland — long indeed before it was carved in English cathedral cloisters by bored choristers or cut on the Sussex Downs by lonely shepherds.

Even today there are periodic revivals, though the English Village Sports Society say it is not played 'seriously' now — except by families like my own who have their own boards: I hesitate to call our sessions 'serious'! Elsewhere it continues in similar fashion — the Germans playing *Muhle*, the Icelanders *mylla* and the Poles *siegen wulf myll*.

Materials and construction

You will need a sheet of good-quality faced ply 16x16⅛in; 17ft of matching or contrasting hardwood strips, ½x⅝in; a pair of card-table hinges; and a clasp.

The board is made up in two mirroring hinged sections which fold together to produce a compartmentalised box for the pieces or 'merels'. The extra ⅛in allows for the saw-cut and cleaning up after completion; thus the contrasting hardwood strips are all mitred and glued in place before the base is sawn and the hinges and clasp fitted. The central strips (D) are separated by ⅛in for the saw.

Prepare and mitre the surrounds (A) first; glue and cramp them in position. Next, mark two more concentric squares of appropriate proportions, together with two diagonals. Measure and mitre the diagonals (B), cutting to meet the centre square, and allowing for the shaped corners. Glue and cramp before preparing and fitting the remainder of the centre square (C). Treat

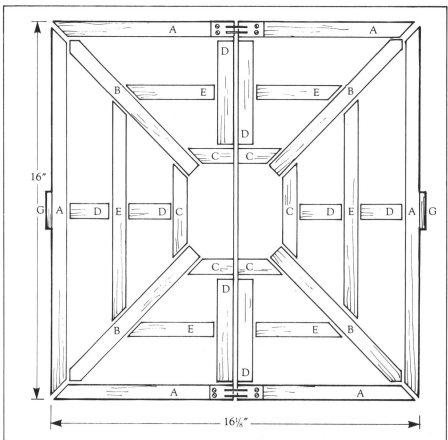

● *To make the nine-men's-morris board,* **1** *glue the strips in order A-E,* **2** *saw in half,* **3** *fit the hinges F, and* **4** *fit the clasp G*

the central strips (D) and (E) similarly.

The next task is to saw the board down the centre, clean up the exposed surfaces and chisel the recesses for the hinges. After these have been fitted, skim the whole top and apply a suitable finish.

Ideally, veneer — again either matching or contrasting — should be laid on the exposed edges of the box. Finally, fit a clasp and (if you want) a handle.

The box completed, all that remains is the making of the pieces. These can be shaped to taste. My own nine men's morris has both square and round pieces, but if contrasting woods — say rosewood and holly, or walnut and sycamore — are chosen, they can all be the same shape. There are nine of each, though it is sensible to make spares while you are at it. They should be an inch or a little more in diameter, and can be left plain or decorated as preferred.

For complete protection, the edges of the box may be rebated and strings of contrasting hardwood glued and cramped in place; but, since this project is essentially about making a lasting and elegant piece with the minimum of difficulty, any embellishment is up to you.

All that is required in construction is care, precision and a little patience. If you exercise these essential woodworking virtues, you will have a game which will never need hiding away in the toy cupboard.

Harold Shenker introduces the traditional round solitaire board

The traditional game of solitaire, played on a board with glass marbles, is an absorbing occupation for a single player. You cover all the holes except the centre one with glass marbles and then take them out by leapfrogging one over the other draughts-fashion. You reduce the number of marbles, putting the discarded ones in the outer groove, and ultimately (you hope!) are left with just one in the centre hole.

I made the board from parana pine, which comes in unblemished boards with a nice grain, and polishes well.

First, of course, you must buy the marbles, which you can get at any good toyshop in various sizes. The sizes of the board and the holes are both decided by the size of the marbles you buy.

I started with a piece of parana pine 10x¾in, and cut out a circle. I marked the centre panel out to a diameter of 7½in and

the outer channel to a width of ⅞in; I cut it with a bowl gouge. It needs to be deep enough to accommodate the marbles, the actual measurement depending on their sizes. Afterwards the decorative edge was cut, but of course this can take any shape you feel like.

The next operation is to mark out the centres for the blind holes. For my marbles I used a ¾in saw-toothed bit, the centres exactly 1in apart. The holes had to be

marked out starting from the centre, and were done while the board was still on the lathe. After sanding and polishing, the base can be covered with self-adhesive Fablon Velour.

Since I made the first board, all my friends have been clamouring for one, and currently I am on my fifth. They get simpler to make. As for playing, we have managed to get down to two marbles, but no one has yet achieved the magic solitaire! ■

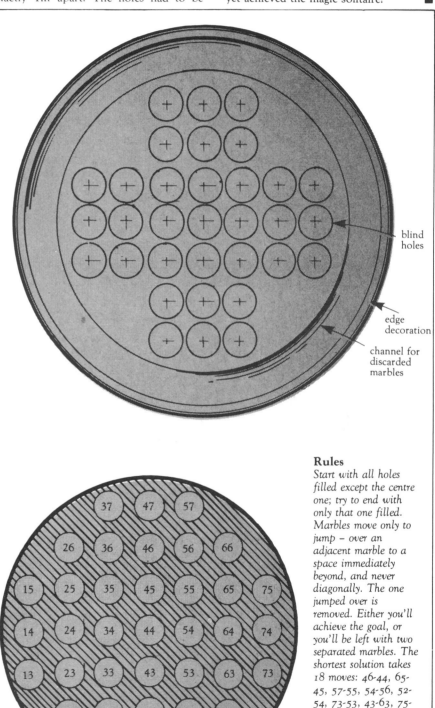

blind holes

edge decoration

channel for discarded marbles

Rules
Start with all holes filled except the centre one; try to end with only that one filled. Marbles move only to jump – over an adjacent marble to a space immediately beyond, and never diagonally. The one jumped over is removed. Either you'll achieve the goal, or you'll be left with two separated marbles. The shortest solution takes 18 moves: 46-44, 65-45, 57-55, 54-56, 52-54, 73-53, 43-63, 75-73-53, 35-55, 15-35, 23-43-63-65-45-25, 37-57-55-53, 31-33, 34-32, 51-31-33, 13-15-35, 36-34-32-52-54-34, 24-44

A PRIMARY PROJECT
EASEL for JUDITH and JAMES

This easel is easily made and can provide hours of absorbing fun, says R. W. Grant who also did the drawing. John Peacock took the photographs showing Judith (5) and James (3) Grant busily engaged with the artistic media of their choice: blackboard and chalks for Judith and paint and paper for James.

The scaled drawing shows the construction of the easel which is based on two A-frames hinged at the top and held apart by two lengths of chain fixed to the inner edges of the frames. The chains will then loop clear as the easel is closed-up for storage.

Ordinary mortise and tenon joints are used to make the frames (haunched on the top rails only) and the requisite splay for the tenon shoulders may be obtained by setting a sliding bevel to 85°.

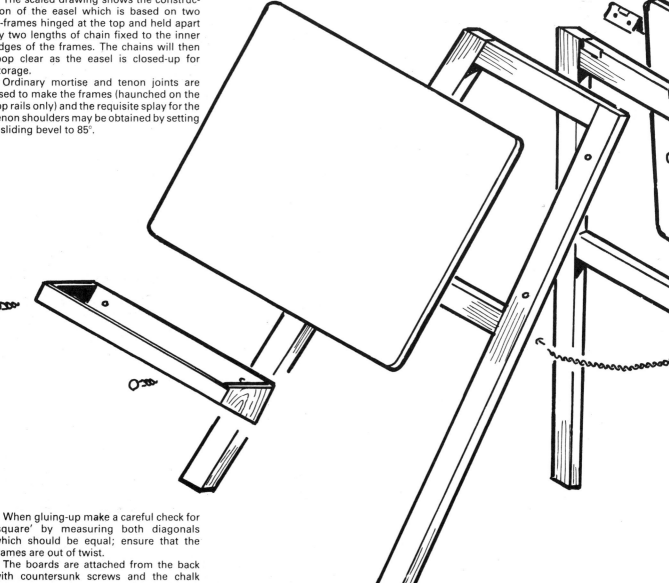

When gluing-up make a careful check for 'square' by measuring both diagonals which should be equal; ensure that the frames are out of twist.

The boards are attached from the back with countersunk screws and the chalk ledge is screwed up from the underneath.

Materials list
Dimensions in in. Net sizes given

No.	Description	L	W	T	Material
4	Legs	42	2	¾	Pine
2	Middle rails	16	2	¾	Pine
2	Top rails	13	2	¾	Pine
2	Boards	24	20⅝	½	Birch ply
1	Chalk ledge	20	2	½	Pine
2	Paintbox ends	3¼	3¼	½	Pine
1	Paintbox bottom	19	3¼	½	Pine
1	Paintbox back	19¼	3¼	3/16	Birch ply
1	Paintbox front	19¼	2	3/16	Birch ply
2	Steel butt hinges	2			
2	Picture chains	13			
	Screws to suit fittings				

The paintbox bottom is rebated into the ends and the ply back and front are glued and pinned on. The assembly is fixed underneath the drawingboard by screwing through the back piece and into the frame legs. It would be as well to bore at least one drainage hole in the base of the paintbox.

**Text and drawing
R. W. Grant
photographs
John Peacock**

The drawingboard may be painted with white emulsion paint while the blackboard is treated with matt black paint with a handful of cement stirred in. This makes paint sufficiently gritty to provide a good key for the chalk. The frames may be clear finished or painted (be sure that it is non-toxic).

Having made and assembled the two frames and their boards the final jobs are to lay the two frames flat and touching at the tops and mark-out and fit the two butt hinges. The easel may then be stood up and the chains fixed with small round head screws through the end links.

Collector's cocktail

This beautiful little chest by Waring Robinson uses no less than four hardwoods; ring your own changes or follow his instructions to reproduce a subtle marvel

U nobtrusive good proportion, fine cabinet work and the feel of the maker is a mix which never fails to excite. This is always how I am affected when I look at James Krenov's books and anticipate the problems his designs suggest. A small chest with a bow door offered an opportunity to try and emulate his principles, and our local art exhibition created the spur to make it.

I decided to make the chest from African padauk and Indian rosewood, which I felt would be a rewarding mixture. The visual effect of recently re-cut padauk is quite startling, and planing the surface exposes the full brightness and colour of the wood. The proportions were established by determining the height which would accommodate the six rosewood drawers (I had some offcuts from a previous piece). I then applied the 'geometric' or 'golden rule' of proportion to find the width and depth of the cabinet.

The construction is interesting and presents some unusual problems associated with the bow door, including the sequencing when fitting the door to the top and base of the carcase, and the correct positioning of the hinges to get an accurate pivot at the top and base of the door. The concave surface allows the door to close and still clear the protruding handles, which in turn complement the visual effect. Continuity is achieved when they form a mitre joint with the drawer-runners.

Construction

Prepare the padauk for the carcase work, which includes finishing the sides and back to the final dimensions. The top and base are left oversize in depth for final fitting at the front.

Cut the four tenons for the top and base, and grooves for the shelves, drawer-runners and back in the two sides. I did this with a router, guide-bush and template. Then I prepared five maple shelves, planing them to correct dimensions and making sure they fit snug in the grooves.

The concave fronts of the shelves were marked out with a template and bandsawed into shape, then finished with a spokeshave and fine garnet paper. Then I glued the shelves to the sides and clamped them in position.

I mortised the top and base to accept the tenons, and cut a groove for the back, then cut the back to size and rebated it to fit in the grooves. I checked the assembly dry with the sides and shelves to make sure I had an accurate fit at the back.

Photos Tim Imrie

● *This delicately proportioned and beautifully designed little piece makes the most of the subtle beauty of a variety of hardwoods. The rose shows scale*

The door

The coopered door is made up of six pieces of padauk, flat and accurately thicknessed. Ideally, these should be quarter-cut and matched for colour and grain. The edges are planed to 88°. Two halves of the door are formed by rub-jointing and clamping the segments individually, ensuring that the surface edges are in alignment. When the two halves were complete I joined them in the same way.

I planed the door to approximate dimensions, using a flat smoothing plane on the convex surface and an old moulding block plane for the inside, which approximated to the concavity. Then I finished the convex surface with a plane, scraper and fine garnet, and when I was satisfied, scribed the edges with a marking gauge to give the thickness. Ideally the concave surface should be finished with an accurately dimensioned plane, but I was able to get a satisfactory result with my moulding plane, a convex scraper and garnet paper held on a wood block which I shaped to fit the curve. I checked both surfaces regularly against accurate templates.

The hinges

Commercial pivot hinges are much too crude for the door, so I decided to make them out of 1.5mm brass, which I found surprisingly easy. The plates are two pieces 34x8mm for each hinge, and the posts are 3.5mm diameter steel rod, which fit in a hole at the 4mm centres. They can be brazed or riveted in position, and an 8mm thin steel washer should be included on the

lower hinge post to act as a spacer. I filed the exposed part of the hinge round to match the washer, and drilled two countersunk holes in each plate for the screws. I finished the brass with abrasives, first paper and then a rubbing compound to produce a polished surface.

Fitting the door

This is probably the trickiest part of the construction, bearing in mind it is the shape of the fitted door which will give the line of the top and bottom front edges, so you have no outside position to work to on the

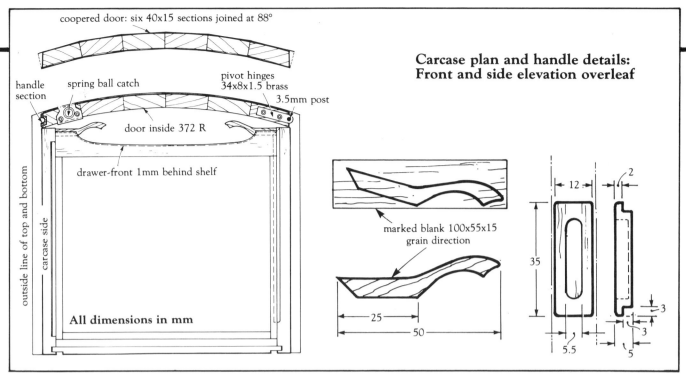

coopered door: six 40x15 sections joined at 88°

handle section

spring ball catch

pivot hinges 34x8x1.5 brass

3.5mm post

Carcase plan and handle details: Front and side elevation overleaf

door inside 372 R

drawer-front 1mm behind shelf

outside line of top and bottom

carcase side

All dimensions in mm

marked blank 100x55x15 grain direction

12

2

35

25

50

5.5

3

3

5

carcase for the door. Krenov describes how to use a 'pivot-positioning jig' so the centre of the hinge post is accurately placed in the top and bottom of the carcase; I followed his advice, although there must be other simpler ways which would work equally well.

Separate the hinge plates from their pivot posts, and mark and scribe the door plates of the hinges into the top and bottom edges of the door, measuring exactly to the centre of the pivot and making sure the hinges protrude precisely the same amount top and bottom. Then cut the 'positioning jig', which is in fact no more than a piece of wood the same thickness as the door. Hold it in the door position against the front edge of the hinging side, and offer the door up to it, marking the exact pivot centre of the hinge. Then, knowing how wide the hinge plate is and how far out the pivot centre protrudes, you can mark and cut the recess for the carcase plates of the hinges in the relevant surfaces of the top and bottom pieces. Once those recesses are cut you can check how the door works, dry-assembling top and bottom again and clamping them up while you check that no adjustment is needed. If it is, be very careful and cheat the thickness of the door a bit. Don't try and re-position the hinges!

I drilled a hole in the bottom edge of the door for the brass ball-catch, fitted it, and closed the door. This left a mark on the wood for the striking plate, which I cut out of 1.5mm brass (commercial ones are too thin) and carefully fitted it in position. I closed the door again and the ball marked the exact position for the hole to be cut. The unobtrusive handle is made from rosewood, fitted into a mortise in the vertical edge of the door.

The outside convex surface of the door is used as a pattern when it's closed to mark the front line of top and base with a pencil. I cut them oversize by the width of the mould detail, made a template and used my router and guide bush to cut the moulding along the front edges, and the same section on the sides. I gave the surfaces a final finish and waxed the door well, polishing to a finish. With the hinges screwed in position, I glued and clamped the top and base in final position. The door closed with a satisfactory click without any chatter.

The drawers

The drawers are made in the traditional way; I completed the dovetailing before shaping the fronts. Accurate marking-out is essential, as the groove for the drawer-runner must be in the middle of the centre pin. The drawer-fronts are marked out to set back 1mm from the shelves. I bandsawed them to shape and finished them with spokeshave, scraper and fine garnet. I fitted the completed drawers, working from the back to the front and then cut the grooves in the drawer side for the runner. Accuracy is essential; having made a template for the size and shelf positions of the carcase, I found it possible to use the same one for positioning the grooves in the drawer sides.

The handles are made out of one piece of wood. I marked out the outline on two edges against a template, making sure the grain ran in the direction of the narrowest section. The shape was carved out, checked for uniformity and then sanded smooth. Finally I sectioned them on a bandsaw and finished them to fit in a groove on the drawer-front, making a mitre joint with the drawer-runner. I glued them in position.

I made the chest over a period of three months in my available spare time. The finish was wax, apart from the drawer handles which I finished with Rustin's plastic coating and then polished them.

The proportions and the colour of the padauk are very satisfying, but a word of warning for padauk lovers. Ultra-violet light is unkind to African padauk and turns it a rather murky brown — so keep it away from the sunlight. ∎

Cutting list

Carcase

Sides (padauk)	2	330mm x	203mm x	13mm
Top (padauk)	1	240	247	19
Base (padauk)	1	240	247	19
Back (padauk)	1	322	210	6.2
Door (padauk)	6	316	40	15
Shelves (maple)	5	210	193	6.2

Drawers

Fronts (Indian rosewood)	6	203	47.5	23
Sides (English cherry)	12	181	47.5	6.2
Backs (English cherry)	6	203	38	6.2
Bottoms (maple)	6	196	172	2.5
Runners (English cherry)	12	175	6.2	6.2
Drawer handles (rosewood)	1 (12)	100	55	15
Door handle (rosewood)	1	35	12	5
Pivot hinges (brass)	4	34	8	1.5
Striking plate (brass)	1	24	16	1.5

cont

Collector's cocktail

Front elevation

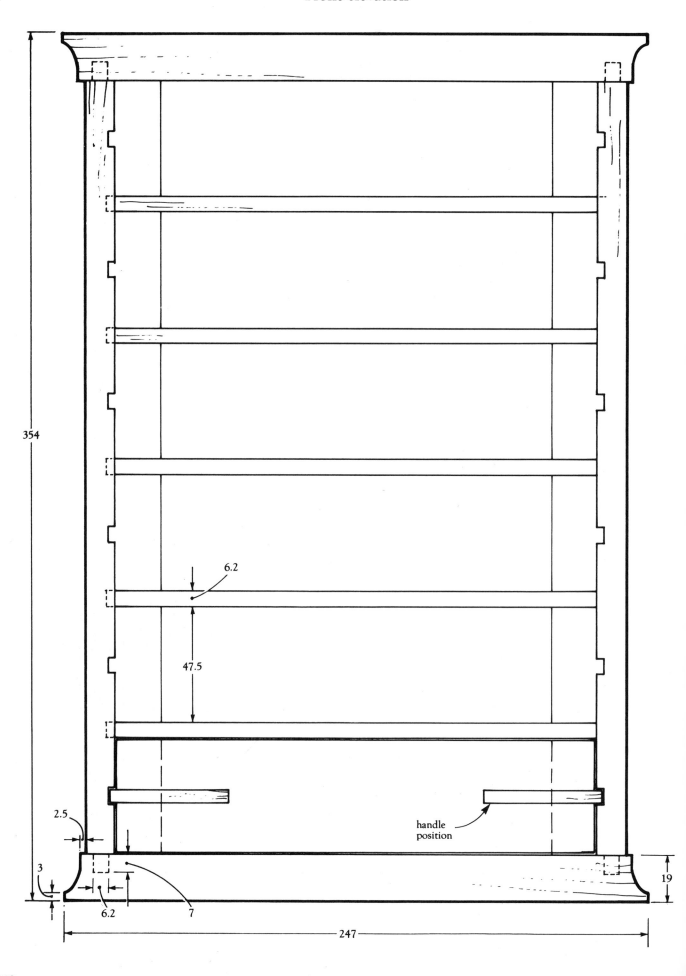

354

6.2

47.5

2.5

3

6.2

7

handle
position

19

247

118

Carcase side — elevation

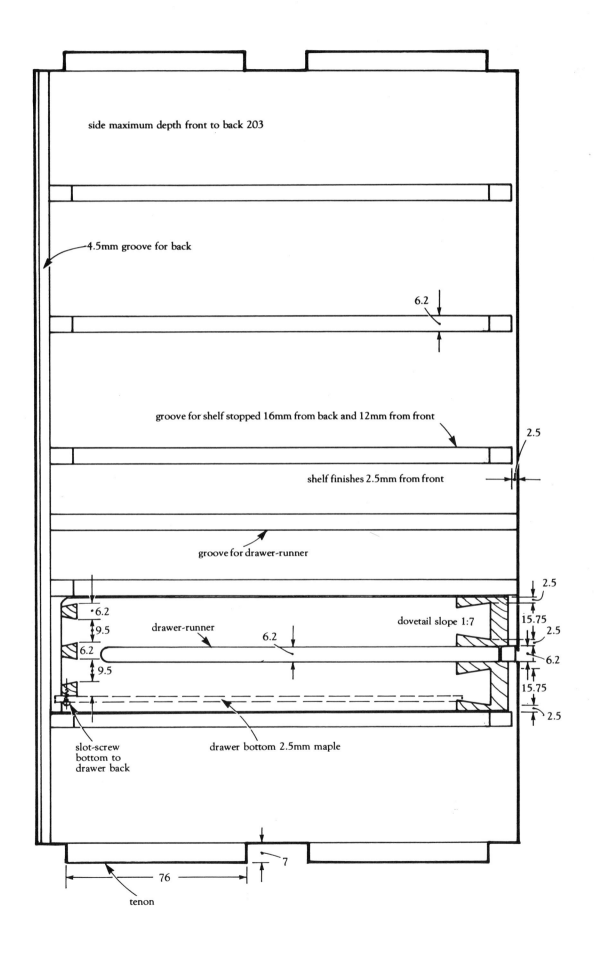

side maximum depth front to back 203

4.5mm groove for back

6.2

groove for shelf stopped 16mm from back and 12mm from front

2.5

shelf finishes 2.5mm from front

groove for drawer-runner

2.5

6.2

9.5

drawer-runner

6.2

dovetail slope 1:7

15.75

2.5

6.2

6.2

9.5

15.75

2.5

slot-screw
bottom to
drawer back

drawer bottom 2.5mm maple

76

7

tenon

Curves in the bathroom

Jim Robinson re-created an early Victorian towel rail to suit his period home

Fig. 1 Front and side elevations

35¼

all dimensions in inches

23¾

12¾

T his design of towel rail is typical of those made around 1860, when our house was built. Obviously everything cannot fit in with this period — otherwise we wouldn't have a bathroom at all. In those days a towel rail would be in the bedroom.

I have used iroko for the construction, chiefly because I already had a large well seasoned piece. You could use ash or beech and, if you are lucky enough to be able to obtain suitable pieces, yew could be a preference as this turns well, polishes easily and mellows to a particularly attractive colour. If you use iroko then inspect it carefully for calcareous deposits which sometimes occur as laminations in the timber; these quickly blunt saw-blades and turning tools. It's also advisable to wear a dust mask when sanding or machining, as the dust can be unpleasant, even harmful to some people with a tendency to allergy. The wood finishes well with an attractive colour and appearance.

The photographs of the complete rail and fig. 1 reveal the construction. Each end consists of two uprights mounted on a base with two feet. The two uprights are then joined at the top with a semi-circular ring and these two ends are joined by five rails.

Bases

Draw the side view to full size, using the square grid on fig. 2. If you are only making one towel rail don't bother to make a template but transfer the shape to suitable 2in thick wood with pencil and carbon paper — or glue paper with the outline on to the wood using a thin smear of contact adhesive (useful with dark wood); this can be easily removed with a cabinet scraper when cleaning up. Make two holes in the top of the base, ¾in diameter and 1in deep; drilled before shaping to ensure that the uprights will be at right angles. Use a flat-bottomed bit. Next cut the two bases to shape using a bandsaw with a narrow blade or a coping saw, though this is more difficult with 2in wood. Smooth by filing and sanding where a scraper can't be used, and carefully put a small radius on all the edges with a file before sanding smooth.

Uprights

Make the uprights from four pieces of 31x2x2in timber. Square the ends and centre for mounting in the lathe between centres. Turn to rough shape using a fairly large gouge, then a large skew chisel for most of the final shaping and finishing, with a smaller skew or beading chisel for the beads. If your lathe has only a short bed you may need to turn each of the uprights in two pieces, joining them in the middle as shown in fig. 3 with a 1½in long pin of ½in diameter, glued into a suitable hole. If the join is made at this position it will be virtually invisible (if you add one or two drops of gravy browning when mixing the glue the lines hardly show). Cut a small groove into the pin to let air and surplus glue escape.

Semi-circular rings

This is the interesting stage and shouldn't be too difficult. The semi-circular ring is made by turning a single ring and then

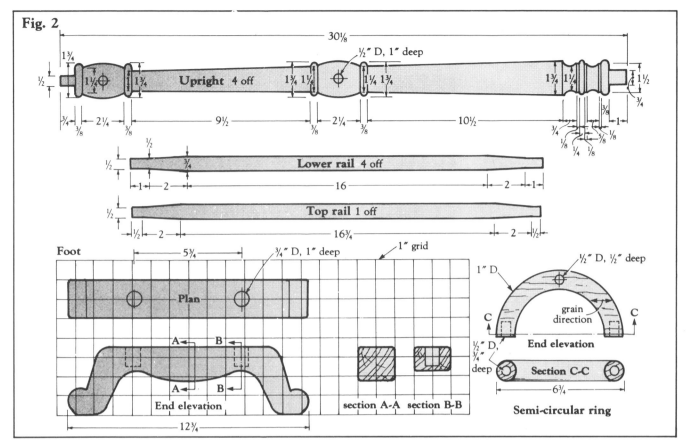

Fig. 2

Upright 4 off

Lower rail 4 off

Top rail 1 off

Foot

Plan

End elevation

section A-A   section B-B

Semi-circular ring

End elevation

Section C-C

grain direction

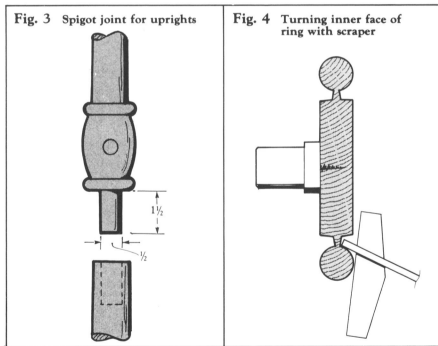

Fig. 3 Spigot joint for uprights

Fig. 4 Turning inner face of ring with scraper

● *Turn the semi-circular end pieces from a single ring and then cut in half*

cutting it in half to form the two end pieces. Select a piece of wood about 7in square and a little over 1in thick to produce a ring of 1in cross-section and 6¾in outside diameter. Cut to a circle using a bandsaw or whatever you have. Find the centre, drill a pilot hole, then mount it on a small screw chuck. I turned the outside of the ring using a bowl gouge on its side to give a slicing

action and the inner side of the ring using a flat scraper to the section as shown in fig. 4; you could do all the turning with a scraper, but light cuts will be necessary to avoid tearing out the grain. Sand in the lathe. If you have to turn the wood over in the screw chuck drill the pilot hole completely through the thickness of the wood, preferably on a bench drill to ensure it is

perpendicular and you have accurate centring from each side. After sanding, you could carry on scraping until the ring is free, but it is less nerve-racking to cut off the thin section with a coping saw.

Clean up the inside with a file, sanding to

continued

Curves in the bathroom

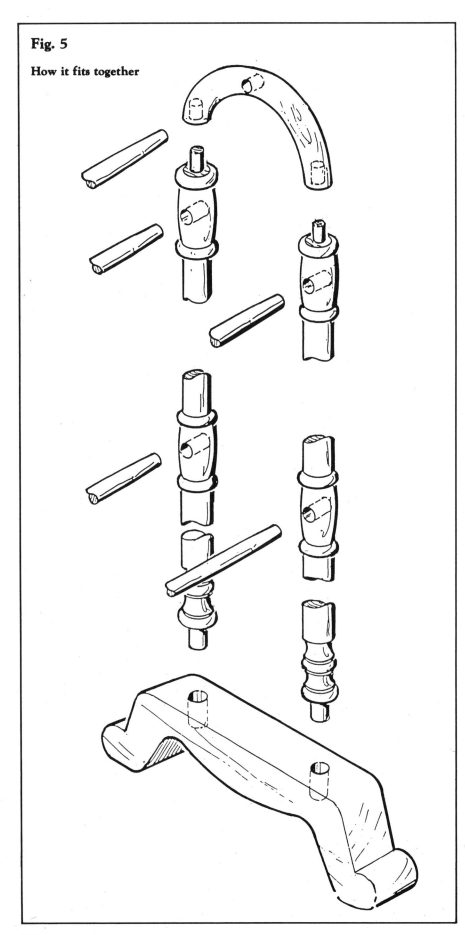

Fig. 5

How it fits together

make it uniformly circular in cross-section. Then carefully saw in half along the grain as in fig. 2. Flatten the ends squarely by holding the half ring upright and rubbing it on a sheet of 80-grit garnet paper laid on a flat surface. Then drill the ½in holes in the ends, putting the half ring in the bench vice, with the sawn surfaces horizontal and level with the bench top and using a brace with the drill aligned in each direction with a square. The single hole in the centre of the curve, to take the top towel rail, is best drilled in a bench drill with a depth stop.

Rails

The design of the rails is fairly straight-forward (fig. 2), though the top rail is slightly different from the remaining four. When turning the rails, take only very light cuts to avoid building up ridges because of vibration caused by their slenderness in relation to their length. You can turn the rails completely with a gouge and sand, or if care is taken they can be finished with a skew chisel. A steady for the lathe will be useful if you have one but I usually steady the work by placing the fingers of my left hand at the rear of the work being turned, keeping my thumb on the gouge.

Drill holes in the four uprights to accept the remaining four lower rails after the rails are made, so they can be used to assist with drill alignment. After drilling the first hole perpendicular to the centre-line of the upright, place a rail in the hole and line up a hand brace in one direction with the rail and a square in the other.

Assembly

I first glued and assembled both ends, using a single cramp with a shaped softwood block cut to the curvature of the top semi-circle. I used carpet underlay to avoid marking the iroko and applied only light pressure. Then I glued into position, again using softwood blocks and felt. If you can't insert the rails easily you could release the pressure on the end cramps to enable the uprights to be twisted slightly to bring the holes for the rails in the correct alignment. I glued it all together in one operation, but it can be rather tricky and it might be easier to allow the two ends to set before gluing the rails into position. If you do this, then insert the rails dry into the uprights in case it's necessary to twist the uprights to get the holes facing in the right direction.

Finishing

Wax finish would look all right but I think a little more protection is needed — the woodwork can be splashed with wet hands when you reach for a towel. I used one coat of Colron Oil Reviver, followed by two coats of Colron Antique Oil which I've found very durable in a bathroom.

Having completed the towel rail all that remains is to get the usual request from the offspring — 'Make me one, Dad'. ■

Pen friend

Bill Walker re-discovers
the traditional writing slope
— a quaint but popular
design which demands
some deft detailing

● *The hinged writing slope becomes an attractive compact box when not in use*

Thousands of these writing boxes were made during the 19th century, many in choice woods, lavishly decorated and internally fitted out. Cheaper boxes were made of pine veneered with walnut or mahogany. They turn up in sales and antique shops from time to time but it's rare to find one that has not been broken inside, probably from impatient or clumsy attempts to find the secret drawer or compartment which the better boxes often featured. I made this box as a present and I found it an interesting piece of cabinet work both to design and make. You can vary the way the box is fitted out to suit your own requirements; this one actually has two concealed compartments, but I have not included them in the drawings.

Before starting this project I experimented a little with the theory of proportion — some rectangles are visually more satisfying than others. I had decided the box would be 178mm high, and using the 'Golden Mean' rectangle gave an end elevation of 178 × 295mm, a bit too wide. So I tried a Fibonacci series rectangle (fig. 1): this gave an end elevation in the ratio 2:3, front elevation 2:5 and plan 3:5 — box dimensions 178x267x445mm which seemed more like it. I drew these rectangles full size but the proportions were still not comfortable to my eye, so I altered them to 178x254x458mm. This looked more satisfying to me. It's purely subjective of course, but try it yourself. The dimensions also had to be considered bearing in mind the internal fitting-out of the box (fig. 2)

I used Brazilian mahogany for the main carcase, good quality 9mm plywood for the top and bottom, darker Cuban mahogany for the interior parts, and crown cut Honduras mahogany veneer for the top.

continued

Fig. 1

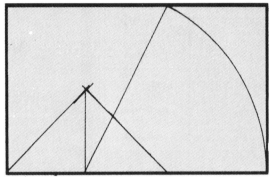

'Golden Mean' rectangle Ratio 1:1.618

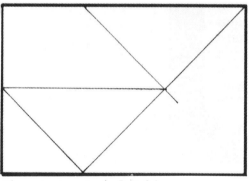

Fibonacci series rectangle. Ratio 2:3

● *Fit for the finest vellum and wax-sealing stamps – even writing the bills could be a pleasure!*

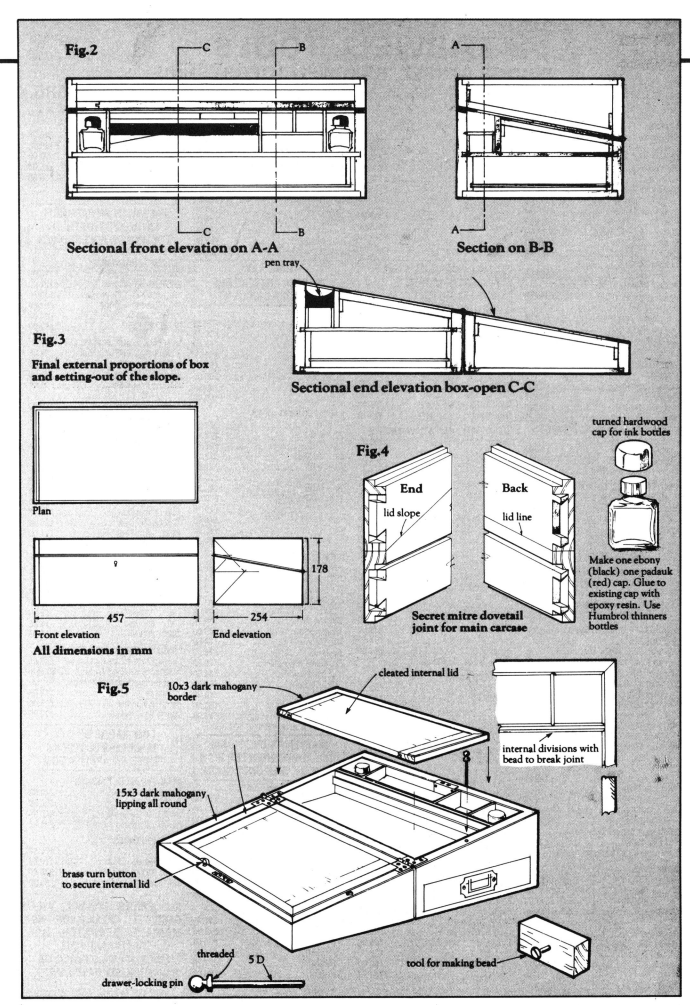

Fig.2

Sectional front elevation on A-A

Section on B-B

pen tray

Sectional end elevation box-open C-C

Fig.3

Final external proportions of box
and setting-out of the slope.

Plan

Front elevation

End elevation

457

254

178

All dimensions in mm

Fig.4

End

lid slope

Back

lid line

Secret mitre dovetail
joint for main carcase

turned hardwood
cap for ink bottles

Make one ebony
(black) one padauk
(red) cap. Glue to
existing cap with
epoxy resin. Use
Humbrol thinners
bottles

Fig.5

10x3 dark mahogany
border

cleated internal lid

internal divisions with
bead to break joint

15x3 dark mahogany
lipping all round

brass turn button
to secure internal lid

threaded

5 D

drawer-locking pin

tool for making bead

Construction

1 Prepare the front, back and two ends from one length of board so the grain will follow around the box when it is assembled, except for one corner which can be at the back. If the timber isn't quarter-sawn, make sure the heart side will be outside.

2 Mark out the rebates, groove and lid cut-off lines. The corner joints are secret mitre dovetails; you could use other joints but they must be strong because the lid section will be heavy and part of one end is cut away to provide the drawer opening.

3 Make top, bottom and horizontal divisions from plywood, veneered both sides for balance. Solid wood was used in the old boxes but often split because of shrinkage.

4 After cutting the corner joints, rebates and grooves, clean up and polish the internal parts. I used clear shellac polish applied with a rubber. Keep the polish away from joints and rebates by masking them out if necessary.

5 Assemble the carcase with the grooved-horizontal division in place and cramp up dry to test for squareness. Before gluing up, saw about 50mm along the sloping lid line on both end pieces; this makes things a lot easier when separating the lid from the box later.

6 When the main carcase has set, you can fit the top and bottom veneered plywood pieces and glue them into their respective rebates.

7 Cut the drawer opening from one end of the box. Use a padsaw to cut inside the marked line, and trim the opening square with a paring chisel. If it's carefully cut out, the piece removed can be used as the drawer-front, but a cock bead will be needed to make up for the wood lost in sawing it from the opening. I rejected this method and cut a drawer front from another piece with near matching grain (don't tell anyone!).

8 Use a fine-toothed tenon or dovetail saw to cut along the lid line to separate the lid section from the box; watch the angle of slope. This is where having started the cut on the ends beforehand pays off. Plane the edges true so that both parts fit together neatly all round. Mitre and glue a lipping 3mm thick around the meeting edges; this allows for the thickness of the leather writing surface and the hinges.

9 Fit the divisions for ink bottles and pen tray in their respective positions with housing joints. A small bead line worked round the interior edges acts as a break joint between the divisions and the

carcase. I used a no.10 csk wood screw in a hardwood block to score this bead (fig. 5).

10 The internal lids or flaps which provide the writing surface are made from solid wood with tongued and grooved cleats each end. Mitre a 3mm thick border around to provide a protective edging for the leather. Using solid wood is better than ply in this case because it can be planed true and flat.

11 The drawer is of conventional construction with lap dovetail joints at the front and through dovetails at the back. The drawer can be subdivided for pencils, crayons or other items but I made a separate pencil box and tray which can be taken out of the drawer in use.

Hardware

The old boxes were often broken at the hinges because the lid is quite heavy. I cut a pair of brass back-flaps into L-shapes to fit on the corners. This gives a broader knuckle which should be stronger than narrow box hinges. One slight disadvantage is that the internal lids cannot be opened through 180° and laid back flat; but this is seldom necessary. The restriction avoids creasing the leather too much along the joint.

I used a turned brass pin to secure the drawer when the box is locked; this is inserted into a hole drilled down the end and part way into the top edge of the drawer front. The lock is a conventional brass box lock. You should make a small brass turn button to secure the internal lid so that it doesn't flap open when the box is opened.

I chose military-chest type handles, one at each end of the box; that is, one let into the drawer front and one at the other end. Take care when cutting them in as a lot of material is removed.

Polishing

I had finished all the internal parts of the box before gluing up. All parts were french polished with transparent shellac (Special Pale) polish to a full-bodied finish, allowing plenty of time for drying between applications and very little white oil to lubricate the rubber. I didn't use a grain filler because the Brazilian mahogany used for the main carcase is very light in colour, almost salmon pink, and this contrasts very well with the darker mahogany used for lippings and the interior divisions. Apart from this contrast the case when closed is devoid of decoration except for the natural grain and colour of the wood used.

Fixing the leather

I purchased the dark green leather tooled with gold border to my specification from the Art Veneers Co. Ltd. in Mildenhall. It arrived on time (14 days after ordering), carefully packed and of excellent quality.

With the box in its open position, glue a piece of brown or green linen over the whole writing surface with scotch glue or one of the 'Clam' adhesives. Make sure that it is well glued down with no bubbles or creases; allow the glue to dry hard. This type of adhesive is best if it's coloured to match the leather or the wood of the box, because it shows along the lid joint when the box is closed. Cut the leather slightly oversize, glue it down on to the linen covered surface and smooth out bubbles from the centre with a cloth pad, but try not to stretch the leather. Cover the surface with polythene, a board and some weights until the glue has dried. Finally trim the edge neatly into the border with knife and straight-edge.

Hey presto, there's your writing slope. ∎

Cutting list (finished sizes)

Front and back	2	500mm x	185mm x	15mm	Brazilian mahogany
Ends	2	300	185	15	Brazilian mahogany
Top	1	500	300	9	Veneered plywood
Middle surface	1	500	300	6	Veneered plywood
Bottom	1	500	300	9	Veneered plywood
Drawer front	1	250	50	15	Brazilian mahogany
Drawer sides	2	450	50	9	Brazilian mahogany
Drawer back	1	250	50	9	Brazilian mahogany
Drawer bottom	1	450	250	4	Plywood
Internal lids	1	800	250	9	Brazilian mahogany
Cleats	1	800	50	9	Cut 4, Brazilian mahogany
Internal divisions	1	450	80	9	Utile (or darker mahogany)
Internal divisions	1	450	80	5	Cut for intermediate parts
Pen tray	1	200	50	20	Utile
Lippings and borders	8	460	15	3	Utile

1 pair solid drawn brass back-flap hinges 1½in wide
1 2in cut box lock
1 pair 2½in brass military chest handles
2 square glass bottles with screw tops
Green leather skiver with gold tooling all four edges, to size of writing surface

NURSERY MACHO

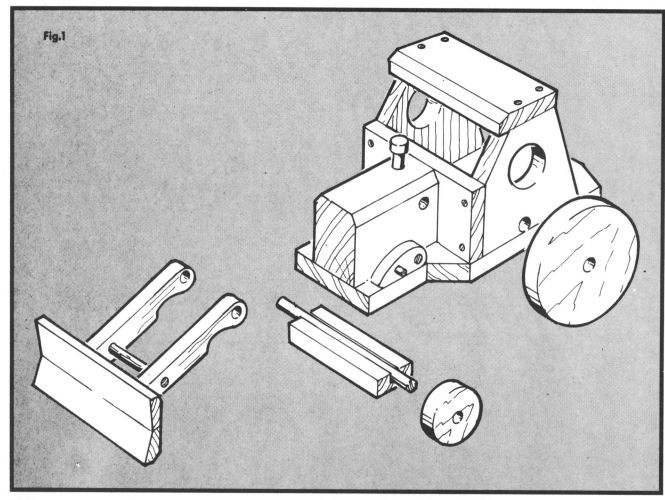

Fig.1

James Wake designed this toy bulldozer to avoid any dangers to children

For me, safety is the paramount consideration in young children's toys. Here's a mechanical toy with a challenging solid wood, glued construction designed for safety and strength. No metal or plastic fittings are involved.

Beech is traditionally the favourite material, for strength, but cost and availability is a factor. You could use other hardwoods, carefully selected softwoods, plywood, laminated board and even chipboard, but the finish, painted or varnished, will be influenced by the choice of material. If painted, make sure you use non-toxic paint. I've found a clear polyurethane varnish, on carefully selected pine, produces a strong, hard-wearing and handsome result.

Joints

The strength of the toy relies upon glued and dowelled joints, which must be tight and well-fitting. It's essential that all structural parts are flat, exactly straight and square-edged, and clean and dust-free — particularly if you're using PVA glue. I strongly recommend using a sanding disc for end-grain. Mark out and pre-drill pilot holes in all the surface parts before assembly, preferably using a drilling machine or drill-stand. The joints rely upon tight fitting dowels, drilling the holes 0.5mm smaller than the dowels' diameter. Saw a groove in the sides of the dowel to provide an escape for air and surplus glue. If this saw-cut is made of sufficient depth, parallel with the surface grain, it provides some 'give', making a tight fitting joint without splitting. When ready for gluing, lay out all the parts, grip the first piece and the gluing jig in the bench vice (fig. 4). Check for accuracy, then holding the pre-drilled part firmly in position against the jig, and using the pilot holes as a guide, drill for the depth of the dowel. Apply glue, insert the dowel and drive into position. Still holding the pre-drilled part firmly, drill the next

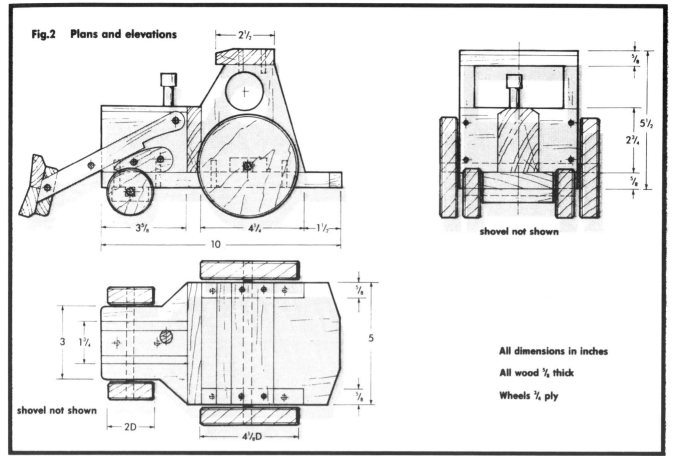

Fig.2   Plans and elevations

shovel not shown

All dimensions in inches

All wood ⅝ thick

Wheels ¾ ply

shovel not shown

hole and repeat the gluing process. Remove from the vice. Because of the tight fitting dowels it is possible, with care, to level off the protruding dowels immediately, and with some ingenuity, use the gluing jig fastened in the bench vice to complete the other corners. Remove all surplus glue.

Wheels and axles

Only wooden parts are used, all glued together. They are resilient to the hard knocks that toys are bound to receive and there are no small components which can be detatched, picked up and swallowed.

The axles are hardwood dowels revolving in a grooved block of wood. Before fixing, a rub of candle wax along the dowels will ensure smooth running, but avoid waxing ends which have to be glued.

If a lathe is available, turn the wheels using ¾in plywood. Without a lathe, I've found the following method very successful:

● Saw wood into squares, slightly bigger than the wheel diameter. Mark the centre and draw the circular size. Drill the centre holes for the dowel axle, such as ⅜in diameter,
● Saw off the corners,
● Mount the wheel on the sanding disc wheel jig (figs 5/6),
● As the wheel is rotated, slide the jig backwards and forwards along the disc table. Remove the waste gradually until the wheel is finished to size.

The look and serviceability of the wheels is much improved if

the edges are bevelled. You can do this easily on the sanding disc by making another jig with the surface tilted to 30° or 45°.

Safety points:

● Don't allow fingers to touch the rotating disc,
● Don't apply too much pressure or the wood will overheat and scorch — not only wood but fingers,
● Sanding produces a lot of dust, so use a nose mask and eye protection.

Construction

1 Start by shaping the chassis base. Drill dowel pilot holes for fastening the cab and radiator.
2 Prepare and shape pieces for the cab. Hold the sides together and bore a hole for the side windows. Drill pilot holes in top and fascia.
3 Shape the radiator block and drill for exhaust pipe.
4 After cleaning and sanding all interior surfaces, use the gluing jig to assemble and glue the cab.
5 Glue and dowel the radiator to the chassis. Holding the cab firmly against the radiator, glue and dowel in position. When dry, clean up and sand the outside.
6 Glue the exhaust, and then varnish the whole assembly, except the underside of the chassis.
7 Prepare the wheels, dowel rod axles, and grooved axle retaining blocks. ▶

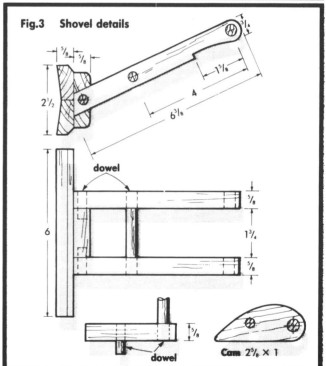

Fig.3   Shovel details

dowel

dowel

Cam 2⅝ × 1

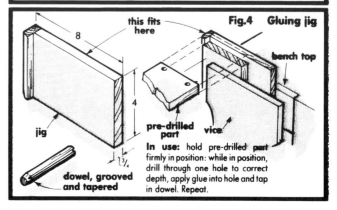

Fig.4   Gluing jig

this fits here

bench top

jig

pre-drilled part

vice

dowel, grooved and tapered

In use: hold pre-drilled part firmly in position; while in position, drill through one hole to correct depth, apply glue into hole and tap in dowel. Repeat.

8 Varnish the inside surfaces edges of the wheels. Wax the axle rods, except the ends to be glued.

Shovel and arms

1 Shape the three shovel parts and glue together. They can be held together with thin moudling pins, which can then be removed when the glue has dried.

2 Prepare and pair the arms and cams. Drill holes for the dowels and glue together, except for the pivoting dowels in the radiator.

3 Varnish these parts.

4 Cut the pivoting dowels to length.

Assembly

1 Place the bulldozer body on its side. Check it is lying square and drill clearance holes for the rear axle.

2 Temporarily position all the wheels and axles.

3 By trial and error, position the cams and shovel, so that the pivoting positions of the holes in the radiator can be found.

4 Again checking the body is square, drill clearance holes for the pivoting dowels.

5 With the wheels and axles glued together, and resting in the groove, glue the grooved blocks, temporarily fastening with moulding pins.

6 Glue the shovel and cams to the ends of the pivoting dowels.

7 Remove surplus glue and give a final coats of varnish to the outsides of the wheels, chassis base and grooved blocks.

So there you have it. A safe, solid wood toy which can't hurt a child of any age, and can give play pleasure for many years. ■

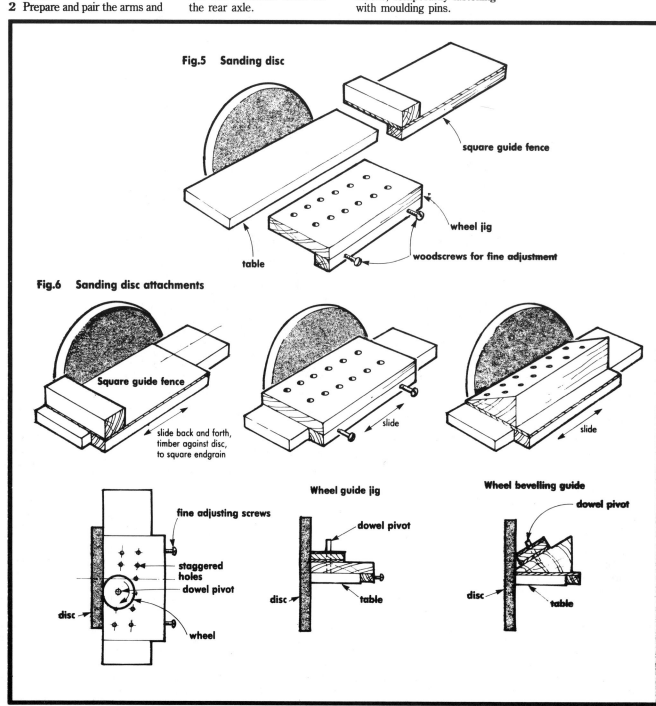

Fig.5 Sanding disc

square guide fence

wheel jig

woodscrews for fine adjustment

table

Fig.6 Sanding disc attachments

Square guide fence

slide back and forth, timber against disc, to square endgrain

slide

slide

fine adjusting screws

staggered holes

dowel pivot

disc

wheel

Wheel guide jig

dowel pivot

disc

table

Wheel bevelling guide

dowel pivot

disc

table

FIX-IT
HOLDALL

If you've followed Brian Porter's ideas on systematic storage, you'll appreciate his hardware holder

ust think how handy it would be to have instant access to an updated inventory of all your hardware at your fingertips. No more searching the shelves in the garage, shed or cellar – or, the last resort, the cupboard under the stairs – for the pair of hinges you know you had left over from the job you did last week.

Once you have a permanent home for all your hand tools – the Porterbox, with variations featured in previous issues – the logical next step is to provide accommodation for all those woodworking hardware essentials. Fixing devices such as nails, screws, nuts and bolts, plugs, mending plates; window hardware such as hinges, fasteners, stays, catches, locks and latches; door hardware and of course door furniture like lever handles, knobs, finger plates and letter plates. There is also security hardware such as tower and barrel bolts, door and alarm chains, door viewers and so on.

If you have a good system already, then of course you should stick to it. But if you like the idea of the Porterchest, why not adapt it to carry your hand-held power tools? Yet another function would be the 'supplementary' tool chest for less used items like moulding planes, carving chisels and jigs or templates.

Requirements

The original brief – to house hardware – required the chest to meet the following conditions.

It had to be large enough to carry the right amount of hardware to meet the tradesman's on-site requirements; it had to be quite light, yet strong enough to withstand hard use and knocks on transit; it should be easy to make, using only basic woodworking joints – with the exception of the trays; it had to be economical on materials, leaving no waste out of a 900×600mm sheet of 9mm ply and a 600×600mm sheet of 6mm (or a 3×2ft of ³⁄₈in and a 2×2ft of ¼in). I chose ply in preference to MDF, because it was easier to get when I was designing the chest, and ply also gives me the option of using a natural finish. Finally, the chest had to be mobile, which meant hand-holds for pulling it and castors on the base for wheeling it round.

To meet the first and most important part of the brief – hardware storage – I designed the chest to be compartmentalised with:

1 A large base compartment, the height of which would vary with the position of the cross-sliding trays.

2 One deep (70mm) compartmentalised tray with a lift-out handle for keeping large nails

Fig. 1

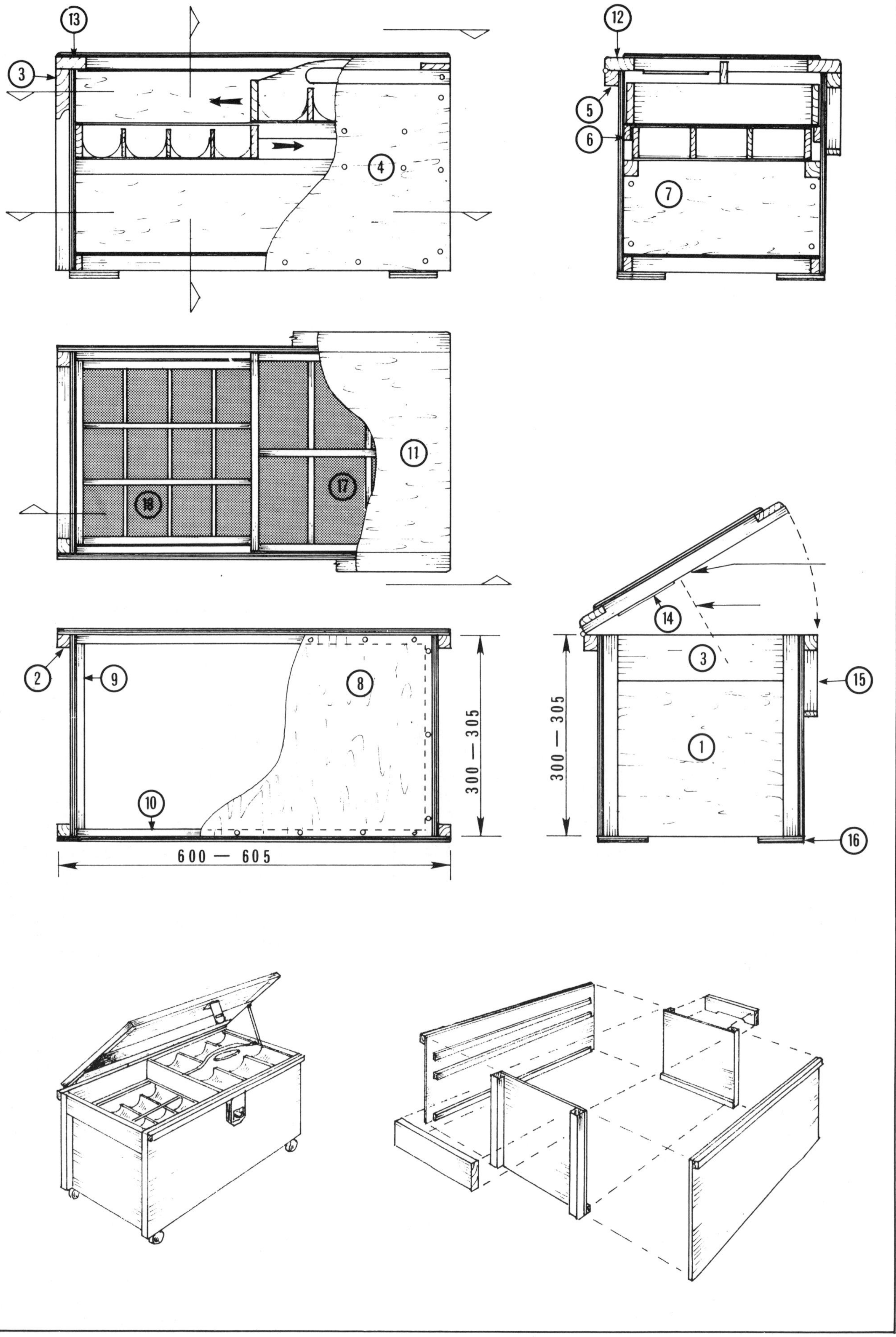

⑬ ③ ④ ⑫ ⑤ ⑥ ⑦

⑰ ⑱ ⑪

② ⑨ ⑧ ⑩ ⑭ ③ ① ⑮ ⑯

300 — 305

600 — 605

300 — 305

and so on separate. You could use a 'scoop' tray for this, made from short ends of 75mm timber, or a piece of 100mm half-round rain gutter, glued to the compartment bottom and sides.

3 One shallow (45mm) compartmentalised tray, to take smaller stuff – again with an optional scoop bottom.

4 A lid compartment for drawings and other bits and pieces of paper.

All the constructional drawings appear in fig. 1. You can of course modify the size and position of the tray compartments according to your needs. The cutting list shows all the component parts with their numbers that appear on the drawings. They are referred to throughout the explanation of how to make the chest, to make reference to the drawings easier.

As you go through the construction, always remember that all inside edges and surfaces

should be cleaned up before you join them to another component.

Rod

Fix a large sheet of drawing paper (lining or wallpaper will do) to a sheet of ply or hardboard, and draw at least two full-size sections through the chest. A vertical lengthwise section (sectional front elevation) and a vertical section through B-B (fig. 1) should include the trays and their compartments. You must decide at this point the depth of the trays, and the size and number of the compartments.

It's important to remember that before you set out a rod you must check the sectional size of the material you have available, and draw the rod to these. I have given standard 'nominal' thicknesses on the cutting list, but of course these are likely to vary.

Once the rod is complete in every detail (double check all

the sizes, but there's no need to write them all on to the rod), you can take all the other measurements and shapes you'll need by laying the uncut timber directly on to the board and marking off with a sharp pencil. As you will have seen if you have used the rods for the Porterbox and accessories, this method of setting out and marking off saves time and materials by dramatically cutting down the risk of mistakes.

Construction

Cut the ends (1) to size from 9mm ply, using the cutting diagram in fig. 2. Tack them together and plane the edges and the corners square. Mark the face side and the face edge, then mark off from the rod the position of the bearers and cleats. Then separate the two ends. Cut the end cleats (2), the end bearers (3), not forgetting the cut-out for the hand-holds, and the bot-

tom bearers (9), and glue and screw the ply to them.

Cut the front and back (4), again using the diagram in fig. 2, prepare them as you did the ends, and separate them. Then cut and prepare the stiffeners (5), tray runners (6,7), the bottom bearers (9,10) and the staple backing cleat. Fix these components to the front and back panels (the staple backing cleat goes on the front panel only) with glue and screws. When you fix the tray runners, tack them on to the ply with a couple of panel pins first before screwing through the ply, to make sure they're accurately positioned.

Cut and plane the bottom (8) to size, using the cutting diagram in fig. 2, and make sure all the corners are square.

You can adapt the internal compartments of the Porterchest to suit your personal requirements

Carcase assembly

Clean up all the inside faces and pre-drill all the fixing points in the front, back and bottom panels. Glue and screw one corner together, then position the bottom panel up against the inside corner on to the pre-glued bearers. When it's square with the sides screw it to the bearers. Joint the remaining corners and fix the bottom panel to all the bearers on the sides. Reinforce the outer top corners by screwing through the ends of the front and back stiffeners into each end bearer.

Fix the feet (16), which will also act as castor blocks, to each corner with glue and screws.

Lid

Prepare the two sets of frame members (12,13), removing any twist by planing. Decide on a suitable corner framing joint – mortise-and-tenon or halving would be best – cut the joints and assemble the frame, checking dry for fit, squareness and wind before you glue up. Dress the joints if you need to with a smoothing plane, then give the frame a light sanding. Cut the lid top (11) to size from the cutting diagram (fig. 2), and bullnose both long edges.

Glue and pin the lid to the frame, and punch the panel pins below the surface. If you are going to have a lid compartment for your paperwork, you should fit it at this stage.

Trays

As I said, the tray arrangement you decide on will depend on the end use of the chest. I have made mine along the following lines:

The tray sides are 12mm thick and the internal compartment walls 9mm, except the handle section which is 12mm. It's best to use slow-grown softwood (redwood or whitewood) or a close-grained hardwood for the handle section, because of the short grain left where you make the cut-out for the hand-hold. You could also use 12mm birch multiply.

House the divisions into the sides, screw the bottoms to the sides and pin and glue them to the divisions. The sides should be dovetailed at the corners, for maximum strength.

Now you can plane the lid to fit the chest top and recess the hinges (19); screw the hinges to the lid, then the lid to the chest. Fix the auto-stay (22); packing in the lid may be required for the bracket, and a runner stop to prevent the trays impeding the stay arm.

Finish

Fill all the nail holes, screw countersinks, blemishes and so on with stopper, and sand the whole thing down to take the coats of paint or varnish you decide on.

Fix the hasp (20) to the underside of the lid and the staple to the backing cleat with through bolts and nuts. Mark your Porterchest with your name, postcode and/or phone number, etching them into the wood on the inside or the underside – preferably both. Traditionally an owner's name or initials should be highly visible, and if you want to make a good show of this you can use stencils or stick-on lettering.

As your chest fills up, it will get heavier, so I would strongly advise that you fix castors (21).

Finally, I should mention that the sliding trays will work more easily if you grease the runners with candle wax. Fixing a strip of plastic laminate to the tops of the runners will also help. ∎

Cutting list

Finished ('nominal') sizes. Part numbers in bold

1	Ends	2	305mm ×	305mm ×	9mm	Plywood	
2	End cleats	4	305	20	20	Softwood	
3	End bearers	2	265	20	70	Softwood – hand hold	
4	Front and back	2	605	305	9	Ply	
5	Stiffeners	2	605	20	20	Softwood – hinge support	
6	Tray runners	2	547	12	22	Hard or softwood	
7	Tray runners	2	547	20	20	Hard or softwood	
8	Bottom	1	547	305	6	Plywood	
9	Bottom bearers	2	305	12	22	Softwood	
10	Bottom bearers	2	547	12	22	Softwood	
11	Lid top	1	605	305	4 or 6	Ply or hdbd	
12	Lid frame	2	605	45	18	Softwood	
13	Lid frame	2	363	45	18	Softwood	
14	Lid pocket	1	547	100	4 or 6	Plywood	
15	Staple backing	1	100	20	70	Softwood – cleat	
16	Feet	4	75	75	12	Plywood – castor blocks	
17	Tray		70mm deep for large nails/screws/bolts etc				
18	Tray		45mm deep for small nails/screws/bolts etc				
			Tray compartments to suit requirements				
19	Butt hinges	2	60			Steel/brass	
20	Hasp and staple	1	100			Steel/brass	
21	Castors	4				Steel/plastic	
22	Auto-stay	1				Steel/plastic	

Fig. 2

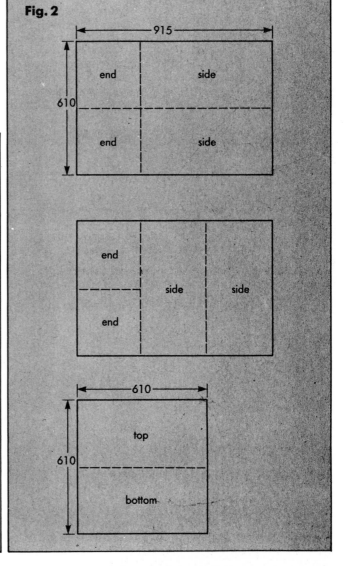

TIME STANDS STILL

John Lester delved back to the Middle Ages for this novel time piece

This unusual exercise in turnery will provide you with the perfect answer to those who insist on showing off the capabilities of their computerised quartz watches. 'I still prefer sundials', you reply, and proceed to demonstrate the portable one you've made, explaining that it has been known over the centuries as the Shepherd's Dial, Pillar Dial, Traveller's Dial or Cylinder Dial. The latter was the name preferred by Chaucer, and for good measure you can throw in the appropriate quotation from *The Canterbury Tales*:

'. . . lat us dyne as soon as that ye may; for by my chilyndre it is prime of day.'

The Shipmannes Tale

Unlike most sundials, the 'chilyndre', tells the time from the height of the sun above the horizon, and not from its direction. For any given hour, this height varies according to the time of year, and so the time-scale on the cylinder consists of a series of curved lines, each of which (apart from the noon line) does duty for two different hours at equal intervals on either side of 12 o'clock.

The height of the sun also varies with latitude. My example

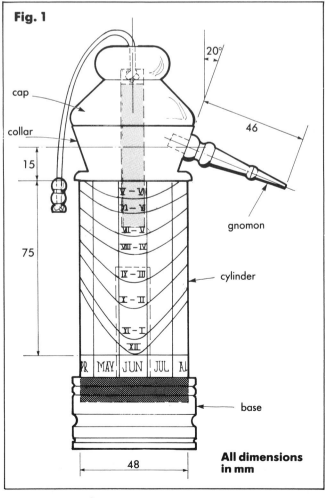

Fig. 1

cap

collar

15

75

20°

46

gnomon

cylinder

base

48

All dimensions in mm

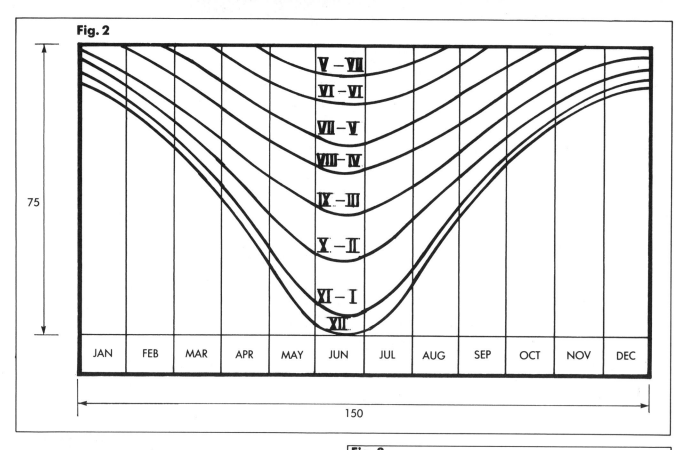

Fig. 2

75

150

JAN FEB MAR APR MAY JUN JUL AUG SEP OCT NOV DEC

V – VII
VI – VI
VII – V
VIII – IV
IX – III
X – II
XI – I
XII

is drawn for Lat 53° 43′, which happens to be the latitude of the Amateur Astronomy Centre in Lancashire, for whom I made a series of these dials. It could, however, be used anywhere in Britain without too much difficulty. If you wish to make a dial for the latitude of your own home town, you'll find the instructions for performing the rather tedious calculations in *Sundials; their Theory and Construction* by A.E. Waugh, Dover Publications 1973.

Apart from a few essential dimensions, a great deal of variety is possible in the design of one of these dials, so you can develop your own ideas (fig. 1). The main part of the instrument is a cylinder marked with the time scale (fig. 2), above which is a rotating collar carrying the gnomon, which casts the shadow. A cap on top of the collar holds it in place, and provides anchorage for the cord from which the instrument is suspended while in use – it must be vertical to work. The cylinder has a hole in the lower end for storage of the gnomon when not in use, and this end is covered by a detachable base.

You can make the cylinder using any available wood if the scale is to be drawn on paper and glued to it. I found this method very effective if the paper is varnished afterwards. If you're skilled in pyrography you may prefer to draw the scale directly on to the cylinder, in which case a light-coloured wood such as lime would be ideal.

First drill an axial hole in the blank to take the wooden rod round which the collar rotates – I made a hole 10mm in diameter and 20mm deep, but this is not critical. When you've done this, remount the blank with a live tailstock centre, in the hole, turning down to a 48mm diameter cylinder. If you leave the diameter slightly larger, nothing will be lost since it doesn't matter if there is a gap between the ends of the hour scale, but it's important that the ends of the scale don't overlap. The length of the cylinder must equal the height of the hour scale (75mm), plus whatever you fancy for the scale of months and the depth to which the cylinder will be recessed into the base. Drill a hole in the bottom end of the cylinder to store the gnomon when not in use. Then glue the hour scale and the calender scale to the cylinder and varnish them, or inscribe them using pyrography.

Hollow out the base with a scraper in the usual way using a screw-chuck, and decorate it any way you please. I used a similar wood for the base, collar and cap, with a contrasting wood for the gnomon and knob on the end of the cord.

I turned the collar and cap as one piece and parted off from one another at the end of the operation. As with the cylinder, I first drilled an axial hole in the blank for the wooden axle around which the collar rotates. This hole needs to be long enough to go through what will become the collar and far enough into

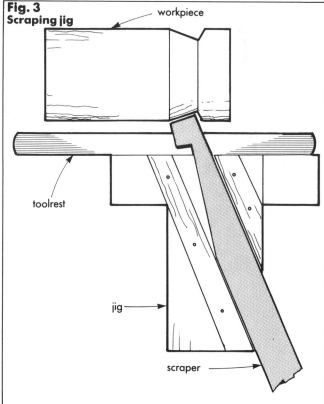

Fig. 3 Scraping jig

workpiece

toolrest

jig

scraper

the cap to anchor it firmly while leaving room for the knot which will be tied to secure the end of the cord. Turn the blank to a cylinder and then you can tackle the most difficult stage in the construction – the hole for the gnomon.

Three things are crucial:
● The face carrying the gnomon must be 20° out of the vertical;
● The centre of the hole forming the socket for

the gnomon must be 15mm above the bottom of the collar;
● At this level the diameter of the collar must be the same as that of the cylinder (48mm).

I didn't feel I had the skill to do this freehand so I constructed a jig to hold a flat scraper at the precise angle required (fig. 3). As the jig was to be positioned against the toolrest, the first essential was to find a method of

Left, using two squares to ensure lathe bed and rest are parallel; right, drilling a perpendicular hole
▼

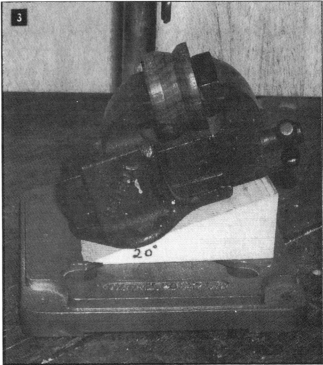

ensuring that the rest was parallel to the bed of the lathe. Using two squares against the front bar of the bed proved suitable for my lathe (photo. 2) but you may need to devise another method for a different machine. A lot of tentative scraping and measuring then follows (photo. 1) until the right dimensions are achieved. Once this has been done, you can shape the remainder of the collar and cap and part off the two components from one another. Before removing the waste piece at the top of the cap it is a good idea to drill the small hole for the cord, otherwise the centre may be lost.

Drill the collar with a radial hole in which the gnomon will fit and as this must be perpendicular to the face in which it is drilled, another jig is needed.

The method I used is shown in photo. 3 but you may have better ideas. The depth and diameter of the hole are not critical.

The axle rod needs to be a push fit in the cylinder and cap, but should allow the collar to rotate without stiffness: a little extra sandpapering of the middle section is enough to ensure this. The rod should be short enough to leave room for the knotted cord inside the cap.

The gnomon has a spigot which plugs into the hole in the collar and the protruding part is 46mm long. The tip should be narrow but the shape of the remainder depends on your inventiveness.

A braided rather than a twisted cord should be used: nylon picture cord is ideal and a free length of 70-100mm is adequate.

Drill the knob with a hole enlarged at one end to take a securing knot.

To finish I suggest you coat the bearing surface with wax: this will not only ensure that the collar turns smoothly but will help to prevent any stray glue causing unwanted adhesion. Glue the axle rod into the top of the cylinder. Thread the cord through the cap and tie a securing knot in the end. Put the collar on its axle and glue the cap on to the axle above it. Thread the other end of the cord through the knob and tie a securing knot in the end. You can finish the dial by whatever method you choose.

To use the cylinder dial, remove the base and extract the gnomon from its storage hole in the bottom of the cylinder. Push

the gnomon fully home in its socket and set the dial by turning the collar until the gnomon lies over the current date as nearly as can be judged. With the instrument suspended by its cord (or standing on a horizontal surface), turn it bodily to face the sun so that the gnomon casts a vertical shadow down the scale. The time is indicated by the tip of the shadow amongst the hour lines. When reading off the time, don't forget that the shadow moves down the scale during the morning and up the scale after noon, and remember too about British Summer Time.

You won't get quartz watch accuracy, but in these days when time is so often a tyrant a little latitude makes a welcome change. ∎

SNACK STAND

Norman Place devised this ingenious fold-up stand for fireside eating

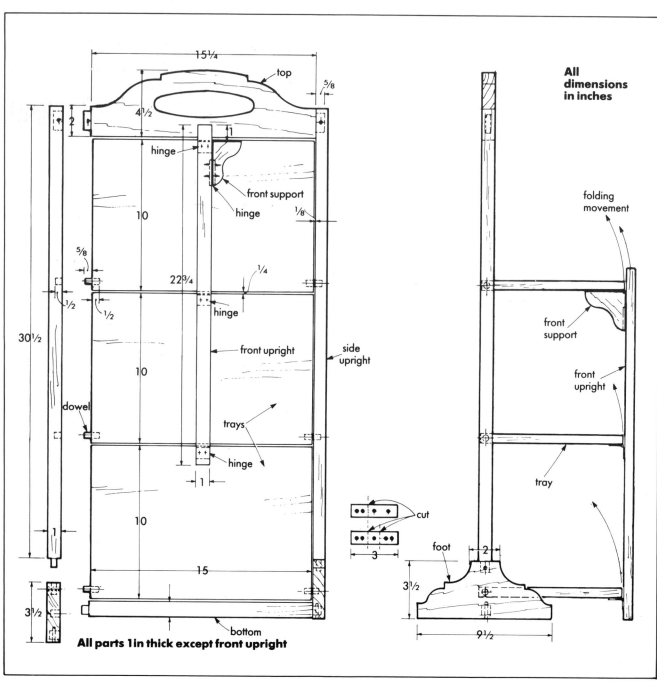

All dimensions in inches

top

hinge

front support

hinge

front upright

side upright

dowel

trays

hinge

bottom

All parts 1 in thick except front upright

cut

foot

folding movement

front support

front upright

tray

Yes, it does look rather like a cake-stand. That's because I adopted the same principle. But I made the supporting surfaces large enough to hold the paraphernalia for afternoon tea or a TV dinner.

You could make the trays from veneered plywood, with beading around the edge. I had some solid oak of suitable size, so I routed out a ³/₁₆in deep recess to form solid wood trays, and I finished with a gouge to have a non-slip surface.

I used dowels to hinge the trays to the uprights; you have to make sure the holes in the uprights are correctly positioned and of suitable depth for the dowels.

I mortised and tenoned the top and bottom to the side uprights, reinforcing the joints with ¼in dowels, since the joints are going to be subjected to a fair amount of strain. I shaped the edges with my router, but you could chamfer them.

Certain areas are going to be difficult to stain if you leave until after gluing up, so I suggest you stain beforehand. The glue-up is all done at once, apart from the feet. Apply candlewax to the dowels on the trap trays so they remain movable.

For the front supports I used 3in brass hinges, sawn as shown. The steel pins slipped out, but I countersank the brass, replaced the pins and burred over the ends of the pins with a nail punch. Then I added further countersunk holes as shown.

I racked my brains trying to think of a suitable method of holding the trays in the stacked position, but my final solution was a simple button.

The whole stand is simple . . . but really useful too. ∎

THE DISK DESK

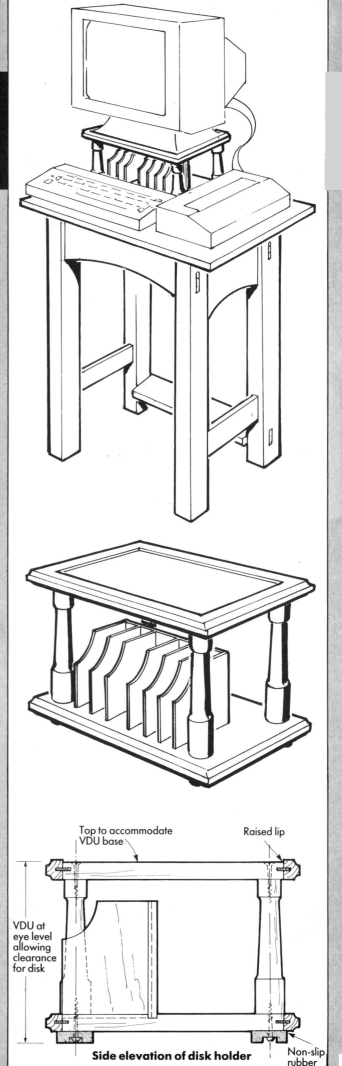

When his wife needed somewhere to keep her floppy disks, Paul Davis came up with this ingenious storage unit

When my wife switched from an electric typewriter to an Amstrad PCW 8256 wordprocessor for her translating work, we were faced with what I imagine is a widespread problem – how to adapt the existing stand to the new equipment. I had made the original table for the secondhand office machine we had before (it was a stout affair in oak to cope with the recoil of the old Olympia's extremely violent carriage return), using a 610 × 450 mm scrap piece of veneered chipboard for a top.

This provided a rather cramped space on which to spread the keyboard, VDU and printer, and to house various loose bits; the drawing shows a stand which was run up with a minimum of fuss, and which elevates the VDU to eye level with a stall arrangement set in.

grooves routed into the base to hold the compact floppy disks. There is storage space for the printout carriage and paper guide bars at the back.

It can be made in just about any material – I used oak and more scrap veneered chipboard to go with the table – and the corner posts can be turned, or have any other suitable section. It would be advisable to add a raised lip to ensure the monitor screen doesn't topple off, while rubber feet will absorb vibration and prevent the stand from sliding around.

It's still rather cramped – the lead from the screen to the keyboard gets in the way when the printer's working, and we need a separate side table for consultation documents – but 610 × 450 mm is a *very* compact storage space for the green-eyed monster. ∎

Top to accommodate VDU base

Raised lip

VDU at eye level allowing clearance for disk

Side elevation of disk holder

Non-slip rubber feet

CRACKING GOOD IDEA

When David Springett was shown a wooden egg that became two egg cups he just had to make one himself

ust at that time when ideas cease, and you've seen it all, a delightful surprise often turns up. This was such a time. A friend brought round an old Austrian painted egg and said that she thought I might be interested. It opened and inside each half there was a close fitting disc of wood. Intriguing. They were difficult to pull out but when removed they were turned stems, upon which fitted the halves of the egg to make a pair of egg cups. Compact, well turned, such a neat idea, I had to have a go.

Fortunately, I had a piece of English walnut the right size for the egg. I had had it for many years; as till now I couldn't decide what to do with it. For the stems I chose yew – it's a wonderful turning timber – and the smell is so good that I turn pieces sometimes just to let the fragrance seep through the workshop.

Before beginning it is helpful to turn a small peg to support the egg, from any hardwood, 12mm long, 12mm diameter for 6mm of its length, and 9mm diameter for the remaining 6mm. If the tailstock centre mark is left on the 12mm diameter end this will be of benefit.

Set the walnut blank, 50mm square and 110mm long, between centres and turn as close to 50mm diameter as possible. Remove the drive centre and replace it with a three-jaw chuck. Set the walnut cylinder in the chuck and bring up the revolving centre. Square up the tailstock face. Drill a 9mm hole, 70mm deep into the end to ease the hollow turning of the inside. That annoying little pip which often forms when turning a hollow with a gouge into a small diameter cannot form for the centre is already drilled out. The hole will take the turned stem or foot to convert the egg into an egg cup. Place the peg in the hole and bring up the revolving centre as support.

A step or rebate on one half of the egg fits snugly into the hollow part of the other. This step or rebate is cut 42mm diameter, 5mm long, 70mm from the faced off end. Part off this half either by sawing with the lathe stationary or conventionally when turning. In either case care is taken to leave 1 to 2mm waste ahead of the step previously turned.

Lay aside the stepped half of the egg. The remaining part still in the chuck is faced off, and again bring up a 9mm bit and drill a hole 40mm deep into the walnut. I like to use a gouge for turning out the centre, it is far more challenging, rather than placing a piece of sharpened steel in the way of rapidly revolving wood and seeing which gives first. Of course that does not mean that there are not times when scrapers are necessary. The satisfaction gained when the gouge hits the right line from start to finish is terrific, not to mention the finer quality of finish produced.

Turn the hollow for the egg shape, carefully, 30mm deep, frequently checking the stepped half into the hollow. When satisfied that the fit is good do not touch that area again with gouge or glasspaper, but continue instead to hollow out the egg shape. Use a cardboard template of the internal profile to check the shape.

When the internal shape is correct, remove the piece from the chuck, replacing it with the other half, with the step facing outwards. To centre this piece place the 9mm drill (still in its drill chuck in the tailstock) back into the drilled hole in the round blank, and carefully tighten the three-jaw chuck around the block.

The internal hollowing of the stepped end can now begin, again using a gouge, care being taken not to run out into the rebate. It might be helpful to make an initial cut with a small square ended 3mm tool to provide an edge upon which the gouge can grip for its first cut. Again use a template to check the internal shape as it progresses.

When the internal shape is complete the half already hollowed can be fitted on. Fit the previously turned plug into the 9mm hole and bring the revolving centre into the centre hole marked. Press the two pieces together for external shaping.

Consideration must be given to the internal shape when turning the outside. Either use another template or judge by eye and sound to decide when the thickness of the egg's walls are sufficiently fine. The whole of the tailstock end of the egg can be turned, allowing the gouge and skew to cut into the plug in the end to produce a clean shape. The headstock part may now be turned, but be aware of the 9mm hole running through, this end of the egg being 39mm away from the joint line. If the whole egg shape is turned and finished satisfactorily it can be parted off with a skew chisel into the 9mm hole, running through.

If before parting off it breaks out into the 9mm hole, prepare a jam chuck, from a scrap piece of wood, into which the stepped end can be fitted and the outside shape of the egg completed.

The stands

Turn a piece of yew 80mm long by 40mm square between centres, to 38mm diameter. Square off the tailstock end with the heel of a skew chisel, leaving a little 'pip'. Begin 2mm in from the squared off end and turn a sweeping curve down to 15mm diameter, finishing 28mm from the start of the cut. At this point if a small part is turned 9mm diameter 5mm long (added on to the 28mm distance) the stem upon which the egg fits will have been produced. To stop the egg slipping down the stem turn a rounded shape 15mm diameter, and bring the diameter on the tailstock side of this shape down to 9mm. A finish curve can now be cut from the point 2mm in from the square off end down to the 9mm diameter at the side of the rounded shape. A skew chisel is ideal for producing the external curves, and a small gouge is best for the concave curves.

Lightly chamfer the end of the stem before parting off, and trim off the 'pip' on the base with a carving gouge so that it will stand evenly. Finish with polyurethane, or paint, as egg cups will need wiping clean. ∎

Stand or foot

9D
15
9
6
28
38

5
50
9
42
44

9
30
39

All dimensions in mm

Template 1
(full-size)

line of step

external curve

internal curve

line of step or rebate

Template 2
(full-size)

Chucking Around

Stephen Jarvis explains how to turn wooden bracelets from branch wood, using two home-made jigs

I t might be thought that turning curtain rings and bracelets is much the same operation, but whereas one can get away with some irregularities on the former, that cannot be said for bracelets. The standard of finish will be closely scrutinized and any imperfection detected immediately. So a different approach has to be used.

Selecting timber

I prefer to make bracelets out of branch wood; especially yew with some of the sapwood incorporated in the finished bracelet. Blanks can also be made by gluing together four pieces of wood 2in square and ¾in thick so that a piece 4×4×¾in is obtained. Gluing is tricky as the joints must be perfect if the ring is to be strong.

The grain can run across the width of the blank, but I prefer the appearance of bracelets where the wood has been cut as a slice across the branch – that is with the wood fibres the short way. This also makes a good finish easier to achieve, as the wood can be more readily scraped. When selecting a branch look out particularly for shakes and other defects which will weaken the bracelet.

The finished bracelet (top) is made using two adaptations of a collet chuck: a four-jaw chuck (centre), and sliding cones (bottom)

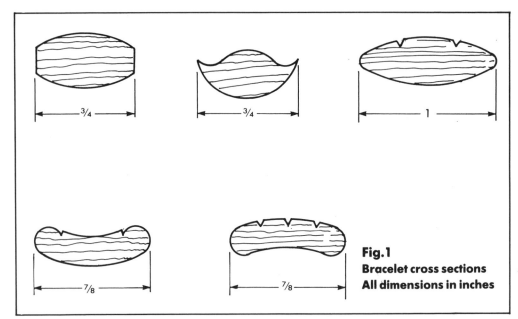

Fig.1
Bracelet cross sections
All dimensions in inches

Dimensions and design

Bracelets tend to start about 2¼in diameter inside and go up to possibly 2⅞in. It is well to decide on the actual size, both inside and out, before you start. If you propose to make a variety of sizes you may need several sets of special jigs.

It is also important to decide on the width and cross section of the bracelets; an oval or curved section is easier to finish than a completely round or rectangular one. The sections can be in various shapes, but life will be less complicated if you concentrate on one size and section to start with, because different diameter sections will need different holding devices.

Cutting the timber

Take a branch of yew some 5in diameter and cut it into slices ¾-1in thick. This is best done on a bandsaw if you have access to a large one; use a cradle to carry the branch so that it does not roll into the saw. This can be tricky and needs care.

Examine the blank pieces carefully and test for strength, as shakes have a habit of hiding and only showing up when the wood is polished – a bit late then! Set a compass for the diameter of the outside of the bracelet some ¾in greater than the internal one, so for the 2¼in bracelet it's 3in and for the 2⅞in, 3⅝in. Finding a centre in each piece of wood which incorporates natural marks and small defects ie sap, knots, twin heart. Cut away some of the surplus wood leaving enough to clean up on the lathe to 3⅝in diameter.

Mount a screw chuck in the lathe, drill a hole in the centre of the blanks and go right through. Place the blank on the screw chuck, and even if the faces are not parallel, screw the wood on until it touches the body of the chuck. Gently skim of the perimeter of the blank – until it is down to the outside diameter of the largest bracelet (3⅝in).

Whilst in the lathe true up the face, and if the face against the chuck needs to be trued, reverse the workpiece on the chuck. Sandwich a disc of plywood between the workpiece and the chuck so that when you part off the parting tool is not damaged.

Decide on the internal diameter of the bracelet and with the parting tool cut an annular groove in the face of the blank; leave enough material to finish the inside of the bracelet to the intended diameter. You can either cut through in one operation or go half-way through and reverse the work to cut through the other half. If you happen to go over your intended internal diameter there is no loss as the ring will come in for the next size.

The blanks all have the same outside diameter because the next move is to make a chuck designed to hold the rings while the inside is shaped. This entails quite a bit of work and could well be a separate project. While the chuck is being made hang the ring on a washing line or dowel in a dry place; pieces cut from branches are seldom dry and you may find some distortions take place. This will not matter unless the distortions are excessive.

Making the chuck

The wooden chuck is designed to be used with the Craft Supplies Combination Collet Chuck. It is simply a cup on a stalk, the cup being slit to make it flexible. The internal diameter of the cup coincides with the outside diameter of the rings. The slits will enable small differences in diameter to be accommodated and the stalk is held in the 1⅞in collet, which provides enough pressure to hold the ring while working on its internal diameter.

Place the ring in the cupchuck and tighten the combination chuck. You may need to spend a bit of time making the ring run true as there is no positive register to locate it. If you decide that all your bracelets are going to be the same shape you could leave a step in the cup to locate the ring, and so eliminate the need for adjustment.

Using a scraper, shape the accessible edge and half-way across the inside of the bracelet. If you are making a number of bracelets it pays to grind a suitable shape in a square-ended scraper, so that you put the same shape on all the inner edges. Alternatively use a straight scraper, but there will be varia-

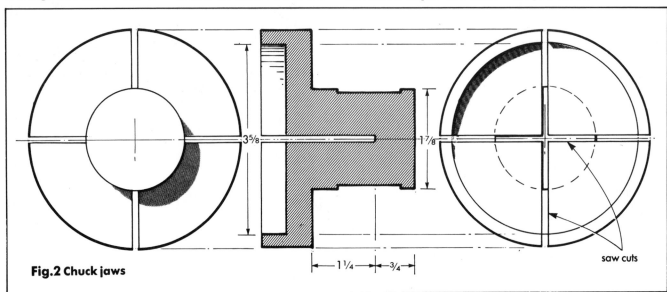

Fig.2 Chuck jaws

saw cuts

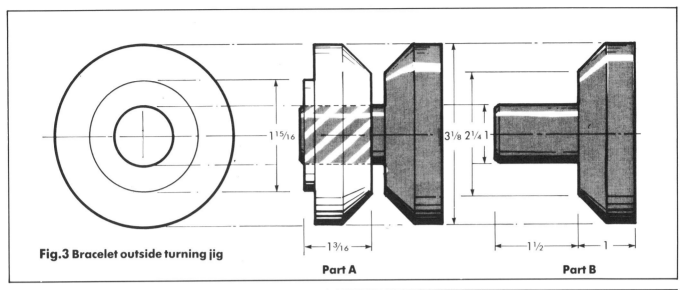

Fig.3 Bracelet outside turning jig

Part A   Part B

tions to the edges of the bracelets which may not be desirable. Sandpaper the internal shape to a finish. Reverse the ring in the chuck and shape the other edges. You should be able to feel the work with your fingers to check if the internal shape is good.

Dilute some melamine polish with cellulose thinners and apply to the inside of the ring, wiping off the surplus with paper tissue. You will need to reverse the bracelet yet again so as to make it accessible for finishing. As soon as all the melamine is dry apply a little carnauba wax and polish up.

The inside of the first bracelet is now finished and as it will be held carefully in another jig the polish will not suffer. You may care to bring a batch of rings to this state before moving on to finish the outsides.

Shaping the outside

To shape the outside of the ring you will need to use another special jig of two parts (fig. 3). One part (A) is a disc with one corner cut off at about 40°, the other part (B) is a disc but has a 1in diameter spigot which must pass freely but not loosely into a matching hole in disc A. More than one of these may be needed for various sizes of bracelets.

The disc with the hole (A) is secured in the collet chuck and the spigot of disc B is passed through the bracelet and into the hole.

Centralise the bracelet and use the tailstock to hold the ring between the two parts. No great pressure is required provided the turning of the outside

Blanks are sawn from branch wood using a cradle to prevent the wood rolling

of the bracelet is done gently. Do not allow the jig to slip inside the ring or the finish will be damaged, so go carefully. Having shaped the outside to your satisfaction remove the bracelet for examination. It can be easily replaced for further work.

Small V-cuts in the outside of the bracelet will be improved by burning. With the lathe in top speed hold an iron wire by both ends and cut into the bottom of the grooves (like a cheese cutter). After a moment the wire will become red hot through friction and will burn its way to the bottom of the groove. Treat each of the grooves the same way. Sand off after this operation before you treat with melamine and wax. Be careful not to drop the red hot wire amongst the chippings! ∎

Find a centre in the blank to include figure and small defects which enhance but won't weaken the bracelet

A walking stick as a present for someone fond of walking seemed a good idea. Then I realised that as the intended recipient always went walking with this wife she should have a stick to match his. But where would they keep the sticks when not in use. They should be worthy of display. I'd have to make a stand as well.

It would not have been possible to contemplate turning a stick if it had not been for the availability of brass connectors (fig. 1) for jointing timber end to end. Instead of attempting to turn a thin piece of timber nearly 36in long I need only tackle the far easier task of turning pieces one third that length. Using

Ralph Sinnott finds that the connectors he uses for making walking sticks have other uses

Sticks

To ensure accurate centering of the connectors it is necessary to bore a section before turning. You may need to improve some means of holding the section to make sure you bore true along its axis. Having drilled the holes, fix a suitably-sized piece of hardwood to a small faceplate on the lathe using a centre screw, and turn a dowel on it (fig. 3) to fit tightly in the hole you have made for the larger end of the connector. Make a shoulder to butt against the squared end of the section. Double-sided adhe-

sive tape used between the shoulder of the dowel and the end of the section helps to keep the section revolving with the dowel. At the other end of the section locate the smaller hole with the tailstock centre.

The diameter of the holes is critical. When they have been bored, insert the connector into the relevant holes, and by twisting the turned sections the connector cuts its own thread in the timber. Make a hole too big and the thread will not hold; make it too small and you will not be able to turn the connector down to its shoulder. Attempting to take the joint apart for correction will result merely in the two parts of the connector unscrewing. It is

Sticks & Stand

connectors has the added advantage that the sticks can be dismantled and packed with luggage, or carried in a bag before reaching the walking area. With connectors used for the stand as well, if the base is not permanently fixed, the whole can be taken apart and packed in a box measuring 12×9×3in for sending through the post, perhaps.

The standard length of a man's walking stick is 36in and a woman's 33in, so in the absence of any special requirements adopt these sizes. Set out the stand and sticks (fig. 2), making the sections equal between the brass parts. The connectors are 25mm and 20mm diameter, and the tip 15mm, which determine the turning. Allow an extra millimetre in diameter, it is better for the brass to be a fraction under rather than stand proud.

I used heads (or handles) of Regency design for the sticks and a ball end for the stand. Other designs available are in the form of animal heads: dog, eagle, duck, goose, horse. Twelve-inch lengths of 1¼in square section timber in various timbers can be obtained from the suppliers of the brass parts. Ash is a traditional material for walking sticks so that was my choice. For the stand I used cherry, which I had in stock.

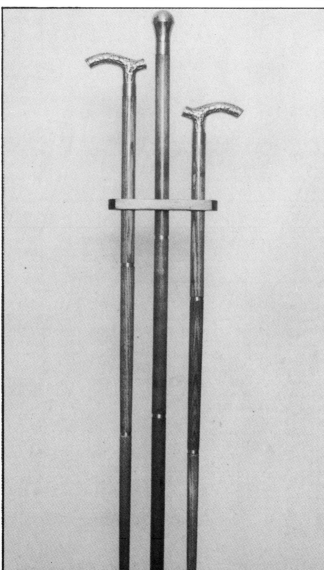

of course, possible to hold the plate of the connector in a vice while twisting the timber but it is difficult to stop the plate slipping round without marking its rim.

Some experimentation is necessary to find the right diameter of hole, which can vary with the hardness of the timber. The ferrule of the head also cuts its own thread so tests are required to determine the diameter of the end of the stick that receives the ferrule.

I put epoxy resin adhesive (Araldite) on the threads of the connectors and on the ferrule when assembling the parts. This has a lubricating action so the adhesive should be applied when trial holes are tested. You may find it necessary to grind the sides of a flat drill bit to reduce it to the required size for the holes.

The tip is not threaded, but fits on to a taper worked on the end of the stick and is secured with epoxy resin.

The stand

On the bottom end of the standard, turn a ¾in-diameter spigot. This fits into the base, which consists of two cross-pieces halved together, surmounted by a round block. Mould the ends of the cross-pieces by paring with gouge and chisel, and finishing with glasspaper. Spalling is likely to occur even though the piece is kept down tight on the paring board, so don't take the pieces to width until moulding is completed. Glue the parts of the base and screw from the underside. Two ¾in-diameter holes are sunk ¼in into one of the cross-pieces to receive the ends of the sticks.

The cross-piece that holds the top of the sticks is bored to

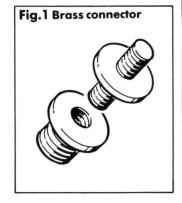

Fig.1 Brass connector

fit over the standard, glued and secured with a brass screw through one edge. As it is impossible to avoid getting surplus glue on the standard have a damp cloth ready to wipe it off immediately.

Finishing

Whether the timbers are stained or left in their natural colour is a matter of choice. I stained the cherry stand darker and the ash sticks to match, as closely as possible. Two coats of polyurethane varnish cut back, followed by wax polishing make an attractive finish for the stand. But the sticks need a weather-resistant coating so treat them with two coats of yacht varnish. ■

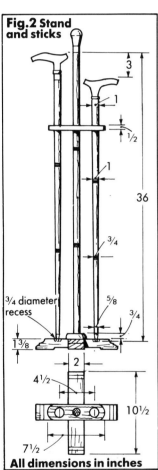

Fig.2 Stand and sticks

3

1

½

1

36

¾

¾ diameter recess

⅝

¾

1⅜

2

4½

10½

7½

All dimensions in inches

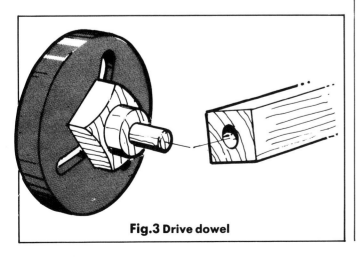

Fig.3 Drive dowel

On the Shelf

Jim Robinson promotes pine for this simple wall shelf

The thought of using pine for furniture in recent times, used to fill many dedicated woodworkers, including myself, with horror. However, in this age, when we are more concerned for the conservation of tropical rainforests, it is not a bad thing to use softwood when we can.

Pine furniture does not have to be plain, it is within the price bracket that young people can afford, it is much more serviceable than veneered chipboard furniture and last, but by no means least, it is solid wood.

This design is for some pine wall shelves which are relatively simple to make but have a little added character in the form of turned pillars at the corners. This use of turned pillars to support shelves was popular in the mid to late 19th century.

There must be many new woodturners reading this project who have made all the bowls, egg cups etc., that the family and friends can absorb, so why not try your hand at using your new ound skills to embellish a piece of furniture.

Softwood can be purchased is sawn joinery grade or planed and square edged (P.S.E). I have recently purchased a Sheppach HMS 260 planer-thicknesser so thought this would be an ideal opportunity to try it out. I purchased my timber as joinery grade sawn timber. This has the advantage of generally being somewhat cheaper than planed and squared-edged timber but probably more importantly, I generally find it to be somewhat better quality.

If, with the exception of the material for the pillars, you buy your timber as 9×1in sawn (225×25mm) then the six inch wide shelves can be cut out economically leaving sufficient width of material from which to cut the two sides and bottom rail. The top decorated rail being somewhat wider will be the odd one out which has to be cut separately. If you are using P.S.E. timber then you might find it more economical to use nominal 6×1in (150mm×25mm) for the shelves. This will necessitate adjusting the finished width to 5¾in but will hardly be noticed. When you are purchasing and preparing your timber large or loose knots and shakes should be avoided but the inclusion of small knots adds a certain amount of character to an otherwise bland timber.

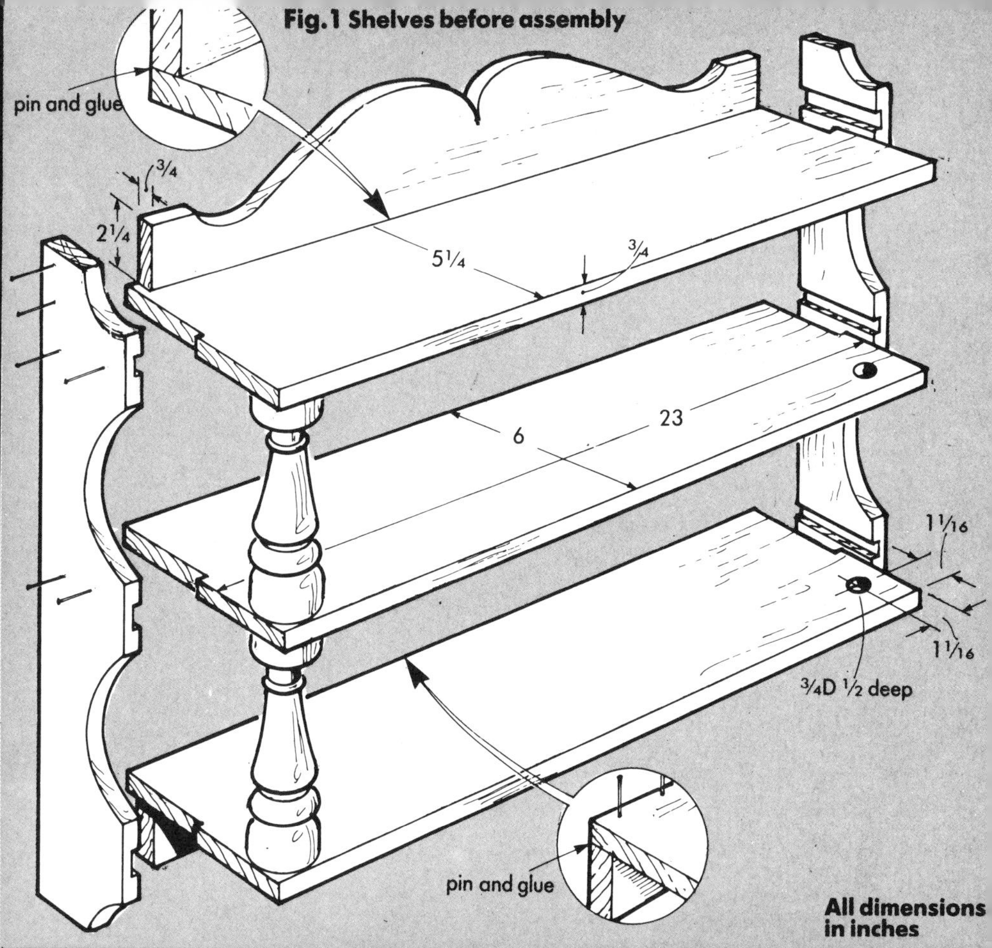
pin and glue
3/4
2 1/4
5 1/4
3/4
6
23
1 1/16
1 1/16
3/4D 1/2 deep
pin and glue
All dimensions in inches

Fig.1 Shelves before assembly

Sides and top

Having planed and prepared or purchased your timber ready planed, to the required thicknesses, the two side pieces and top can be cut to shape using a bandsaw if one is available, or alternatively a coping saw or bow saw. If this outline is transferred to a piece of cardboard or plywood offcut and then cut to shape for a template, it is easy to draw the required outline. A centre line should be drawn across your timber, then the template can be turned over after drawing one half to complete the shape required.

I next removed as many of the saw teeth marks as I could with a belt sander. The front roller of the belt sander was used for the convex curves but it was still not possible to sand all the top decoration at the centre. The remaining marks can be removed with a file and garnet paper but instead of a file I used a very sharp cabinet scraper held at an angle of about 45° across the saw tooth marks. After completing this shaping, sanding to a finish was left until the rest of the work was complete.

The housing joints for the shelves were cut next with a router to a width of ¾in and a depth of ⅜in. If you do not have a router then these joints are fairly simple to make by hand. A saw cut can be made each side of the required depth and the waste removed with a chisel. It is probably a good idea to clamp a square piece of wood in position along each line to guide your saw. To complete the decorative top, two holes for fixing need to

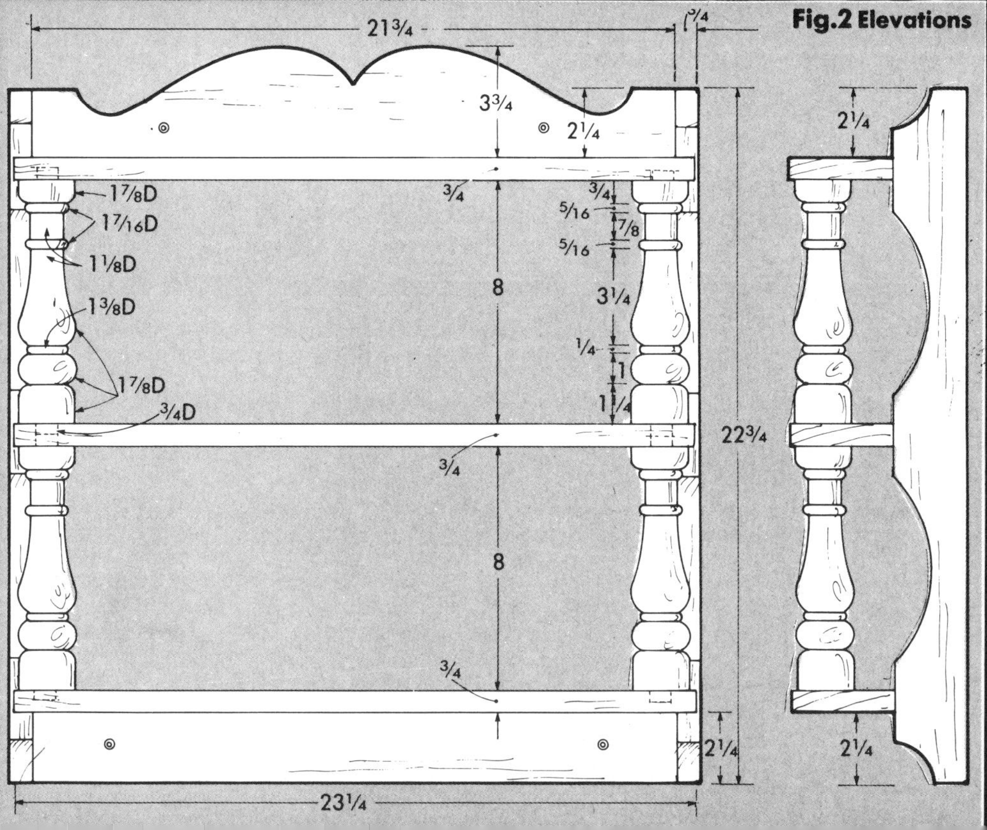
21 3/4
3/4
3 3/4
2 1/4
1 7/8D
1 7/16D
1 1/8D
1 3/8D
1 7/8D
3/4D
3/4
3/4
5/16
7/8
5/16
8
3 1/4
1/4
1
1 1/4
22 3/4
3/4
8
3/4
2 1/4
23 1/4
2 1/4
2 1/4

Fig.2 Elevations

be drilled and countersunk to the required screw size, which will probably need to be a No. 8 or No. 12 gauge.

Bottom support rail

The bottom support rail has a length of 21¾in and is ¾in thick; these are the same measurements as the top. It is perfectly plain except that two fixing holes are required similar to those in the top.

Shelves

The three shelves are identical in size and shape. The first stage is to cut them square, with a length of 23in and a width of 5in. I next used my bandsaw, with the fence and depth stop in position, to form the cut-outs, which fit into the housings cut in the side pieces, and with this method marking out on the timber was not necessary.

Holes to take the pillars were next drilled in the shelves. If you have a ¾in drill, this is a good size to use, but if you use a different size then remember to turn the pins on the pillars to match. I have only a very old hand bench drill so I prefer to use my lathe to drill the holes. The wood to be drilled is held flat against a faceplate screwed to a morse taper adapter, which fits into the tailstock.

A machine type saw-tooth bit was then mounted in a chuck fitted to the headstock. This method ensures that the holes drilled are square to the face of the timber and their depth can be ensured by adjusting the travel on the tailstock. The hole position can be marked out with a marking gauge. Set the gauge to 1 1/16in and square off from the front and sides of the shelves. The holes in the top and bottom shelves are drilled ½in deep, the middle shelf has the hole drilled right through. In practice though, I kept the lathe settings the same and drilled the hole from each side, which avoided having to place a piece of scrap wood at the back to save damaging the drill against the faceplate, also it ensured a clean hole free from splintering at each face of the wood.

The turned pillars

The four pillars were turned from timber sawn 2in square. The pins at each end are shown to be ¾in in length though

these will have to be adjusted to fit the holes drilled in the shelves. The top and bottom shelves have holes drilled to ½in depth but the middle shelf has to accommodate pins from the top and bottom pillars, so if your shelf has a finished thickness of ¾in then the pin at the top of the lower pillars and the pin at the bottom of the upper pillars can of course only be ⅜in in length. The timber selected for the pillars should be cut square and their centres marked by drawing diagonals ready for turning. After mounting between centres a ¾in square-ended roughing gouge was used to turn the wood to a cylinder before smoothing to finish at a diameter of 1⅞in with a large skew chisel.

The pillars were next marked out to the length of 8in, after

Fig. 3 Profiles of top back and sides

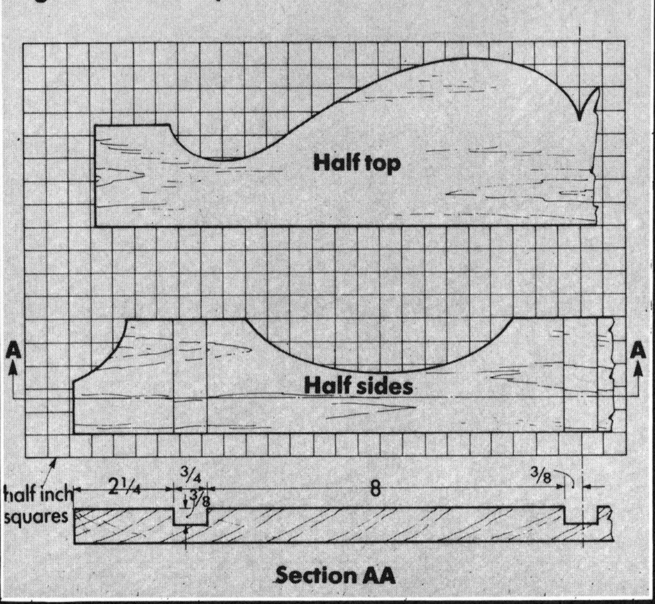

Half top

Half sides

half inch squares 2¼ ¾ 1⅜ 8 ⅜

Section AA

starting with a small V cut made with the point of the skew chisel. The pins at each end were turned to ¾in diameter with a parting tool. The face was then trimmed flat with the long point of the skew.

After marking the position of the beads etc., the rest of the work can be carried out entirely using a skew chisel, even the very slightly concaved shape on the stem. It will help though if some of the bulk waste material, to bring the stem down to the diameter of the beads, is first removed with the roughing gouge and it may be necessary to use a small skew to finish between the small beads at the upper part of the stem.

Before removing the work from the lathe, sand down to 320 grit using garnet or similar paper. Remember when sanding on the lathe and changing down to a finer grade of paper to ensure that there are no pieces of grit left remaining from the courser paper that can become embedded in the finer paper and cause scratching.

Assembly

Before starting to assemble the components together sand down all surfaces to 320 grit to provide the same standard of finish as the pillars. Next cut a small V

groove in the pins of the pillars, to allow surplus glue and air to escape which would otherwise make assembly more difficult due to piston effect. Since gap filling properties were not required of the glue I used the waterproof grade of Evo-Stick wood adhesive, mainly because this glue requires no mixing.

Apply glue to the bottom face of the top decorated rail and then fix to the bottom shelf with four panel pins 1½in in length. Similarly glue the top face of the bottom rail and pin to the bottom shelf. The pins should be punched just below the surface with a small punch, then filled with a pine woodfiller.

The pillars can next be glued

On the Shelf

into place. If the pins are a good tight fit, sash cramps may be needed to lose the gap but protect the shelves from damage with softwood blocks. Once cramped together the pillars should stay in place if the cramps are moved. It is a useful tip to fix softwood blocks to the cramps with Sellotape, so that one pair of hands is sufficient. To complete the assembly, glue and pin the side pieces to the shelves. Fill all nail holes and sand smooth as previously.

Finishing

I do not like the new pine look but much prefer the more mellow appearance of stripped pine, so I use a pale brown or stripped pine look stain. When dry it may be necessary to sand the end grain very lightly, if this has been raised by the wetting. The shelves were next polished, using medium brown (P7) Briwax. An easy way of applying this, particularly to the turned pillars and into the corners is with a 2in paint brush which has had its bristles cut short to about 1in in length. The wax can be applied with a piece of Scotchbrite denibbing cloth to the end-grain.

After the wax polish has been applied it can be buffed up and I use a 'Pine Brush' mounted in an electric drill for this purpose. Further depth to the finish can be achieved if a second light application of the wax polish is made, followed by buffing up with a soft cloth.

Now that you have completed this set of shelves, why not try a few alternatives ie. the distance between the lower shelves could be increased to say 10in by increasing the length of the sides and pillars. The extended pillars would look more in keeping with the others if their stems were extended and possibly two beads spaced about 1in apart were worked instead of the single bead. Another possibility would be to make the bottom and middle shelf wider than the top shelf, then step back the top set of pillars. Also of course alteration in the length of the shelves could be made to suit the available space, with an alteration to the top decoration.

STEPPING UP

For a simple project, which incorporates traditional pegged, mortise and tenon joints, Douglas Curtis explains how to make a stepped stool

I made this little step stool for the kitchen as the top cupboards were too high for convenient access, and I did not want aluminium steps, as they'd be out of keeping with the hardwood fittings. So I made an ordinary kitchen stool with an extension step on the side, in hardwood to match the kitchen; thereby having a dual

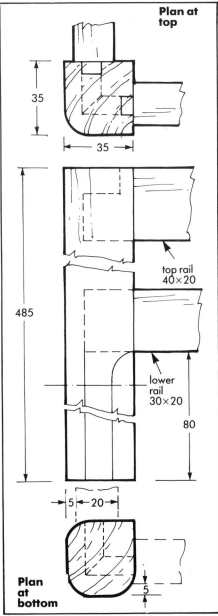

Plan at top

35

35

top rail
40×20

485

lower
rail
30×20

80

5 20

Plan at bottom

5

Fig. 1 Isometric drawing of stepped stool

300

300

28   28 60

485

35 sq.

242

440   80

Details (right) of plan of leg at top (top); section through leg to rails (middle) and plan of leg below lower rail (bottom)

All dimensions in millimetres

Note the rounding below the bottom rail and pegged joints

purpose item, taking up little more space than an ordinary stool.

Construction is simple, with the main frame of 35×35mm material, and the top rails of 40×20mm, and the other rails of 30×20mm, all positioned 5mm from the front face. Use a 9mm mortise throughout, with the same setting for all the mortises, and pin all the completed joints with 6mm dowels for traditional effect. The rails all have a small round on the outer edges, and when the framing was glued up it was easy to run a largish round on the outer edges as

detail, with a router. Which parts to decorate is a matter of choice but I moulded the four outer corners from top to bottom, and short, stopped rounds on the inner corners, from floor to underside of bottom rails.

The top overlaps 5mm all round and is secured from underside of top rails, screw holes oversize to allow a little movement. The step treads are screwed from the top with rust-proofed screws. The whole job is given two coats of polyurethane, rubbed down carefully between coats, and fits in well with the existing units. ∎

Cutting list

Back legs	2	500×	35×	35mm
Front legs (bottom)	2	250	35	35
Front legs (top)	2	275	35	35
Centre rails	2	450	35	35
Top rails	4	300	40	20
Bottom rails	2	300	30	20
Bottom rails	2	440	30	20
Top	1	320	320	20
Step	2	320	28	20
Step	1	320	60	20

All dimensions are overlong, allowing for trim

Power of the press

Solid and simple in concept,
Chris Coupe's flower press
design has a couple of
challenging features to
get right before you flatten
the flourishing flora

I f, like me, you live in an area where
there is an abundance of wild flowers,
you may be interested in making this
simple-but-strong flower press — for your
own enjoyment, or perhaps to give the kids
an unfair advantage in Nature Study!

All the information you need is in the
drawings; construction is really quite
straightforward. Make the platens first,
from pieces of 16mm chipboard laminated
together, with ply inserts set into routed
grooves for strength.

Cut a recess in the centre of the top, or
moving platen — it is 4mm smaller in width
than the base platen, note — for a piece of
3mm mild steel plate which will take the
bottom of the threaded rod and washers
which provide the rise-and-fall. The detail
on the drawing shows how they fit together.

Then assemble the cross-beam and the
nut-retaining piece, which is counterbored
to take an M16 nut, glued in with epoxy. I
cut the recess with a router. Once the nut is
well fixed in its recess, glue the support
piece to what will be the underside of the
beam. Use your piece of M16 studding,
threaded through a 16mm hole in the centre
of the cross-beam and the nut-support
piece, to make sure the holes line up
accurately when you are gluing. It is best to
leave them oversize until you have fixed the
two pieces together.

The cross-bar is set into full-size mortises
in the tops of the sides, and the base platen
is fixed to the bottom inner edges of the
sides with a 6x12mm ply tongue, plus glue
and screws.

I used iroko for the cross-bar, nut-
retaining piece, handwheel and sides, but
any dense and stable hardwood would do.
Turn the round components to the sizes
indicated, and screw the handle to the wheel
through an oversize full-depth hole. The
washer and split-pin arrangement at the
bottom of the studding is straightforward
once you have turned the studding down at
the end, but where the studding goes into
the handwheel at the top you need to make
sure you won't suffer from 'drift'. I got
round this by cutting a recess for the M16
nut in the centre of the wheel, screwing the
nut on to the studding, then 'lockwiring'
them together by drilling a 3mm hole
through both and pushing a piece of wire
through. Then I glued the nut and studding
into the recess with epoxy. 'Loctite'
adhesive alone without the wire may be
enough, but if you want to make doubly

● *This sturdy press can flatten a surprising number of flowers at one go if you layer
them between sheets of plywood and blotting paper*

sure I think the lockwire is a good belt-and-
braces solution.

I finished all the surfaces with linseed oil,
except for the pressing surfaces of the
platens, which I varnished to prevent
sticking. You can press quite a quantity of
flowers at one time by sandwiching them
between sheets of 3mm ply and blotting

paper; go in the order: ply, blotting paper,
flowers, blotting paper, ply, blotting
paper, flowers, blotting paper, ply and so
on. Depending on how many flowers you
use, you can get a drying time as short as
three days.

Now all that remains is for you to be out
and about in the summer hedgerows . . .■

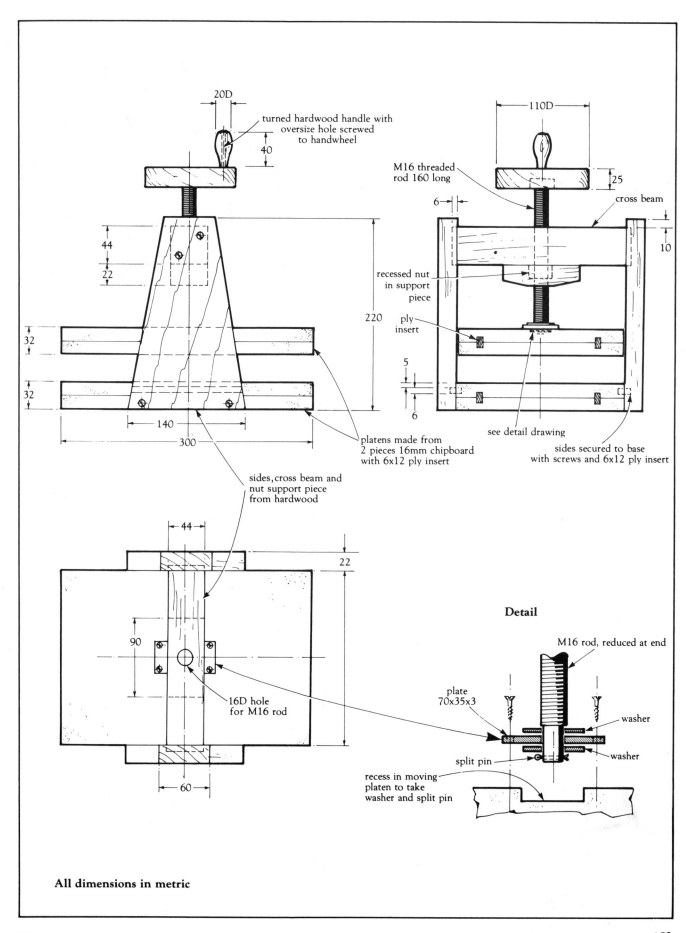

20D

turned hardwood handle with oversize hole screwed to handwheel

40

110D

M16 threaded rod 160 long

25

cross beam

6

10

recessed nut in support piece

44

22

ply insert

220

see detail drawing

32

5

32

6

140

300

platens made from 2 pieces 16mm chipboard with 6x12 ply insert

sides secured to base with screws and 6x12 ply insert

sides, cross beam and nut support piece from hardwood

44

22

90

16D hole for M16 rod

60

Detail

M16 rod, reduced at end

plate 70x35x3

washer

washer

split pin

recess in moving platen to take washer and split pin

All dimensions in metric

MUSIC STOOL uniquely your own

Well-known for his early keyboard instruments Donal Garrod MBE MA is author of the series on single manual harpsichord construction published in WOODWORKER during 1973-4. Here he gives information on making a music stool explaining that 'although joints should fit exactly and certain basic proportions should be adhered to, the rest is a matter of individual judgement.'

'How to use your WOODWORKER' is a subject brought to my mind by queries from readers about apparently inconsistent measurements in articles I have written for previous issues. Always I have assured readers that although joints should fit exactly and certain basic proportions should be adhered to, the rest is a matter of individual judgement.

A careful reproduction of someone else's work may involve exact craftsmanship but something is lacking — and depending upon the excellence, or otherwise, of the original may be very disappointing.

The photograph and drawings of the music stool could be a good example of what I mean. It was made for quick assembly and dismantling, without wing nuts or bolts which would have been out-of-character. For a stool like this all I should need to know is the basic construction which consists of stretcher B through a mortise in each side member. This stretcher is clamped to both side members by tapered pegs as at A. This lower stretcher should be wide enought to take shoulders to fit against the inside of the side members. (It was 2½in wide in this case.)

The top stretcher is glued down the middle of the underside of the seat. It is the same length as the lower stretcher and drops into mortise slots in the upper edges of the side members. It is similarly fixed by wooden pegs. (I attached the curved wooden brace because the seat showed a tendency to curve width-wise; however, the brace might not be necessary.)

The base was added to give greater stability and the width is unimportant as long as it looks right. The sides were stepped down for decorative effect. The stool was upholstered in this case but, depending upon the wood you are using, the top could be polished and used with a cushion. The height is a matter of convenience depending upon the height of the instrument and the length of the musician's legs.

Although the stool should come apart easily it must be stable when it is up. This depends upon the pegs being tight in the holes.

If you use only the basic idea in a plan and alter or adapt the rest to your own requirements, the end result should be a piece which you can take pride in as uniquely your own.

Right: Music stool similar to the one described in the article.
Below left: One of the tapered pegs used for clamping the stretcher.

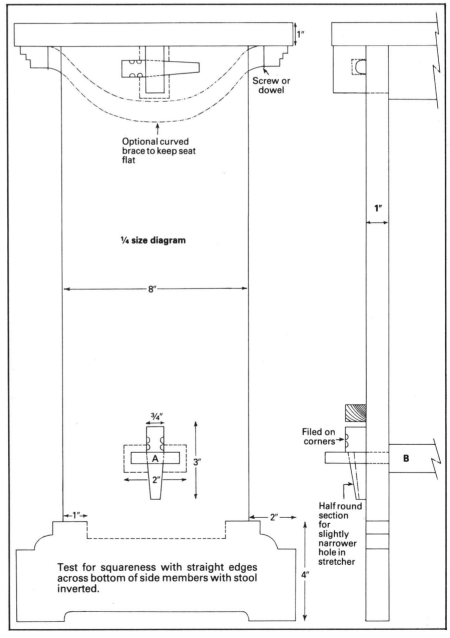

1"

Screw or dowel

Optional curved brace to keep seat flat

¼ size diagram

8"

¾"

A

3"

2"

1"

1"

Filed on corners

B

Half round section for slightly narrower hole in stretcher

2"

4"

Test for squareness with straight edges across bottom of side members with stool inverted.

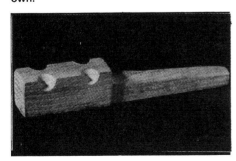

Essential Equipment...

Here are two tools no woodworker should be without, *Woodworker* and *WoodWorks* magazines.

Generations of craftsmen have gained expertise, advice and ideas from Woodworker magazine. This quality monthly continues to bring unrivalled projects, plans and inspiration to all woodworkers and its success has paved the way for a totally new type of magazine...*WoodWorks.*

With the same no-nonsense approach as *Woodworker*, *WoodWorks* really shows you 'how-to' build stylish, practical home and garden furniture that you'll be proud to show off!

This superb new quarterly magazine guides you through making your own furniture with advice on tools, techniques, materials and workshop safety. With as many as 10 projects in every issue – we've covered everything you could want to know about making quality furniture – on a budget!

Both *Woodworker* and *WoodWorks* are available from all good newsagents or by our superb *Direct Delivery Service*. We deliver every issue to your door for 1 year and we pay for the postage anywhere in the U.K. You just relax and enjoy a truly constructive read!

Essential Savings 10% off

If you subscribe to both *Woodworker* and *WoodWorks* with this advert, we'll give you a discount of over 10% off the total price, that's a *saving of over £3.30!*

Woodworker
Britain's best-selling woodwork magazine
AN ARGUS SPECIALIST PUBLICATION
July 1993 £1.90 Founded in 1901

WoodWorks
PRACTICAL PROJECTS FOR THE HOME WOODWORKER
ISSUE ONE £2.50

TEN HOME PROJECTS TO MAKE
COMPLETE STEP BY STEP INSTRUCTIONS WITH PLANS AND DIAGRAMS

Stylish fall-flap DINING TABLE in solid Ash and Walnut

Solid Pine PLAY HOUSE for the kids

ONLY BASIC TOOLS NEEDED

DRAPER TAPE MEASURE 3m/10ft Made in Great Britain 3ME/16

DIRECT DELIVERY SERVICE